The Tech-Savvy
Real Estate Agent

GALEN GRUMAN, REALTOR

The Tech-Savvy Real Estate Agent

Galen Gruman

Peachpit Press
1249 Eighth Street
Berkeley, CA 94710
510/524-2178
510/524-2221 (fax)
800/283-9444

Find us on the Web at: www.peachpit.com
To report errors, please send a note to
errata@peachpit.com

Peachpit Press is a division of Pearson Education
Copyright © 2006 by Galen Gruman

Project Manager: Suzie Nasol
Editor: Carol Person
Production Editor: Becky Winter
Copyeditor: Anne Marie Walker
Compositor: Diana Van Winkle, Van Winkle Design
Indexer: Rebecca Plunkett
Cover Design: Aren Howell
Interior Design: Diana Van Winkle, Van Winkle Design

Image Credits

All photos and illustrations are copyrighted by
Galen Gruman, except for the following, which are
copyrighted by their owners and used with permission:

Part dividers: iStockphoto.com and gettyimages.com

Page 7 photo courtesy of Belkin Components.

Pages 28 and 29 illustrations by Arne Hurty reprinted
from the December 1994 issue of Macworld.

Pages 120 (top) and 128 photos in the screen images
by Sylvia Chevrier.

ISBN 0-321-41366-0
9 8 7 6 5 4 3 2 1
Printed and bound in the United States of America

To Carol Person:

*For years, we managed a great organization together
and enjoyed a deep friendship, then found our business paths
diverge. It's been a real pleasure to partner again
on this project, and to discover that we both are
now in the real estate business.*

Acknowledgments

Marjorie Baer, Peachpit's executive editor, came up with the basic concept for this book, then gave me the wonderful opportunity to explore it and make it real. Several people and organizations— Sylvia Chevrier, Andres Enriquez, Arne Hurty, Belkin Components, Eurekaware, Mac Publishing, Prudential California Realty, and 3DVista—were kind enough to provide permissions to include their software or images in this book.

CONTENTS

Chapter 3: Working with Electronic Media 53

PART 2

Marketing Yourself More Effectively . . . 77

Chapter 4: Effective Web Sites 79

INTRODUCTION

Technical Opportunities in Real Estate

As many surveys show, more and more buyers are turning to the Internet to research their home purchases—about two thirds, according to recent surveys by the National Association of Realtors (NAR). And sellers are also increasingly using the Internet to gauge the potential selling price of their properties.

This fact shouldn't surprise anyone, given how common online shopping has become. In the last decade, Americans have become comfortable using computer and Internet technology at home, work, and school, with shopping and product research among the most common activities. In fact, many clients now expect their providers—including their real estate agents and brokers—to use the Internet to provide information. This is particularly true of younger buyers and sellers, who use technology routinely in their lives: e-mail, the Web, digital cameras, cell phones, iPods, and so forth. They expect the people who serve them to work at the same technology level.

Some members of the real estate industry have quickly adopted these new technologies. For example, in California, about 90 percent of agents have high-speed Internet access at home, according to a recent California Association of Realtors survey. NAR's surveys show that most agents now access the Multiple Listing Service (MLS) over the Internet, rather than connect through special computer setups at the office or rely on the old paper books stored at the office. Most Realtors associations have made active listings available to the public via their own Web sites, through their brokers' and agents' Web sites, and through aggregation sites such as www.Realtor.com. Thanks to this technology adoption, tens of thousands of people can now explore current listings to better understand the market. Savvy agents and brokers encourage this, since better-educated customers usually don't waste your time looking at places that don't fit their basic budgets or criteria.

Despite this Internet adoption for MLS data, many agents and brokerages still tend to be low-tech. There's an understandable reason for that: You don't have the skills, time, or inclination to develop and then implement a technology strategy—after all, you're an agent, not an engineer. You're focused on the bread-and-butter activities of finding clients and then helping them sell or buy properties instead.

But in a world that is increasingly technology-oriented, you'll have to make the time to adopt current technologies to serve those clients well. Otherwise, your efforts will become less efficient—and often more expensive—than your competitors' processes. If your service begins to fall behind that of your competitors, you'll lose many of your clients over time and find it harder to get new ones.

Does that mean you must become a technology expert? No, but it does mean you should judiciously apply technology to serve your clients and market your services. Because real estate is such a local business, there's no single answer to what technology a particular agent should use. But a savvy agent can craft her own strategy by using the techniques and tools described in this book—and improve your customer service, business operations, and overall success. If you're a broker, you too should craft a strategy that meets your local business needs and customer requirements, keeping your firm ahead of the competition.

Just as not investing in technology can hurt your business, so can inappropriately investing in technology be bad. Agents quickly learn that there are hundreds of companies trying to sell services, sales methods, and technologies. You'll go broke spending money on every possible "solution." The real estate business has many demands on agents' pocketbooks, and the tech-savvy agent also knows when *not* to spend on technology.

All technology used *must* serve a purpose worth its investment. When creating your technology strategy, first ask yourself *what* you want to do, *why* it is worth doing, and finally *how* to do it—assuming your analysis says that it still makes sense to do. Don't get caught up in using technology just because you think you have to, because "everyone else is doing it," or because the technology looks "cool." Technology can be a great help to your business, but only if it actually improves your business.

How to Use This Book

Whether you are an agent or a broker, achieving the right technology strategy means assessing several parts of your real estate business: marketing yourself more effectively, facilitating communications, and managing transactions more effectively.

This book is organized around those key aspects of your business, with sections that show you how various technologies can improve your business and how you can actually use them. The first section covers the technologies themselves, while the rest of the book focuses on how to use the technologies in the practice of real estate.

Once you understand the possibilities, it's up to you to decide which technologies to use. To help you do that, the book provides handy checklists of what to look for in various technologies and services. You'll also find "The Bigger Picture" sidebars that help you understand a related issue. The CD that accompanies this book includes links, demo software, and templates to help you act on the advice; summaries in each section of the book list the related resources on the CD, which will save you time hunting for Web addresses and other contact information. There are also multiple-choice quizzes on the CD to use in a training or classroom environment. See Appendix E, "The CD," for detailed information on how to use the CD and its contents.

Note that the book is written largely for agents, but much of the advice equally applies to smaller brokerages (those with no IT expert on tap). Also note that because real estate is such a local business, there are often many ways to accomplish your business and technology goals. Local laws, requirements, standards, customs, and expectations also affect your decisions. As you read through this book's advice and tips, be sure to think them through within your local context. Some advice simply might not work for your specific situation, but that's fine: What really matters is that you think through your needs, understand the appropriate options, and then figure out the best way to implement them. This book will help you do just that, even when the specific technology options or how-to advice doesn't apply to your situation.

Even with that caveat, you can expect to use a lot of the hands-on advice in this book. While many real estate issues are local and specific to each individual, many are common to all agents and brokers, and even local norms and requirements are usually based on a wider issue or need.

My deepest hope is that this book will help you act smartly to make your real estate business more successful and easier to manage.

Creating the Right Work Environment

PART 1

The Right Office Tools

CHAPTER 1

IN THIS CHAPTER

ISSUES COVERED

- What kind of computer, printer, fax machine, and software do you need? And what options are available for each?

- How should you set up your office for safety and comfort?

- How do you get technical support when you need it?

The romantic notion of a home office quickly disappears when you actually work from one. That kitchen nook really isn't appropriate, what with the food splatter, constant interruptions by family members, scrunched workspace, and the awkward tangle of cables afoot.

And make no mistake about it; if you're an agent, you're working from a home office. Most brokers don't provide agents with a dedicated desk and equipment. Instead, you probably have a desk assigned to you for floor duty or other shifts. And even if you do have a dedicated space at the office, the nature of real estate is such that you'll work from home during the evenings and weekends to better serve your clients rather than head back into the office.

Your brokerage probably provides basic equipment such as copiers, fax machines, and printers. There might be computers as well, but it's easier to use your own computer that has all your files handy and is configured the way you work. So you'll likely bring your laptop computer into the brokerage and connect to the office printers via a network connection. Most agents use a laptop as their main computer whether at the office, at home, or on the road. Thus, no matter what your broker provides, you'll want the right technology for your computer and home office.

CHECKLIST

YOUR COMPUTER SYSTEM

Your basic computer hardware should include the following:

- ☐ A middle-of-the-road processor—there's no need to spend lots of money on the fastest systems

- ☐ At least 512 MB of RAM (computer memory)

- ☐ An internal hard drive with at least 60 GB capacity

- ☐ For laptops, built-in 802.11g wireless network connectivity—buy a laptop with this connectivity built-in rather than one that uses a plug-in card, because you might need that slot for other peripherals (see Chapter 2, "The Right Connections")

- ☐ Also for laptops, an extra mouse and power cord to carry with you, plus a docking station for home

- ☐ For desktop PCs, a 17-inch or larger LCD flat-panel monitor

- ☐ A backup hard drive and a CD or DVD burner drive—for external drives, make sure they use the USB 2.0 or FireWire connectors

Choosing the Right Hardware

At the center of your technology needs is a computer. Selecting a computer is a key decision, but it's just one piece of your whole technology environment. The rest of this section identifies what you should consider for your technology environment, starting with choosing a computer.

Selecting a PC

The first decision you make when choosing a PC is whether to buy one that runs the Microsoft Windows operating system or the Apple Mac OS X operating system.

Although Macintosh PCs are easier to use than Windows PCs, you'll likely choose a Windows PC because some real estate software and some MLS Web sites run only on Windows. If you don't need Windows-specific software, or if the software is Mac-compatible, by all means consider a Mac. (Microsoft also offers software called Virtual PC that runs Windows programs on a Mac, but it's slow, so make sure you test it before relying on Virtual PC as your method for having a Mac and Windows, too.)

Whether you buy a new PC or are using one you already have, I'll assume for the examples and recommendations in this book that you're using the Windows XP operating system or the Mac OS X 10.3 (Panther) or 10.4 (Tiger) operating system on it. If you have an earlier version of the operating system, please upgrade it. The newer versions have much better security features, which is critical if you use the Internet.

After you select the desired operating system, choose either a desktop PC or a laptop (also called notebook) PC. Desktop PCs are cheaper than laptops, but they're not mobile. Most agents work in several locations—your home office, the broker's office, and perhaps at open houses, coffee shops, and client sites—so a laptop usually makes the most sense.

If you decide to buy a laptop, be sure to get one that has at least a 14-inch screen and 802.11g wireless access built in. I prefer the so-called thin-and-light notebooks, which weight less than 5 pounds, because they're easier to carry and take less room in my computer bag, leaving room for other items. You should also carry an extra mouse in your computer bag (it's easier to use a mouse than the built-in trackpads) as well as an extra power supply and cord.

I also recommend a docking station for your home office, because unplugging and again plugging in all the various cables each time you leave or come back to your office is a real pain. A docking station eliminates that problem because all the cables connect to the dock, leaving just one cable for you to mess with between the laptop and the docking station. (Note that not all laptop companies make docks for all their models, so be sure to check that a dock is available for your preferred laptop before making a final decision.)

If you purchase a desktop PC, I recommend that you get at least a 17-inch LCD flat-panel monitor. LCD monitors take up less desk space and are easier on the eyes than the traditional CRT. Quality brands include Philips, Samsung, Sony, and ViewSonic.

Whether you buy a laptop or a desktop PC, you need at least 60 GB of hard drive space and 512 MB of RAM (system memory). Processor (also called CPU) speed is less critical, because modern computers handle business computing needs well. My best advice is to get a middle-of-the-pack processor, which should last you several years and provide the most bang per dollar spent.

The brand of PC you choose also makes little difference these days, since most computers are actually made by a handful of companies, no matter what brand label is on the case. You can safely buy a desktop or laptop PC from Dell Computer, Gateway, Hewlett-Packard, or Sony—or from your local computer store that builds its own PCs (these non-branded PCs are often called "white box" systems). Laptop buyers can also safely choose from Acer, Fujitsu, Lenovo (which bought IBM's ThinkPad line), Toshiba, or WinBook. (If you want a Macintosh, your only choice is Apple Computer.)

For do-it-yourselfers, the Cnet Shopper service is a great place to find online retailers for specific products. I've consistently found good deals and selections at Mac Connection and NewEgg. RAM Seeker is a great place for Mac memory, while NewEgg usually has the best deal for PC memory.

CD RESOURCE: For PCs, links to Acer, Apple, Dell, Fujitsu, Gateway, Hewlett-Packard, Lenovo, Sony, Toshiba, and WinBook. For Virtual PC, a link to Microsoft. For computer upgrades, links to Cnet Shopper, Mac Connection, NewEgg, and RAM Seeker. For LCD displays, links to Philips, Samsung, Sony, and ViewSonic.

THE BIGGER PICTURE

THE UPGRADE OPTION

Chances are you can upgrade an existing PC for less than buying a new one. For example, you might get a larger hard drive, a new motherboard with a faster processor, a more recent version of the operating system, and/or more memory.

Chain stores such as Best Buy, Circuit City, CompUSA, Office Depot, and OfficeMax sell upgrades. Or consider buying from an online retailer. Online retailers are often less costly and usually have a wider selection of upgrade options.

If you don't feel comfortable upgrading your computer yourself, CompUSA is a good place to start, because it will install the upgrade for you (for a slight charge, of course). An even better source is your local computer repair shop, where you can build a long-term relationship and get personal attention.

Selecting Additional Drives

You should also have two additional drives on your PC: a backup hard drive and a burner drive.

Agents rely tremendously on their PCs to store all their transactions, financial data, photographs, contact lists, and so forth, yet very few of us take the steps to protect that data by making a backup copy. Keep in mind that if your PC is disabled by a disk failure or a virus, the lack of a backup can hurt your business.

You should buy an external hard drive whose capacity at least matches the size of your PC's internal hard drive. Windows comes with its own basic backup utility called Backup, which is accessible via the Start menu (Start > Programs > Accessories > System Tools), but Mac OS X does not.

You might want to use full-featured backup software to get more control over your backups and file recovery than Microsoft Backup can provide. For example, Microsoft Backup can't remind you when you haven't backed up in a while or let you choose certain types of files to back up or ignore. For Windows, EMC Dantz's Retrospect or Symantec's Norton Ghost are good full-featured backup tools, while on the Mac, you could use CMS's BounceBack Express or EMC Dantz's Retrospect. The simplest solution is to use the backup software that comes with some external hard drives.

Be sure that whichever external hard drive you get that it uses either a FireWire (also called IEEE 1394) connector or a USB 2.0 connector—these are fast enough to make backup times tolerable. Note that FireWire connectors come in two shapes that are not interchangeable, so make sure that you get the right cable for the kinds of connectors you have. Similarly, there are two incompatible shapes for USB connectors, so be sure you get the right cables for your equipment. In either case, it's very possible that you'll need one connector shape for your computer, and the other shape for your hard drive.

A CD or DVD burner drive lets you create CDs for archiving files and to provide files for your clients. (I give each of my clients a CD with copies of all the papers they signed and information they received. The CD includes all their real estate information in one convenient place that doesn't take a lot of room to store.) Many PCs come with such drives, so chances are you don't need to add one.

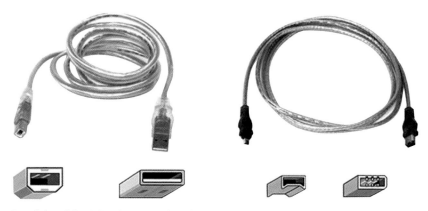

From left to right: USB A plug, USB B plug, FireWire 8-pin plug, and FireWire 6-pin plug.

Several types of burner drives are available: CD-Rs can write to a recordable CD just once, CD-RWs can write to a rewritable CD several times, DVD-Rs can write to a recordable DVD just once, and DVD-RWs can write to rewritable DVDs several times. (The "R" means you can write just once to the disc, while the "RW" means you can write repeatedly.) As with PCs, the brand matters little.

Because a CD holds about 650 MB of data, all you really need is a CD-R drive. (A DVD stores about 4.7 GB—eight times as much.) If the price difference between a CD-R drive and a CD-RW, DVD-R, or DVD-RW drive is small, get one of the more-capable drives, because you might need the extra capabilities in the future.

Disc Compatibility

Drive Type	Can Read	Can Write
Dual-layer DVD-RW	CD-ROM, CD-R, CD-RW, DVD-ROM, DVD-R, DVD-RW, dual-layer DVD-R, dual-layer DVD-RW	CD-R, CD-RW, DVD-R, DVD-RW, dual-layer DVD-R, dual-layer DVD-RW
DVD-RW	CD-ROM, CD-R, CD-RW, DVD-ROM, DVD-R, DVD-RW	0CD-R, CD-RW, DVD-R, DVD-RW
DVD-R	CD-ROM, CD-R, CD-RW, DVD-ROM, DVD-R, DVD-RW	CD-R, CD-RW, DVD-R, DVD-RW
DVD-ROM	CD-ROM, CD-R, CD-RW, DVD-ROM, DVD-R, DVD-RW	none
CD-RW	CD-ROM, CD-R, CD-RW	CD-R, CD-RW
CD-R	CD-ROM, CD-R, CD-RW	CD-R
CD-ROM	CD-ROM, CD-R, CD-RW	none

Windows and the Mac OS typically come with basic software to write files to a CD, but if you want to create more custom discs, such as those that work equally well on Windows and Mac OS X, you'll need to purchase CD burning software. For Windows, two good choices are Nero's Nero and Roxio's Easy Media Creator. For the Mac, Roxio's Toast is the gold standard.

 CD RESOURCE: For backup software, links to CMS, EMC Dantz, and Symantec. For burning software, links to Nero and Roxio.

Faxing, Printing, Scanning, and Copying

Real estate agents work with a lot of paper—tons of it. That's why you want fast, high-quality output at your home office. I recommend you purchase a multifunction device that can print, copy, scan, and send and receive faxes. Not only does a multifunction device save you desk space, it will save you money as well. A multifunction device typically costs less than buying a separate device for each of the four essential functions.

A flatbed model should have a glass window on which you can lay papers to be scanned and copied. The device should have an automatic document feeder as well, so you can feed in a stack of disclosures or other papers rather than scanning each page individually.

Multifunction devices—like printers—come in two basic forms: inkjet and laser. Inkjet printers are slow and cheap initially, and they print in color. But the cost of ink for a color inkjet really adds up over time. A laser printer (including variants such as LED printers) is much faster and costs less to operate over time but usually only prints in black and white.

If you really need color, you can get a color laser printer, but as of early 2006, there are no color laser multifunction devices that do all four tasks equally well. Instead, consider getting an inexpensive color inkjet printer for your color jobs (such as open-house flyers) in addition to your workhorse, black-and-white multifunction device.

As inkjet printer prices have dropped, so has quality, so don't expect many models to last more than a couple years. Also look for a model that uses separate ink cartridges for each color. With an all-in-one cartridge, you end up throwing away unused ink each time you replace the cartridge—considering how expensive ink has become, you don't want to do that.

You can get a decent low-cost inkjet from Canon or Epson. Note that Hewlett-Packard and Lexmark printers have had a mix of good and bad quality ratings for both output and reliability in recent years.

My favorite multifunction device by far is the Brother MFC-8840DN, which also works on a network of multiple computers, so you can share it with family members or, in a brokerage, with office mates and staff. Plus it can do two-sided (duplex) printing automatically and scan and print legal-size (8.5×14-inch) sheets. There's a cheaper version, the Brother 8840D, if you don't need network connectivity. A second choice would be the Hewlett-Packard LaserJet 3380, for which you can buy a network interface if needed. (Note that the HP 3380 does not do automatic two-sided printing.)

The Brother MFC-8840DN multifunction device is my favorite tool for printing, faxing, scanning, and copying.

Another great feature of Brother's mutifunction devices is that they include ScanSoft's PaperPort software, which lets you scan in a set of documents from the device's document feeder and automatically create a PDF file of the entire document. (The Portable Document Format, or PDF, is a very handy format for transmitting documents electronically, since anyone can get the software to read and print these files for free, plus this software now comes with most Web browsers.) As you'll see in Chapter 9 "Communicating Better with Clients," providing documents in the PDF electronic format can greatly improve your service to buyers and sellers. (If you have a multifunction device or scanner with a document feeder, you might want to buy PaperPort software to add the automatic PDF-creation capability. Although PaperPort comes bundled with several scanners and multifunction devices, it's also available separately. You can also directly scan documents if you own Adobe's Acrobat Professional software, as Chapter 3, "Working with Electronic Media" explains.)

*CD RESOURCE: **For multifunction devices and printers, links to Brother, Canon, Epson, and Hewlett-Packard. For PDF creation software, links to Adobe and ScanSoft.***

Selecting a Digital Camera

An indispensable tool for any real estate agent is a digital camera. With it, you can easily add photos to your listing materials as well as show buyers what prospective homes look like when you are previewing properties for them. I keep mine in my car's glove compartment, along with a spare battery.

Although many cell phones now come with built-in cameras, use a separate digital camera. The image quality is much better, and you don't need a special cell service plan to access the pictures.

The price range of digital cameras varies greatly and is essentially based on three factors: memory storage, image resolution, and lens quality. I recommend using a moderate quality camera because top-notch resolution just isn't necessary for most real estate work. Most of your real estate images are typically posted on the Web, displayed on a low-resolution PC, or printed to create flyers with photos typically just a few inches in size. A camera with an image resolution of 3 to 4 megapixels—the entry level—is just fine. If you plan to publish the photos in a glossy real estate magazine or on photo-quality flyers (typically for high-end homes), you'll need a much higher resolution—in the 7-megapixel range. But at that quality level, you'll probably want a professional photographer to stage the pictures and photograph them, not do it yourself.

Cameras are personal devices, so look at several models to see how well they fit your hand, how easy the controls are to use, and how well you can see what you are photographing. The two most common camera types are SLRs—which look like a 35mm camera—and pocket cameras. The SLRs usually have better lenses as well as a preview LCD and a viewfinder, but they're bigger and heavier than the pocket type. The pocket format is easy to carry in a purse or fit in a glove compartment and is lighter, although the smaller, cheaper lens usually restricts zoom settings and image quality for close-ups.

Also look into the type of memory card used to be sure it is a common type (CompactFlash and Secure Digital are the most common, and most Sony equipment supports Memory Stick) and check the cost of the batteries. You'll likely want an extra battery for the road.

There are many good manufacturers of digital cameras—Canon, Casio, Fujifilm, Kodak, Leica, Nikon, Olympus, Panasonic, Pentax, and Sony—so look less for the brand than for the features you need at the price you're willing to pay. (However, do note that the Canon cameras consistently come out top in magazine reviews.)

To make digital cameras easier to use, get a memory card reader for your PC. Although most cameras come with a USB cable you can connect directly to a PC, you usually need to install the connectivity and image-viewing software that comes with them before you physically connect the camera. (That's so the PC has the right resources to connect and communicate with the camera when it is physically connected via the cable.) On a desktop PC, the USB jacks to download your images from your camera to your PC are usually at the back of the PC, making them difficult to access.

Memory card readers help solve these connection problems, since they don't usually require special software to read the cards, and on desktop PCs, they let you place the reader in a convenient location. External memory card readers typically plug into a USB port. There are also models that go inside your computer's case that connect to the internal USB connector. (Note that you can't install an internal reader on a Mac.) Either way, get a reader model that supports multiple types of cards so you can easily access photos from other people's digital cameras' memory cards as well as your own.

Examples of internal (top) and external memory card readers. The external models come in all sorts of shapes, colors, and sizes.

Memory card readers tend to be made by small companies you probably haven't heard of (two exceptions are Adaptec, which makes a range of storage products, and Belkin, which also makes computer cables and wireless adapters), so it's best to look for card readers at your local computer store or at an online retailer such as NewEgg.

CD RESOURCE: For cameras, links to Canon, Casio, Fujifilm, Kodak, Leica, Nikon, Olympus, Panasonic, Pentax, and Sony. For card readers, links to Adaptec, Belkin, and NewEgg.

CHECKLIST

YOUR SOFTWARE

When shopping for software, be sure to consider the following types of programs. In some cases, you might prefer to hire a specialist to do certain tasks for you:

- Office productivity—word processor, spreadsheet, and presentations programs
- Basic system utilities—anti-virus, antispyware, backup, and compression programs
- Page layout and PDF creation and editing programs
- Photo retouching or image-editing program, and perhaps illustration, video, and/or animation software
- E-mail client and Web client software
- Contacts and schedule manager—these also handle to-do lists and calendars
- Bulk e-mail delivery program
- Web creation and editing software
- Accounting and tax software
- Real estate forms software
- CD creation software

Choosing the Right Software

With the hardware in place, let's turn our attention to the software that runs on it. After all, software is what does the actual work on your computer, from checking e-mail to creating flyers.

There are several classes of software you should consider having. Unlike your hardware choices, your software choices are usually more flexible. For example, rather than lay out your own business cards or flyers, you might hire a graphic artist to do so. Or you might hire someone to design and perhaps maintain your Web site. So as you go through my software recommendations, always keep in mind the tasks you want to do yourself and the tasks you're willing to pay someone else to do. In some cases, you can hire someone to create the basic materials—such as a flyer template or Web site—and then handle modifications and updates yourself. But it's a very rare agent who does it all.

When you're shopping for software, you'll find that prices are pretty much the same wherever you go, although you'll find that certain categories of software—particularly system utilities—regularly go on sale or offer rebates. A few online sites—Atomic Park Software and NewEgg, most notably—often have discounts on major software programs. So do shop around.

CD RESOURCE: For online software vendors, links to Atomic Park Software and NewEgg.

Selecting Office Productivity Software

Perhaps the most widely used software is office productivity software. Most people know it in the form of Microsoft Office, which includes the Word word processor, Excel spreadsheet, and PowerPoint presentation programs. A variation of Microsoft's suite also includes the Publisher page layout tool. All the Office suites include Microsoft's Outlook, a combination e-mail client, schedule manager, and contacts manager. (On the Mac, Outlook is called Entourage.)

There are competing programs such as Corel WordPerfect Office for Windows and AppleWorks or iWork for Mac. (Note that iWork has no spreadsheet program.) But most people use

Microsoft Office applications, so it's usually easier for you to use them as well. Plus, Office comes installed on most new PCs, so you likely already own it.

You use office productivity software mainly to create letters and other documents such as seller presentations. You'll most often use a word processor (like Microsoft Word), but sometimes you might want to use presentation software (such as Microsoft PowerPoint) to create a more dynamic presentation to give to your potential clients. Also part of an office productivity suite is a spreadsheet (like Microsoft Excel), which is very handy for doing quick budgets and other calculations, whether for yourself or your clients.

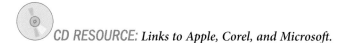 **CD RESOURCE:** *Links to Apple, Corel, and Microsoft.*

Selecting System Utilities

There are certain software tools everyone with a computer should have, yet they're easy to overlook because they don't help you produce specific items like flyers or presentations. System utilities typically keep your system running smoothly and help you manage files more easily.

In today's Internet-connected world, PC users face an insidious threat of malicious software, or "malware," that includes viruses, adware, spyware, Trojan horses, worms, and other exotic varieties. Some of these threats monitor your actions and deliver only certain ads based on the Web sites you visit, while others destroy your data, use your PC as a virus-spreading engine, or capture your financial and other private records and send them on to thieves.

You need at least one program that protects your computer from viruses and other malware, and make sure this software is set to run continuously to intercept any threats. In fact, you should really have a couple of programs, because no single program can catch everything. (This is particularly true on Windows, which malware writers target. The Mac is a safer venue for computing because its small market share makes malware authors less interested in writing their destructive software.)

Your antivirus and antispyware programs continuously monitor your system. On a Windows PC, look for the programs' icons in the Taskbar (the row of icons that also contains the Start button). If you don't recognize the icons shown, using your mouse, hover over the icon to display a pop-up description.

Norton Antivirus and the full SystemWorks suite from Symantec are the best known protection tools. Unfortunately their popularity has also led to malware authors figuring out ways to disable their protection when attacking your system. So I recommend that you don't use Norton Antivirus but instead use an alternative tool like McAfee's Internet Security Suite or Avanquest/VCom's well-regarded Fix-It Utilities for Windows, or Intego's Virus Barrier X for Mac. (It's perfectly fine to use Symantec's other utilities, such as Norton Disk Doctor.)

Not all protection tools safeguard your PC from all forms of malware. For example, not all tools yet deal with a newer type of threat called spyware. So you may need a separate tool to detect and eliminate spyware. For Windows, you should consider Lavasoft's Ad-Aware, Microsoft's Windows Defender, PC Tools' Spyware Doctor, Trend Micro's Anti-Spyware, or Webroot's Spy Sweeper. (Note that Fix-It Utilities also includes spyware protection along with its virus protection.) For Mac OS X, the only real option is Intego's NetBarrier X3. Even if your protection software blocks spyware, it's usually a good idea to get a separate antispyware program anyhow, as an added layer of security.

As mentioned earlier, you should routinely back up your data, using a built-in tool such as Microsoft Backup or a third-party tool such as EMC Dantz's Retrospect or Symantec's Norton Ghost for Windows, or CMS's BounceBack Express, EMC Dantz's Retrospect, or Intego's Personal Backup for Mac OS X.

A third type of utility that compresses and decompresses files is especially helpful when you're downloading or e-mailing large files. Two popular compression formats in use are Zip and StuffIt. Zip compression is used on both Windows and Mac OS X PCs, while StuffIt compression is used almost exclusively on the Mac. WinZip's WinZip for Windows handles Zip files, and Allume Systems' StuffIt software handles both Zip and StuffIt files, with versions for both Windows (called ZipMagic) and Mac OS X (called StuffIt).

CD RESOURCE: For antivirus and antispyware software, links to Avanquest/VCom, Intego, Lavasoft, McAfee, Microsoft, PC Tools, Symantec, Trend Micro, and Webroot. For compression software, links to Allume Systems and WinZip. For backup software, links to CMS, EMC Dantz, Intego, and Symantec.

Selecting Page Layout Software

Many people use Microsoft Word, WordPerfect, AppleWorks, or iWorks Pages to lay out simple flyers and documents. Each can do the job, and if your needs are simple, go ahead and use any of these programs. But to produce professional-looking flyers or marketing materials—open-house flyers, neighborhood mailings, business cards, listing presentations, stationery, and so on—you need a real page layout program, or you need to hire a graphic artist who uses one.

You can use Microsoft Publisher, a Windows-only page layout tool, for a whole range of documents without knowing a lot about design. Professional publishers typically use Adobe Systems' InDesign or, less and less frequently, Quark's QuarkXPress, both of which come in Windows and Mac OS X versions. Although harder to learn, they can do much more than Publisher. InDesign, for example, can help you assemble electronic flyers that include slide shows or movies to help you create a virtual-tour flyer.

You can create flyers in several programs. For example, the left flyer was created in Microsoft Word, and it's perfectly serviceable. The right flyer was created in InDesign, which allowed more column choices, more control over image placement and text wrap, and more control over font and style choices.

As you might expect, the professional tools are much costlier, although Adobe sells the Creative Suite, which includes Photoshop image editing, Illustrator illustration, and InDesign page layout programs, for a discounted price.

No matter which tool you use to create your documents, you'll need a good selection of fonts to create a distinctive identity and showcase your higher-quality work. The fonts that come installed on Windows and Mac OS X are so widely used that they carry little design impact. But many sources for fonts are available, including Adobe, Agfa Monotype, FontSite, International Typeface Corp. (ITC), and MyFonts.

CD RESOURCE: For page layout software, links to Adobe, Microsoft, and Quark. For fonts, links to Adobe, Agfa Monotype, FontSite, International Typeface Corp. (ITC), and MyFonts.

Selecting PDF Creation Software

A related type of software handles PDF creation and editing. PDF is a common format used to display documents electronically. It's practically a standard. Anyone can open these documents and view or print them using the free Adobe Reader software. But just reading and printing PDF files is only part of what you'll need. You should also be able to edit and create PDF files.

Some programs, such as Adobe's Creative Suite applications and QuarkXPress, let you create PDF documents from within the program, but most applications do not. Using Adobe's Acrobat Professional software or Docudesk's DeskPDF software, you can create PDF documents from almost any Windows or Macintosh program, by simply "printing" your file to PDF rather than to an actual printer. And as mentioned earlier in this chapter, software such as Adobe's Acrobat Professional and ScanSoft's PaperPort lets you automatically convert documents scanned in from a scanner or multifunction device to the PDF format.

To edit PDF files, you'll want to use Acrobat Professional or Docudesk DeskPDF Pro as well. Note that editing PDFs is not the same as editing other documents: You're limited to changing text line by line, and you can't move or delete items on the page. Instead, you can only fix small errors or make small changes to an existing PDF document. (Chapter 3 covers techniques for creating and editing PDFs in more depth.)

For example, the MLS system I use lets me create PDF flyers from listings in its database. So I create PDFs from the MLS for my office's listings so I can include links to them on my Web site. Because I am not the seller's agent for these listings, I need to edit the MLS flyers slightly. Using Acrobat Professional, I add "buyer's agent" after my name, so it's clear what my role is. I also edit the contact information to indicate that agents and buyers with agents should contact the main office—after all, the whole point of publicizing these office listings is to find prospective buyer clients. In addition, it's a waste of my time and against NAR rules for me to try to answer questions from other agents or from buyers who already have agents, since I'm not the seller's agent.

Acrobat also lets you attach electronic sticky notes for comments. I like to use this feature to make notes on disclosures I provide to clients. Using the sticky notes, I can explain what confusing text might mean or highlight where they need to sign or initial a page.

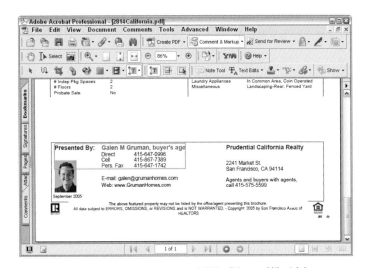

A PDF editing tool like Adobe Acrobat Professional lets you make small changes to PDF documents. Here, I'm adding "buyer's agent" to my name in the flyer produced through my MLS system.

CD RESOURCE: For PDF software, links to Adobe, Docudesk, and ScanSoft.

Selecting Image Editing Software

When working with digital images—typically, photos of houses and their interiors for properties you're listing—it quickly becomes apparent that not all photos look that great. Sometimes, you'll need to reshoot a bad photo, but in some cases you can fix it on your computer. That's where image editing and photo retouching software comes in.

Many digital cameras come with photo retouching software, such as Adobe's Photoshop Elements (based on Photoshop but designed for nonprofessionals), Corel's Paint Shop Pro, Google's Picasa, Microsoft's Digital Imaging Suite, Roxio's PhotoSuite, or the camera maker's own software. (Of these programs, only Photoshop Elements comes in a Mac OS X version, though Apple's iPhoto for Mac also includes photo retouching capabilities.) You can also buy photo retouching software separately.

Photo retouching software lets you lighten, darken, change contrast, straighten, rotate, crop (cut out the parts you don't want), and adjust color balance for photos. Some software also lets you "stitch" together multiple images to create a panorama or create a slide show from multiple pictures.

To do more than retouching, you'll want a professional image editor such as Adobe Photoshop (for Windows and Mac OS X), Apple Aperture (for Mac OS X only), or Corel Photo-Paint (part of the Windows-only CorelDraw suite). A professional image editor gives you finer control over your images' resolution, size, and color balance as well as sophisticated editing features such as creating multilayer images. But, honestly, these features are overkill for most agents. Most of us just need a photo retoucher to brighten dark pictures, correct color imbalances, and crop out the neighbor's tree, not a professional image editor.

CD RESOURCE: *For photo retouching and image editing software, links to Adobe, Apple, Corel, Google, Microsoft, and Roxio.*

Selecting E-Mail Client and Web Client Software

A big part of being an agent is staying in touch—with clients, with other agents, and with the MLS's data. That's why every agent needs an e-mail account and needs to check it at least daily. You also need Web access to view the local MLS and other resource sites.

Today's computers come with built-in e-mail client software and Web browser software. Windows PCs typically have Microsoft's Outlook (or Outlook Express) e-mail client and Internet Explorer Web browser installed, while most Macs come with Apple's Mail e-mail client and Safari Web browser.

E-mail and Web client programs are all similar, although their interface differences do tend to make people love or hate individual ones. For example, in Windows, I find Microsoft's Outlook e-mail client too complex, because of its other features such as contact management, so I use the free Outlook Express instead. On the Mac, I find Apple's Mail is too simplistic, so I use Microsoft's Entourage instead. Other choices include Mozilla's Thunderbird and Netscape's Messenger, both of which have Windows and Mac versions.

For Web clients, you will need Internet Explorer on your Windows PC or Mac, because there are some sites—including many MLS sites—that use Microsoft-specific technology and thus require you to use this specific browser. (And many of these sites require that you access them from Windows.)

Internet Explorer is a frequent target of virus and spyware attacks, so using Internet Explorer extensively could compromise your computer's security—particularly on a Windows PC. Many people instead use an alternative such as Mozilla's Firefox, Opera's Opera, or Netscape's Browser, all of which have both Windows and Mac versions. (I prefer Firefox.) If you use these programs, you'd still use Internet Explorer occasionally, when visiting sites that only work with Internet Explorer.

CD RESOURCE: *For e-mail and Web clients, links to Apple, Microsoft, Mozilla, Netscape, and Opera.*

FAX OPTIONS

You might wonder why there's no category for fax software in this chapter. The reason is that a multi-function device can handle your faxes for you; it even lets you fax directly from applications like Microsoft Word, as long as your PC is connected to the device. Also, Windows and Mac OS X come with built-in fax software to send or receive faxes on your PC computer if you are connected to a phone line. You just choose the fax option when printing.

There are services you can subscribe to that provide a virtual fax: You get a phone number that when dialed converts the incoming fax into an image file that is e-mailed to you for printing. Some of these services also let you fax documents to your regular office phone number to convert them to PDF files. This is usually part of the phone and answering service your broker sets up at the office for all agents. The benefit of these virtual fax services is that you can receive faxes anytime you have an Internet connection. But the downside is that the files are fairly large and require a high-speed connection to access the files in most cases. Plus, these faxes take a fairly long time to print, and the printouts are usually not as readable as the files you generate from a multifunction printer or scanner using the Adobe Acrobat Professional or ScanSoft PaperPort software recommended earlier in this chapter.

These virtual fax services are fine as a backup service if you can't get to your home office or the broker's office. My broker provides such a service, called MongoFax, as part of the monthly desk fees. Check to see if yours does as well.

THE BIGGER PICTURE

E-MAIL ACCOUNT TECHNIQUES

Many of us have both personal and professional e-mail accounts to keep our private and business lives separate.

Most e-mail clients let you manage multiple e-mail accounts from one computer, placing messages in separate folders and offering the ability to reply from the correct account (based on the account the message was sent to).

I like having the ability to respond to my e-mails no matter which e-mail address they were sent to, but sometimes it's hard to manage. To be efficient, you need to set up folders and message rules properly to keep the various e-mails separate.

Consider using two e-mail clients: one for your professional e-mail and one for your personal e-mail. By using two programs, you'll never confuse the two types of messages.

You also might want to use a free e-mail account service such as Google Gmail, Microsoft MSN Hotmail, or Yahoo Mail as a third account. This way, you could use the service for your online shopping, newsletter subscriptions, and other transactions, so only one address becomes the address spammers discover, leaving your private and professional e-mail addresses less likely to be polluted with come-ons for porn, mortgage loans, low-cost software, and other dubious spam. And when the free account gets overloaded with spam, close it and open a new one.

Selecting Contact and Schedule Management Software

Some people are very organized. The rest of us are not. A big challenge for any agent is tracking all your contacts, appointments, and to-do items, especially because many contacts are specific to a particular transaction, while others are contacts you'll talk to repeatedly.

The best way to manage contacts, appointments, and to-do items is difficult for me to suggest, because everyone has such personal approaches to this kind of work. But there are plenty of tools available—including paper-based standby tools like Rolodexes, appointment books, file folders, and notepads—to use after you figure out your own system.

As mentioned earlier, Microsoft Outlook (and its Mac counterpart Entourage) comes with tools to schedule appointments, get alerts so you don't miss them, track to-do items, and manage contacts. An advantage to Outlook's integrated approach is that your phone, e-mail, and mailing-address contact information can be in one place, so you don't have to maintain a separate e-mail directory from your phone directory.

If you do use Outlook, consider a real estate-specific add-in like Eurekaware's Real Estate Contact Manager, which adds fields to help you track current prospects, past clients, and so forth within Outlook.

Some people—especially those with lots of sales experience—prefer full-blown contact management systems such as Sage Software's Act for Windows and Now Software's Now Up-to-Date and Contact suite for Windows and Mac OS X. The newest version (8) of FileMaker's FileMaker database for Windows and Mac OS X also adds such capabilities.

For me, a simple contact manager and scheduler work best. I use a Handspring Visor (a version of the well-known Palm Pilot)—a portable organizer that holds schedule and contact information—to maintain my appointments list and frequently called numbers. This device comes with a desktop program that lets me access the same information on my computer, so whether I'm at my office or in my car, I have the same information available. (Outlook lets you accomplish this as well, if you use a Microsoft-compatible organizer device such as the Hewlett-Packard iPaq.) I store transaction-specific information in client folders (both paper and on my computer), keeping a notepad of contacts in my car. Using this strategy, I can keep my contacts list manageable, so only long-term contacts are in my organizer.

The key is to use your preferred system for managing your information, and then figure out where to keep it. Knowing what works best for you will guide you toward the technology (paper and/or electronic) you need.

CD RESOURCE: For contact and schedule managers, trial software from Eurekaware is on the CD, as well as links to Eurekaware, FileMaker, Microsoft, Now Software, Palm, and Sage. For handheld organizers, links to Hewlett-Packard and Palm.

Selecting Bulk E-Mail and Campaign Management Software

If you have a large client base or a large farm (a neighborhood or other area in which you focus to cultivate clients), you probably send regular postcards, letters, holiday cards, or other materials to advertise your services and remind past clients that you're still in business to assist them and their referrals.

But mailing printed materials is expensive. To lower your costs, you can stay in touch with prospects and clients for much less via e-mail if you use bulk e-mail software. This software lets you create e-mail messages—complete with graphics, essentially as a small Web page—and send them to all your contacts. (Chapter 5, "Online Marketing Techniques," explains how you can manage campaigns, including how to abide by recent laws meant to protect recipients from spam.)

MANAGING CAMPAIGNS FOR LESS

In addition to sending individual e-mails, you might want to manage campaigns. You can set up e-mails to be sent based on events, such as a "How is your new home?" message a month after escrow closes or an "I just wanted to touch base" e-mail a week after a potential client signs up on your Web site.

Campaign management systems such as FNIS's AgentOffice and Top Producer Software's Top Producer are expensive, and you need a lot of clients to justify their cost.

A campaign system's goal is admirable—but you can accomplish the same thing by using your scheduling software to remind you when it's time to send your messages. You can also use a bulk e-mail program to send your preformatted messages when it's time to do so. And version 8 of the FileMaker database lets you set up bulk e-mail delivery based on contacts' characteristics and schedules of your choosing.

THE BIGGER PICTURE

If you've attended free technology seminars sponsored by training companies, you've probably been pitched some expensive campaign management software or subscription service. Maybe these make sense for a medium to large brokerage that sends messages on behalf of all its agents, but the software or services I've seen are overkill for individual agents and small brokers.

If your client e-mail list is small, you can use your e-mail software to send bulk messages, but bulk e-mail software makes more sense. Bulk e-mail software lets you manage your client lists by categories, and it allows you to personalize your messages (such as insert their names in the "Dear so-and-so" lines).

One of the easiest to use—and affordable—bulk e-mail programs is G-Lock Software's EasyMail Pro. Other programs aimed at sole proprietors and small offices include AtomPark Software's Atomic Mail Sender and LmhSoft's e-Campaigner.

CD RESOURCE: For bulk e-mail software, links to AtomPark, G-Lock, and LmhSoft. For campaign management software, links to FileMaker, FNIS, and Top Producer.

Selecting Web Creation and Editing Software

Having your own Web site is one of the most powerful marketing efforts you can make, as Chapter 4, "Effective Web Sites" explains. But laying out Web pages and linking them together is not a simple task, especially if you aren't a geek.

Although many brokers give you your own page on their site, you can't showcase your skills, listings, or services your way. That's why you'll still want your own Web site.

One option is to create your Web site's pages yourself, using Web creation software. This gives you complete control over how your site's content is arranged and presented.

Or you could subscribe to a Web service that creates your site's pages automatically based on templates and that lets you use menus and dialog boxes to update the pages without actually working with the underlying HTML code. (The Hypertext Markup Language, or HTML, is the programming language in

WEB SITE REQUIREMENTS

To have a Web site, you need more than the software to create it. You need a place to put it and a way to put it there.

The first step to creating your Web site is getting your domain, or Universal Resource Locator (URL). That's your Web address. Several companies, called Web registrars, can register a domain (after checking to see if it's available). Two that I like are GoDaddy and NTT Verio, both of which have good prices and clear interfaces. You can register a domain for just $10 per year if you pay in advance for several years.

The next step is to get a space on the Web for your Web pages. A company called a Web host provides this space on its servers and then makes sure those servers are connected to the Internet. When someone types in your URL, they'll see your pages on the Web host's server. There are hundreds of Web hosts out there, and many of the cheap ones provide terrible service. I've had better luck with mid-priced Web hosts like Pair Networks that are still pretty affordable ($15 per month or so).

Finally, you need a way to transfer the Web page files you created from your computer to the Web host. The Web host usually has transfer capability built into its Web site (using something called a control panel), but it's easier to use a file-transfer protocol (FTP) program like Fetch on the Mac or Ipswitch's WS_FTP Pro on Windows because they have easy-to-use interfaces. (If you use Microsoft FrontPage, FTP is built in, but you do have to make sure your Web host enables FrontPage compatibility.)

I recommend that you also set up an e-mail account that uses the same domain name as your Web site, to provide a consistent name for clients. For example, my Web site is www.grumanhomes.com, and my email address is galen@grumanhomes.com.) Note that the URL is the whole Web address, such as www.grumanhomes.com, while the domain name is the part of the Web address after the www., as well as the part of your e-mail address after the @ symbol, such as grumanhomes.com.

which Web pages are written. Web browsers then use that code to produce what you see on the screen, which is why Web pages often look slightly different from one computer to the next.)

Or you could hire a Web designer to create a Web site for you, which either you or he maintains (such as updating listings).

There are pros and cons to each option, which boil down to three factors: required knowledge, time and/or money spent, and control over the end result.

If you create and/or maintain your own Web site, you'll need HTML editing software to create and edit the pages. Such software typically gives you a layout view—where you can work on pages visually much like you would in a word processor or page layout program—and a code view, where you can edit the actual HTML code.

If you're new to Web design, consider Microsoft's FrontPage, a Windows-only program that does a good job of shielding you from the HTML code, so you can fairly easily create a decent-quality Web site and maintain it without excessive effort. If you're more experienced—or adventurous—get a full-blown HTML editor such as Adobe's GoLive or, my favorite, Adobe's Macromedia Dreamweaver. Both programs require more skill, but you can make much better sites if you're willing to learn the software.

You'll also need an image editor, which I covered earlier in this chapter, to work on the images you place on your Web site. (Chapter 3 provides tips on using Web creation and image editing software.)

CD RESOURCE: For Web creation and editing software, links to Adobe and Microsoft. For file transfer, links to Fetch and Ipswitch. For domain registration, links to GoDaddy and NTT Verio. For Web hosting, a link to Pair Networks.

Selecting Accounting and Tax Software

When considering the tools you'll need as an agent or broker, it's easy to overlook the tools necessary to manage your business. Many of us dislike managing money, such as tracking costs and calculating taxes. But even if you use an accountant to do the nitty-gritty work, you should have some method of tracking your income and expenses so your accountant has accurate information. If you're more proactive in managing your finances, you might find you can do more with your money, such as saving more in tax-deferred retirement accounts or setting money aside for vacations or your own property investments.

There are three basic ways to manage your finances: using paper, using a spreadsheet program, or using accounting software.

Accounting software, such as Intuit's QuickBooks and Sage Software's Peachtree Accounting, are probably overkill for individual agents, although such an application might make a lot of sense for small-to-medium brokerages.

For individuals, a program like Intuit's Quicken or Microsoft's Money is probably more appropriate. And if you have rental properties, consider Intuit's Quicken Rental Property Manager. But some users have found that the data entry is so time-consuming that they get out of the habit of keeping their records up to date, making the software useless.

However, you track your income and expenses, so keep in mind that you also need to manage your taxes. Most agents are self-employed independent contractors and must pay quarterly taxes. Yet none of the tax programs, such as Intuit's TurboTax or H&R Block's TaxCut, calculate quarterly taxes; they're just designed to figure your taxes at the end of the year. Remember, if you underpay your quarterly taxes in any quarter, you'll likely owe a penalty. A good accountant can figure your quarterly taxes for you (or you can try to use the IRS's complicated forms), but that means for most of each quarter you won't really know how much to set aside for your taxes.

One way to track your expenses and your estimated taxes as the year progresses is to use a spreadsheet. If you're not a spreadsheet jockey, you can use a spreadsheet template for Microsoft Excel such as the Zango Group's ZangoTaxQ.

CD RESOURCE: For financial management software, trial software from the Zango Group, as well as links to H&R Block, Intuit, Microsoft, Sage Software, and the Zango Group. For tax information, links to relevant IRS Web pages and publications.

Selecting Real Estate Forms Software

In many parts of the country, agents can use Realfast's Realfast or RE FormsNet's Zipforms software to complete all transaction forms on their PC. (In California, the Zipforms software is called Winforms.) Typically, the state or local Realtors association has contracted with one of these two companies to provide its forms, so you usually do not have a choice.

The software uses the standard transaction forms for various states and local Realtor associations. Using your computer and the software, you fill out all the forms for each transaction, ensuring a clean copy for your client to read and sign with no hard-to-read handwriting to confuse matters. You never have to worry about not having enough forms. Plus you always have an electronic copy if you need to print extra copies later. (Zipforms has an option to complete transactions over the Internet, which is handy if you don't happen to be at a computer with the Zipforms software installed.) The only flaw with Realfast and Zipforms is that they do not work on the Macintosh, even over the Internet.

Some local associations might use forms that are not available via Realfast or Zipforms. However, they may be available directly from the local association in PDF or other computerized format, so be sure to ask. And TrueForms sells individual forms for several states in electronic format for use by agents, sellers, and buyers. Depending on how savvy the form's creator was, you can fill in the blanks onscreen and print some of the PDF forms, but some forms only let you print them out for completion by hand.

Brokers and agents are so used to working with the printed forms that often no one bothers to mention that electronic versions are available.

If your real estate business includes property management and rentals, there are a few places you can get standard lease and related forms in electronic format. These include Kaktus Productions, Socrates, and local apartment owner associations. A good place to start is with the Apartment Owners Association, which can direct you to any local chapters.

Remember: There are many state and local laws that these forms might not address. Because they are typically written for the entire country, make sure you understand all the local requirements and have a local real estate attorney make all the required adjustments. If there is a local landlords or apartment owners association in your area, the chances are excellent that it has the localized versions of the forms you need, created by its lawyers, will be available.

CD RESOURCE: *For real estate forms, links to Realfast, TrueForms. Winforms, and Zipforms. For rental property forms, links to the Apartment Owners Association, Kaktus, and Socrates.*

Selecting CD Creation Software

It's a good idea to use recordable or rewritable CDs or DVDs for archiving transactions and disclosures. You also might want to create CD "flyers" to use at open houses or for prospective buyers who stop by your office. These CDs could contain a PDF flyer, video tour, photos, disclosure documents, and/or other materials.

Both Windows and Mac OS X let you write ("burn") CDs by copying files and folders onto them. If you want more control, you should consider using disc-creation software. This type of software helps you create and edit music and video, as well as produce discs that work on both Windows and Macintosh PCs. In Windows, two good choices are Nero's Nero and Roxio's Easy Media Creator. For the Mac, Roxio's Toast is the gold standard.

CD RESOURCE: For burning software, links to Nero and Roxio.

Making Your Home Office Safe and Comfortable

Repetitive stress injuries (RSIs) such as carpal tunnel syndrome and tennis elbow are the number one causes of disability claims, but most people have no idea that RSIs exist or what to do about them. Office workers—including people who work from their home offices—are particularly susceptible to damaging their arms and shoulders because of poor ergonomics in their workplaces. We real estate agents may be especially susceptible because we often work in several locations, including our brokers' offices where desks and computers are set up for "one size fits all" and at home where we likely have carved out a space for a desk and computer equipment.

Raising a laptop on a platform brings its screen to a comfortable viewing level. Using an external keyboard and mouse helps keep them at comfortable levels as well. (And the platform that raises the laptop doubles as storage for things like staplers and tape).

Be sure to seriously think through the following considerations when setting up your home office:

Good posture is essential for avoiding repetitive stress injuries. Try sitting in the "good table manners" posture shown in the screenshot to minimize stress on your body.

- **Correct body posture:** Correct posture is very important, as incorrect posture leads to extra strain on the body, which leads to injuries that can limit or destroy your ability to type, write, drive, or even brush your teeth. You should sit in "good table manners" posture: back straight, arms at your side, forearms and hands parallel to the floor, thighs parallel to the floor, lower legs straight down (knees at a 90-degree angle), and feet flat on the floor. Adjust the height of your chair and desk or table to ensure this posture. (You might feel uncomfortable at first, but after you let your body adjust for a few days, the potentially harmful leaning-forward posture most of us have will instead feel wrong.) You might want to get a chair that lets you adjust the height of the arm rests and distance from the seat, seat height and tilt, seat back angle, and lumbar support.

- **Correct head posture:** When working on the computer, you should face straight ahead and not angle your neck down or up to get a better view of the screen. If you draw an imaginary line horizontally a third of the way down from the top of your screen, that line should be at the same elevation as your eyes when looking straight ahead. You might need to raise your monitor to make this work correctly. If you use your laptop's screen, consider raising the entire laptop and plugging in a separate keyboard and mouse so you can type easily without craning your neck to see what you are doing.

- **Good lighting:** You need to have sufficient light so you are not straining to see. Ideally, the light is indirect, coming through a translucent window shade, for example, or from an overhead light with a diffuser such as a nontransparent glass globe or plate. You do not want light shining directly on your monitor, because that causes glare that in turn results in eye strain.

- **Tools within reach:** Make sure the tools you use regularly are within easy reach, or that you can easily move them into reach while working.

Arrange frequently used items in your workspace so they are within easy reach to minimize arm strain. Also, make sure your monitor is at eye level, so you don't strain your neck. "Eye level" means just that: if you're looking straight ahead, your eyes should be level with an imaginary line a third of the way down from the top of the screen.

CD RESOURCE: A PDF version of the defining article on how to avoid RSIs, "Safer Computing" by Dr. Franklin Tessler, a former colleague of mine, from the December 1994 issue of Macworld. The article's recommendations remain as valid today as they were when it was first published, and they apply to Windows as easily as to the Macintosh.

Getting Effective Technical Support

One of the biggest frustrations when using computer equipment happens when things go wrong. Manuals rarely exist any more, and those that you can get are often mere recitations of the user interface or written in incomprehensible language. Phone technical support is usually an intensely maddening experience with long hold times and nonexpert technicians who go through canned laundry lists of "solutions" from a database rather than really understanding your issues. And at the end of an inconclusive call, technicians often claim that another product is at fault, recommending you call the other company instead.

As technology prices have plummeted, perhaps it should come as no surprise that the expensive human support systems have been cut way back. But you can take a few measures to help the technical support process along:

■ Don't call in a panic or in a rush—the process requires your time, patience, and good humor.

■ Before you call, make sure you know what steps led to the problem. The more you can narrow down the circumstances of the problem, the faster the support technician can get to the likely cause—and the greater chance of avoiding wild goose chases caused because you happen to mention something vague or irrelevant that the technician got stuck on.

■ Also before you call, make sure you've done some basic troubleshooting that will help eliminate wild goose chases. Disconnect any newly installed equipment (new hardware might be the source of the problem, due to a conflict), and for the same reasons uninstall any software that was installed right before the problem occurred. Check your antivirus and antispyware software logs or status displays to make sure they are not blocking your software or Web pages because they are detecting a possible risk.

■ Never reformat your hard drive, even if told to do so by a technician. The "reformat your drive" advice is a last resort by desperate technicians who don't know what the real problem is. Reformatting the drive wipes out everything on your computer—usually including the problem. But by then you've lost all your data unless you have been rigorous about backing up. Reformatting is almost always the wrong solution.

- If the technician blames other software or hardware, ask for specific reasons why he believes that to be the case. If the technician can't give you a good answer—one you'll need when you call the other company and ask for its help—then he's probably clueless as to the cause and is just trying to get rid of you.

- If you sense that the technician doesn't know how to help you, ask for a supervisor or another technician. Don't waste your time with someone who can't help.

- Keep logs of your calls, including the names of the people you spoke with. Difficult problems often take several calls as you try different possible fixes, and it's almost guaranteed that whoever answers your call the next time won't be the person who helped you the first time. A sign of good technical support is when the original technician gives you a way to contact him directly for follow-up. If he doesn't provide his contact information, ask if there's a way to follow up with him directly if the suggested fix doesn't work.

More and more companies rely on e-mail technical support, which can be very frustrating because of the delayed responses and because there's no way to have a real conversation that results in a quick resolution. And chances are good that you're getting canned responses, not real support. If after a couple rounds of e-mails you don't have a resolution, ask for someone you can call directly. If you don't receive that level of service and you're having problems with a new product, consider returning it and trying another company's product. (When customers accept bad service, they only get more of it.)

Some companies use electronic chat systems, which give you the immediacy of a phone call and the ability to have more of a conversation, so you and the support technician can have a real dialog to get closer to a useful response. These can work well once you get the hang of the slight pauses as you wait for the other person to finish typing. But note that some chat systems don't work well on the Macintosh or on browsers other than Internet Explorer, so be sure there is an alternative contact method if you're not using Windows.

Because technical support is often mediocre or just plain inferior, you should get your own technical support network. It's a cliché, but it's true: a smart kid often can figure out problems

THE PRICE OF TECH SUPPORT

Because of the cost of delivering effective technical support, many companies now charge for the service. The problem is, you don't know if the support is worth the money until after you have spent your money. And at $25 or more per incident, or several dollars a minute, the costs can really add up.

Worse, most companies do not provide a satisfaction guarantee on their support, meaning even if they can't solve your problem, you still pay. Charging for tech supports protects the company against truly clueless users, but it harms those who have a legitimate problem.

My advice: Avoid paid support unless the fees are waived if your problem is not resolved. If you must pay for support, try a local computer repair shop where you can establish a real relationship.

quickly and take care of them for you. (If you call this kid repeatedly, be sure to pay her or otherwise reward the person for her time and effort.) You might have a geek or two in the family or among your friends. Ask for their help, but again be sure to compensate them somehow for their time and expertise—a nice dinner, perhaps?—if your requests become frequent.

Additionally, look for a neighborhood computer repair shop. They're increasingly common, but usually in parts of town where the rents are cheap. Check the phone book or search for "computer repair" and the name of your town in an online search engine such as Google. You can also try the Geek Squad national service, but its folks come and go more often than the local shop's staffers, so you don't get the same personal service and long-term relationship. A computer repair shop is much like an auto mechanic—someone you need to trust and one who knows your needs and issues.

 *CD RESOURCE: A link to the Geek Squad.*

CHAPTER 2

The Right Connections

ISSUES COVERED

- What kinds of phones do you need?
- What kind of Internet connections do you need?
- What mobile and wireless technologies should you consider?
- How can you work well in multiple locations?

Real estate is very much a business of networking, developing personal and professional relationships that introduce you to possible clients. But modern real estate also involves the other kind of networking: the kind that connects computers and information together.

Clients expect you to have information on listings and the real estate market at your fingertips, and they expect you to be able to work on contracts and disclosures at their office, their home, or properties they're interested in, not just at your broker's office. Most real estate agents need to be "road warriors," professionals who use technology to do their jobs on the road.

Several technologies support mobile professionals such as you: the cell phone and voicemail, e-mail and Internet access through a variety of methods, and data synchronization. A tech-savvy agent will use several of these technologies to remain productive no matter where she happens to be. But connectivity technologies are also rife with over-promised, undelivered benefits and frequently changing standards. Those realities suggest you not leap into latest and greatest gadgets and services when they first become available—you could easily spend precious time and money on dead ends if you move too fast. After all, a key issue with connectivity technology is that it requires all involved parties to use the same technology, so being ahead of the pack may simply isolate you. Instead, rely on established technologies when putting together your connectivity toolkit.

Choosing the Right Phones

A telephone is probably the most used piece of technology by real estate agents. You probably have several: a cell phone, a home office phone, and a brokerage office phone.

Phone technology isn't as simple as it used to be, so there are several issues to consider for both your desktop and cell phones.

Working with Multiple Phone Lines

The foremost issue is that you'll need a separate phone line at home for your business. Having a dedicated line helps keep business separate from family life, so your kids don't misplace client messages, and you can let your voicemail pick up when you're having dinner. You might also want a separate line for your fax machine, which means a third line.

Adding a second (or third) line is usually not difficult. A handyman or knowledgeable relative can probably do it for you, while hiring the phone company is usually the costliest option. If you want to do it yourself, read on; otherwise, skip to the next section in this chapter, "Selecting Phone Equipment."

PHONE TECH GOTCHAS

It's the thing that goes on behind the scenes that can cause the most frustration when you're working with technology. Be sure you don't overlook the following issues when setting up your phone system:

- If you use the telephone company's voicemail service rather than your own answering machine, note that the special tone it uses to tell you that you have messages usually interferes with the ability of fax machines, modems, Supra lockbox-key cradles, and other devices to dial out. You'll need to connect those devices to a different line.

- If you have DSL high-speed Internet service, be sure that each jack to which a device is connected has a DSL filter installed. These filters typically come with your DSL service and let you connect line splitters to them so multiple devices can all be connected to the same DSL filter. Check with your DSL provider for details. (You don't need a DSL phone filter for your phone jacks if you have cable modem Internet service.)

- Avoid 2.4 GHz cordless phones if you have a wireless network at home—they use the same radio frequency and thus can interfere with each other. Instead, opt for a 5.8 GHz phone to get good range and avoid interference. Or consider a 900 MHz cordless phone for its low price and interference avoidance—but understand that its range is usually limited.

- Be sure to turn the ringer off on your home fax machine—otherwise, you might be awakened in the middle of the night when a fax arrives. Likewise, if your home office line is audible outside your office, you might turn its ringer off after hours.

THE BIGGER PICTURE

Most newer homes are wired for two phone lines: Each jack usually has enough wires to serve two phones, and a two-line phone is designed to use those wires. (You'll of course need two phone numbers from your telephone company.) Regular phones are designed for just one number, so they ignore the extra wires as well as the signals for that second line. In most cases, you can plug a two-line phone into a regular jack.

You can tell if a room is wired for multiple lines by counting the number of wires in its phone jack or box. There are two wires per phone line, so if you see four wires, your wiring can support two phone lines. (Six wires will support three lines.) Note that these individual wires are usually contained in one cord, so they look like a single wire. But the individual wires are exposed where they connect to the jack or box. Remember that each jack that you want to support multiple lines must be wired for those multiple lines.

Normally, your primary line—your home phone—is set as the first line, and your business phone is set as the second line. You might want to reverse the order in your home office and make the primary line the business line. It's easy to do. Just reverse how the home and business wires are connected: If red and green are the wires for the home line and yellow and black are the wires for the office line, just swap the red and yellow wires and then the green and black wires. Now the jack will treat the business line as the primary line *for that jack.*

Also, where the telephone service enters your house, there's usually a box or plate with several metal screws, called *posts,* that all phone jacks in the house connect to. (The phone company's outside wires, which bring in the phone service, also connects to these posts, which act like a bridge between the inside and outside wiring. The phone company will connect just one external wire to each post.) Each pair of posts serves one phone line, so if you have two pairs of posts with inside wires attached to each pair, you're wired for two lines.

Remember that what is wired from the outside might not match what is wired on the inside: For example, you may have four posts (which support two lines) with inside wires hooked up to all four posts, but outside wires hooked up to just two posts (one line). That means your house is wired internally for two lines, but the phone company has connected your service for just one line. In that case, see if there are outside wires available that have not been connected to the second set of posts. If so,

A two-line phone splitter has three jacks: One that passes both lines to the device, one that passes just line 1, and one that passes just line 2. For example, you might connect a two-line phone (so you have access to your home and office lines from one phone) to the first jack, the answering machine for line 1 to the second jack, and the answering machine for line 2 to the third jack. Or you might connect a two-line phone to the first jack and your fax machine or computer modem to the third jack (for line 2).

On the left are the posts where the telephone company connects its wires to your inside wiring. In this photo, there are two pairs of posts, supporting two lines, although only one set of posts (on the right side) is connected to the phone company's wires (the orange and white wires); thus, only one line is active. To make the second line active, you need to attach two unused wires from the phone company, one to each post on the left side. On the right is a common surface-mount phone jack that shows the four individual wires (red, black, yellow, and dark blue) connecting to the jack, which supports two phone lines. If there were only two wires connecting the jack to the posts, the wiring would support just one line.

the phone company brought the wires in but did not connect them. You'll need to connect those wires so the second line works after the phone company activates it. Or you could pay the phone company to come in and connect those wires, but because it's so simple, try to do it yourself.

Older homes might be wired for a single line, meaning that there are only two wires in the phone cord. In that case, you'll usually need to run a second set of wires between the posts and the phone jack in the rooms where you want to activate the second line. (There are phones with special power plugs that can use your house's electrical wiring to transmit the voice signal to another phone on a jack whose wiring is connected to the posts. They make wiring each phone jack to the posts unnecessary, but these phones tend to have lower voice quality and suffer from signal interference. It's fine to try these phones, but make sure you can return them if they don't work well.)

Selecting Phone Equipment

Once your home—or at least home office—is wired for multiple phone lines, the next step is to connect a phone to them.

You'll typically need a two-line phone, so you can answer both business calls and personal calls from your office. Two-line phones connect to a standard jack and automatically detect the two lines.

If you connect single-line devices to the additional line, such as a fax machine or modem, you will likely need a splitter, but it depends on how your jacks are wired. Without a splitter, any single-line device will automatically use the primary line for the jack it's connected to. If you want the device to use a different line, you need to connect it via a splitter, which separates each line to its own jack.

You have plenty of choices for your home-office phone, whether you want a single-line or two-line phone. You first need to decide on whether you want a corded phone or a cordless one. I prefer a cordless phone because I can easily move around my office or home while talking on it, although it's not unusual for me to forget where I left it!

WORKING WITH THREE OR MORE LINES

Your third (or fourth) line is usually used for a fax machine and for devices such as the Supra lockbox-key cradle that must dial out periodically to keep their service active.

Because few homes are wired for more than two lines, chances are you'll need to run additional lines from your phone posts to the jacks in your home office. To do this, you might have to use the crawlspace under your house or run the lines through the attic and drop them into the walls. So you might need to hire someone to do this wiring work.

In your office, you'd need to install a jack box or wall plate that has multiple jacks, and you would wire no more than two lines to each jack. (Even though you can wire a jack to handle three or more lines, most equipment is not designed to detect more than two lines.)

The photo shows such a setup, with the home and business lines wired to the top jack (which has a splitter attached), and the fax line wired to the bottom jack.

THE BIGGER PICTURE

If you get a cordless phone, I recommend a 5.8 GHz model because of its greater signal reach. Don't get a 2.4 GHz cordless phone if you have or plan to get a wireless network in your home: Such phones use the same frequency as wireless networks, leading to signal interference that degrades the voice quality on your calls and slows down your wireless access.

For my home office, my two-line cordless includes an answering machine, which I've enabled for my office line. But I use a separate answering machine for my home line, which I placed in the family room for everyone to use. That's my solution for keeping my office and personal phones—and space—separate.

Because phone models change so frequently, I can't recommend specific models. But look for easily readable displays, jacks for headsets (so you can check out MLS listings on the computer when talking to a client, for example), and big buttons for easy dialing. Look for a simple, intuitive interface for common functions, so you don't have to think about your phone to use it, and other ease-of-use options such as a blinking light on a cordless phone so you know if you have messages even if you're not near the base station that contains the answering machine.

CD RESOURCE: For two-line phones, links to AT&T, General Electric, Panasonic, Polycom, RCA, Uniden, and Vtech.

Selecting Cell Phones

A cell phone is a must for any agent, so you can talk to clients and other agents while looking at homes or in transit. Cell phones come in a mind-boggling array of features and styles, much of which caters to teenagers and twenty-somethings. For working adults, most cell phone features are overkill.

What your cell phone needs to do is let you talk with clients, other agents, and people involved in transactions. So talk time, price, and coverage are the three top issues you should consider when selecting a phone and service provider.

After that, the necessities get personal. Because I'm in my 40s, a clear, readable screen and decent button size are very important. If you get a flip-phone, be sure it displays the number of the incoming caller without needing to be opened—so you can tell at a glance if you need to answer the call. The number display prevents you from being rude when talking to someone in person, since you can quickly glance to see who's calling without interrupting your in-person conversation. Likewise, the message indicator should be visible when the phone is closed.

I don't think most agents need or really use cell phone features like cameras, text messaging, e-mail, or Web browsing. (Your kids might disagree, but it's not their phone.) Phone cameras' images are typically low quality, so you'll need to use a regular digital camera for any photos you show clients or include in flyers or on the MLS. Text messages can cost you (or your clients) real money—both recipient and sender typically pay for each text message after a certain number—and typically, text messages don't transmit that much information because of the cell phones' tiny screens. Similarly, it usually costs money to send or receive e-mails on a cell phone. In any event, you'll likely use your laptop for examining listing data and communicating details with your clients. Web browsing on a small screen is simply painful; again, use a laptop for the Web.

There are devices that offer PC-like functionality plus cell phone capabilities together in a handheld size, such as the Research in Motion BlackBerry, Hewlett-Packard iPaq, and Palm Treo. I think these are overkill—not too mention too pricey—for most real estate agents, but only you can make that determination. As with any device, make sure you'll actually use the features it offers and that you can justify the price (of the device and monthly service) in your business. And if you want the latest technology for its own sake, that's fine—as long as you're aware of the price.

Now that I've confirmed myself as a cell phone Luddite, there is one cell phone technology that you should consider: a cellular modem card for your laptop PC. (See the sidebar "The New Wireless Internet Option" elsewhere in this chapter for more information.)

CD RESOURCE: For cell service, links to AT&T Wireless/Cingular Wireless, Sprint Nextel, T-Mobile, and Verizon Wireless. For organizer/cell phone combinations, links to Hewlett-Packard, Palm, Research in Motion, Samsung, and Siemens.

CELL PHONE ACCESSORIES

When you buy a cell phone, there are a few items you should get with it. Some of these items might come with your phone, while others you'll need to buy separately:

- **Spare charger for your car:** You'll need a model specific for your phone or a universal charger that accepts specific adapter connectors for your phone.

- **Adapter storage:** If you use a universal charger to charge your cell phone, iPod, and perhaps digital camera, be sure to get a bag or other container for the adapters you'll need to keep in the car. (Store the bag in the glove compartment or console.) Adapters can get lost easily and can cost about $10 each to replace.

- **A hands-free headset:** A headset lets you talk while driving yet keep both hands on the wheel. Many localities and some states now require headsets if you use your phone while driving.

- **Voice-activated dialing:** If you use the phone while driving, even using a headset won't eliminate the need to take your hands off the wheel and eyes off the road to dial a number. Voice-activated dialing can reduce that kind of interruption by letting you say someone's name and have the number dialed for you. (Voice-activated dialing works only for stored numbers, so it's not a complete solution.)

- **A belt clip:** A belt clip keeps your phone handy, although sometimes having your phone attached to your belt can do more harm than good. For example, your phone might get crushed when you sit down or might get caught in your seat belt, damaging the case when you try to get out of the car.

Before you buy a cell phone, note that stores like Best Buy, Circuit City, Office Depot, OfficeMax, and Radio Shack usually charge high prices for accessories. In many cases, they make more profit on the accessories than they do on the phone itself. Be sure to shop online, both at online retailers and at places like eBay, to make sure you find the best deal.

THE BIGGER PICTURE

Choosing the Right Internet Connections

Once your phone system is under control, it's time to think about your Internet access. Today's agents rely heavily on the MLS database to track local listings and even download disclosure packages and other documents. Furthermore, e-mail is a handy way to exchange information with clients and other agents, especially electronic copies of disclosure packages and other items that you would otherwise need to pick up in person from your office or another agent's office.

High-Speed Access at Home

In much of the country, high-speed Internet access is now available to homes, making it much easier to have a home-based business yet be well connected to the rest of the world. Having high-speed Internet access is a must for real estate agents, so they can quickly search the MLS database, receive and send large disclosure packages, and stay in touch with clients via e-mail.

DSL versus Cable Access

You have two basic choices for Internet access for your home office: cable and DSL. Whether you choose DSL or cable, you'll get a device called a modem in your home to which you connect your computer(s). If you have just one computer, it generally connects directly to the cable or DSL modem. If you have several computers, you'll connect the computers to a broadband router, which in turn connects to the modem. Either way, that modem attaches to your cable line if it's a cable modem or to your phone line if it's a DSL modem.

The cable TV company and the phone company are vying to expand their offerings into new areas such as Internet access, so both offer discounts if you bundle Internet service with their other services. (Some cable companies even offer phone service.) Bundling services can make good sense, as long as the service meets your needs in terms of reliability and customer service.

As of early 2006, cable Internet service costs around $45 per month, while DSL service costs about $20 per month. Either could be cheaper or costlier in your area, depending on how much competition there is where you live, but as a rule cable costs more. That's because cable Internet speeds are usually three to six times faster than DSL speeds. Do you need that speed? Most of the time, no. At least not for real estate. A 1 MBps connection—a common DSL speed—is fine for e-mail, Web browsing, and transmitting attachments. You'll certainly notice how much faster everything is with cable service, but only you can decide if that's worthwhile.

What might tip you in favor of cable is if your family is also using high-speed Internet access. The benefit of the higher cable speeds really becomes evident as multiple people use the Internet at the same time. And although you can have cable service for the family and DSL service just for your office, chances are the cable service can provide enough speed for everyone, so having an independent provider for your business Internet use is just not necessary. (If you deduct your Internet service from your business taxes, be sure that you figure out how much of the Internet cost is for business use and deduct just that portion.)

Of course, if you work mostly out of your broker's office, you can use the Internet connection there. In that case, a dial-up connection at home might be fine for occasional, limited use—and DSL service would certainly be sufficient—if family Internet access isn't an issue.

MANAGING YOUR PHONE LINES

I strongly recommend that you have a dedicated home-office line to keep your personal and business lives separate. But that business line of course could be a cell phone instead of a landline. Landlines are usually much cheaper than cell phones, but the convenience of a cell phone can outweigh its higher cost, especially when you're not in the office.

The questions then become whether the price of the additional minutes is cost-effective and whether you want all business calls to go to your cell phone. (I find it harder to manage interruptions when using a cell phone, since I usually don't have paper, pencil, or other resources handy. That's why I have a home-office landline whose number I use in my ads, cards, and other outreach methods. I keep my cell phone number more private, using it only for active clients and so on, so I'm less likely to get solicitations, dinnertime or late-night messages from other agents, and general inquiries on it.)

Of course having a cell phone—either as your primary business line or as a secondary business line—raises the question of whether you should have a separate cell phone for personal calls and one for business calls. Theoretically, I'd say yes, but in practice, the cost of multiple cell phones, not to mention the inconvenience of carrying them around and remembering which phone is for what is just too high. But you can use features like caller ID that are typically included with your cell phone plan to screen calls, helping separate business and personal use.

THE BIGGER PICTURE

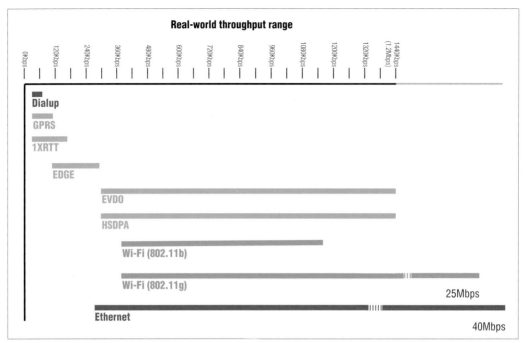

Throughput speeds vary widely based on how you connect to the Internet, as the chart shows. Wired technologies are in violet, cellular technologies in orange, and other wireless technologies in green.

Wireless versus Wired Access

With your Internet service selected, the next question is how to connect your computers to the Internet. You can use a wired (Ethernet) connection or a wireless (Wi-Fi) connection. Ethernet connections are faster—at least twice as fast—as Wi-Fi, but require running the Ethernet cables from each computer to your router or cable/DSL modem. Wi-Fi connections don't use any wires except to connect the Wi-Fi access point to the modem or router. And some routers and modems come with Wi-Fi built in, so there is no separate access point to connect.

You'll also need an Ethernet or Wi-Fi adapter in or attached to your computers, printers, and any other devices you want to connect to the Internet and to each other. Most laptops come with Wi-Fi and Ethernet connections built in, and most desktop PCs come with Ethernet connections built in. For other devices, Wi-Fi adapters cost $30 to $75 each, which can quickly add up, while Ethernet adapters typically cost $10 to $75 each. (The highest prices are typically charged for the adapters, called print servers, used to connect printers to the network.)

Of course, you can have both wired and wireless connections on the same network—just connect a wireless access point (or a wireless router that can function as an access point) to your wired router. If you use a wireless router connected this way, be sure it is set to operate as an access point and that it is connected from a regular LAN port on your wireless router, not from the WAN port—otherwise, it might not work. (Don't worry about what WAN and LAN mean—just check the labels on your equipment or the manual to be sure you make the right connections.) Check your router's instructions for details on how to connect a wireless router to a wired router and then set them up to work with each other properly; there is no standard method.

CD RESOURCE: For wired and wireless routers, links to Belkin, Buffalo Technology, Cisco Systems, D-Link, Hawking Technology, Linksys, Netgear, and SMC Networks.

High-Speed Access on the Road

When you're away from the office, accessing the Internet is trickier. Chances are you'll use one of three methods: connecting via dial-up modem from someone's phone line, connecting via someone's network, or connecting through a subscription to a Wi-Fi hot spot service.

In your laptop bag, be sure to carry a phone cord (also called an RJ11 cable) and an Ethernet cable (also called an RJ45 cable), so you can connect to the Internet via a dial-up or a network connection. I suggest you get a cord that automatically spools the wire to save space in your bag.

You'll need a dial-up account to connect via modem: Most companies that provide Internet access for your home provide a free or low-cost dial-up option when you're traveling, so be sure to ask about dial-up options before spending money on a separate account from a company like AOL, EarthLink, MSN, or PeoplePC.

WATCH OUT FOR WI-FI VARIANTS

Like everything else when it comes to technology, Wi-Fi wireless networking—also known as 802.11—comes in several variations.

The best is 802.11g, because it's pretty fast and widely compatible. An 802.11g device runs on both the 802.11g and the slower 802.11b networks. Likewise, an 802.11g network lets both 802.11b and 802.11g devices access it (although if it detects an 802.11b device, an 802.11g network will make all devices run at the 802.11b device's slower speed).

The 802.11a technology is not compatible with 802.11b or 802.11g, so you should not buy an 802.11a device. But if 802.11a comes at no extra cost as one of several technologies on the same card or access point—such as an 802.11a/g combination—it does no harm.

Definitely avoid all the proprietary technologies offered by wireless vendors—those with labels like Super G, G Plus, SRX, MIMO, 108, and pre-N—because the extra speed they promise only occurs if all the equipment on the network comes from the same vendor *and* uses the same special technology. That's a big if, and is essentially just a tricky way to get you to pay more than you should.

THE BIGGER PICTURE

Using Networks at the Broker and Elsewhere

If you connect over someone else's network—such as your broker's—you need to configure your laptop to work properly. Changing the configuration can get complicated, so you might need some help.

The basic issue is that networks have a router that manages all the connections, and your laptop needs to find this router. Routers have a unique network address, which may or may not match the one at your home. (Routers in different locations can have the same address because the address is seen only in that specific network, not across the Internet.) If the network address is different, you might need to tell your laptop where to find the router you want to connect to. Also, most routers automatically give your laptop its own temporary address when connected to them. But some routers expect your laptop to have a predefined address, called an IP address. So you might need to set this IP address as well when you switch networks.

In Windows XP, choose Start > Settings > Network Connections > Local Area Network, then click Properties to open the Internet Protocol (IP) Properties dialog box. Scroll down the list until you see Internet Protocol (TCP/IP), select it and then click Properties. Normally, both Obtain an IP Address Automatically and Use the Following DNS Server Addresses should be selected, letting the router figure out the best settings.

But if choosing these automatic options don't work, first try to change the router address by clicking the Advanced button in the Internet Protocol (IP) Properties dialog box. Then adding a new gateway (router address) in the Advanced TCP/IP Settings dialog box that appears by clicking the Add button and entering the router address provided by the network manager.

If manually entering the router address doesn't do the trick, you might need to change the IP and DNS settings in the Internet Protocol (IP) Properties dialog box, using settings provided by the network manager. You'll probably need an IT person's help at this point. Just so you know, IP Address is the laptop's address, Default Gateway is the router's address, and DNS Servers are the addresses for using the Internet from that router.

In Mac OS X, choose > System Preferences > Network. In the TCP/IP pane, the Configure IPv4 pull-down menu should normally be set at Using DHCP, which lets the router and laptop figure out the right settings automatically. If the automatic settings don't work, select Manually in the Configure IPv4 menu and enter

An automatically spooling Ethernet cable (top) and phone cord (bottom) are great space savers. You can find them in most consumer electronics shops, as well as at online retailers and auction sites.

the IP address (laptop address) and Router settings as instructed by the network's manager. For access to the Internet, you might also need to enter addresses in the DNS Servers area.

Accessing the Internet Using Wi-Fi Hot Spots

Additionally, you can access the Internet through a Wi-Fi hot spot. Using a hot spot requires having an 802.11 wireless radio or card in your laptop, which is now all but standard equipment. (Several versions of Wi-Fi technology are available, but the only one you want to buy new is 802.11g, although if you already have 802.11b equipment, that'll work, too.)

Wi-Fi hot spots have a range of a few hundred feet and are typically found in cafés that are happy to rent you a table, either by charging a daily or monthly Wi-Fi access fee (as Starbucks does) or by hoping you'll buy enough coffee and snacks to make it worth your taking up their table space (as many local coffee shops do). More and more, cities are providing free or low-cost wireless hot spots in downtown and other dense areas to encourage business usage. And brokerages are increasingly installing Wi-Fi hot spots for their agents, because it's often a lot easier and cheaper to install a wireless network than it is to install individual network jacks at each desk.

Wi-Fi hot spots use the same technology as a wireless network in your home. Thus, you'll have the same connection requirements for a Wi-Fi hot spot as you do at home (described later in this chapter), plus you might also have to log in to your Wi-Fi account from your Web browser to get Internet access.

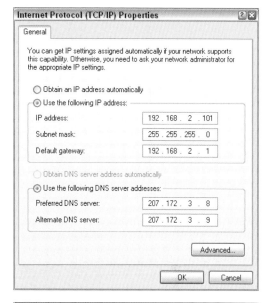

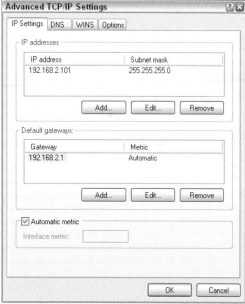

The two network setup panes in Windows XP let you override the automatic address management when that doesn't work. Get the correct settings from the network's manager.

CD RESOURCE: For 3G cellular service, links to AT&T Wireless/Cingular Wireless, Sprint Nextel, and Verizon Wireless. For cellular modems, links to Novatel Wireless, Sierra Wireless, and Sony Ericcson.

Securing Your Connections

However you connect to the Internet, you need to protect your computers from hackers (who try to steal information from your computer) and malware (software that can damage your computer, steal your financial account information, or do other nefarious things). Chapter 1, "The Right Office Tools," covers software tools for your PC such as antivirus and antispyware, but you should have more protection than that.

Make sure your computer's firewall—which blocks many intruders and malware—is turned on. In Windows XP, do so in the Security Center (Start > Settings > Control Panel > Security Center). In Mac OS X 10.3 (Panther) or later, do so in the Sharing system preference (> System Preferences > Sharing, then go to the Firewall pane). For other operating systems, you can buy an Internet security tool such as those from Symantec and McAfee. Also, be sure your router or modem has a hardware firewall built in—and ensure that it is turned on. (See the manual that came with your hardware for details.)

If you use a wireless connection, be sure to turn on wireless security—it's usually off by default—and require the use of a password for connecting to the Internet. Follow the instructions that came with your access point. The best type of password is secured using a technology called WPA-PSK (or just WPA), although older equipment and operating systems won't support it. In that case, use the older WEP technology for password security.

You also need to make sure your laptop's wireless hardware is set to use the same security settings as the wireless access points or routers you are connecting to. (Your home office network may use different settings than your broker's does.)

In Windows, either use the software that came with your wireless card or notebook, or use Windows XP's settings. Be forewarned: Windows' network management controls are hard to find and provided through a series of dialog boxes and tabbed panes, making it hard to follow the instructions that follow. (Feel free to complain to Bill Gates about the incredibly bad user interface his company created for these settings.)

In Windows XP:

1. Choose Start > Settings > Network Connections > Wireless Network Connection, then click View Wireless Networks.

2. Click Change Advanced Settings, then select the wireless network connection to change.

3. Click the Properties button to set the security type and, optionally, enter your password for automatic log in later.

Fortunately, you can save these various settings as profiles and switch among them as needed. I recommend you save profiles for those connections that you make often, such as for your home or broker's office or for a Wi-Fi hot spot you frequent. To create and save this profile, use the software that came with your wireless card or use Windows's built-in settings:

1. Choose Start > Settings > Network Connections > Wireless Network Connection.

2. Click View Wireless Networks.

3. Choose Change Advanced Settings.

4. Go to the Wireless Networks tabbed pane and click the Add button.

5. Complete the connection and security information.

6. Click OK to save the profile.

The profile's name will be the same as the SSID you entered when creating that profile. (The SSID is the name the router was given by the network manager, and it will appear in the list of available networks automatically.)

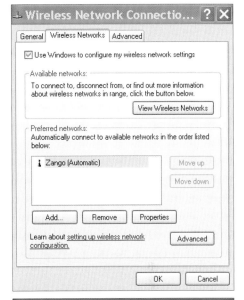

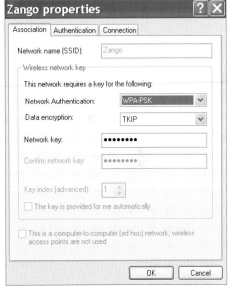

The two wireless network setup panes in Windows XP let you set up security settings for your laptop (click Properties to display the pane at the bottom) and save connections as profiles for easy selection later (by clicking Add in the pane at the top).

On the Mac, you'll be prompted for a password when it detects a new wireless connection; if the Mac doesn't detect the security protocol (such as WPA or WEP) in use, you can manually select the protocol in the Wireless Security drop-down menu. You can store passwords in the Keychain utility by selecting the Add to Keychain checkbox in login dialog boxes, such as when you connect to a network.

Working in Multiple Locations

With all the technology you have in place to stay connected from home, from your broker's office, and points in between, the next question becomes how do you keep track of everything?

Centralizing Your Connections

The answer is to keep it simple for yourself and your clients by centralizing wherever possible. That means:

- **Don't have too many phone numbers.** Keep the number of phone numbers you provide to the public (on your Web site, in your flyers, and on your business cards) to a minimum. You'll likely have lots of real estate-oriented phone numbers to manage—home office, cell, broker's office, personal fax, broker's fax, and broker's voicemail—but don't burden other people with that task. Providing too many options just confuses people and increases the chances that a message will slip through the cracks. Even if you have an office or voicemail line at your brokerage, don't give it out. Instead, make your home office and cell phone numbers the only ones you publicize—and the ones you check regularly. Leave messages on your other numbers referring people to your home office number.

- **Give out just one fax number to the public.** Choose your broker's fax or your home fax (if you have one). If you go to the office a lot, you might as well use the broker's fax. Otherwise, have faxes sent to your home, where they won't get mixed up with other agent's faxes and where you can get them easily.

- **Use one e-mail address for your business.** If your brokerage provides you with an e-mail account on its system and you have your own personal business e-mail account, set up one to forward to the other. For example, set up the brokerage e-mail account to forward all messages to your personal account. (The process for doing this varies from e-mail system to e-mail system: after you log in, look for a menu labeled Options or Settings that offers a forwarding capability, or ask the IT department.)

- **Use autodial features and stored numbers.** Almost every cell phone lets you store numbers and autodial them, and so do many desk phone, fax machine, and other devices. Using this feature ensures that the numbers you use are readily available on whatever device you happen to be using. Consider keeping your master contact list on either your laptop using a program such as Microsoft's Outlook or Now Up-to-Date and Contact, or use a paper or electronic organizer. The idea is to have one master list on a device you keep with you.

THE NEW WIRELESS INTERNET OPTION

A new technology began sprouting up in late 2005 that could be a great service for real estate agents and other mobile professionals. Called 3G—for third-generation cellular technology—it provides the equivalent of low-level DSL speeds over the air.

Two flavors of 3G technology now exist in the United States: EVDO and EDGE. EVDO is provided by Sprint Nextel and Verizon Wireless; EDGE is provided by AT&T Wireless/Cingular Wireless (the two recently merged). The EVDO technology is far superior, providing about 200 Kbps to 400 Kbps performance, versus 100 Kbps or so for EDGE. (For comparison, a dial-up modem runs at about 48 Kbps, while DSL service runs anywhere from 384 Kbps to 1.5 Mbps, with 1 Mbps being the most common speed. Note that 1 Mbps is the same as 1024 Kbps.) If you're an AT&T/Cingular customer, consider waiting until it offers the forthcoming HSDPA 3G service—probably in 2007 or 2008—because HSDPA works at least as fast as EVDO. (The fourth major cellular carrier, T-Mobile, doesn't yet offer 3G service of any sort.)

The beauty of 3G is that you can use it almost anywhere you get a cell signal. It's not limited to small areas like Wi-Fi hot spots at Starbucks and other places. So, equipping your laptop with a 3G card would give you moderate-speed Internet access from almost anywhere. Plans start at about $70 per month, so consider it only if you really need that access a lot when you're away from home and your brokerage.

THE BIGGER PICTURE

Working with Multiple Computers

Use a laptop as your central computer. This way, your files, e-mails, and so forth are all in one place. If your broker has PCs for you to use at the office, use your laptop when working there as well.

If you must use multiple computers, set your e-mail client on each computer to store messages on the server after you've read them. If you don't save messages to the server, the message will appear only on the computer that first downloaded the message, making it unavailable to your other computers. That in turn makes it very hard to track your messages. (Note that if you check your e-mail over the Web by going to a Web page to read your mail, your messages are usually automatically left on the server. But check the mail settings just to be sure.)

To make sure every computer can access all the e-mails you've received, follow these steps:

■ In Microsoft Outlook or Outlook Express in Windows, choose Tools > Accounts, then click Properties and go to the Advanced pane. Check Leave Copy of Message on Server. To keep your server from getting clogged up, I suggest you also check Remove from Server after Days, and enter a value like 15 or 20.

■ In Apple Mail on Mac OS X, choose Mail > Preferences, then go to the Advanced tab. Change the menu under Remove Copy from Server after Retrieving a Message from Right Away to After One Month.

■ In Microsoft Entourage for Mac OS X, choose Tools > Accounts, then double-click your e-mail account. In the Edit Account dialog box that appears, go to the Options pane and check Leave a Copy of Each Message on the Server. To keep the server from getting clogged up over time, I suggest you check Delete from Server after Days, and enter a value like 15 or 20.

■ For other e-mail clients, look for similar options, and check the manual or online help if necessary for instructions.

Managing Messages

Remember that any e-mail you read in a program like Outlook or Apple Mail on a specific computer is stored on that computer even after it's been deleted from the e-mail server it's kept until you delete it from the e-mail program itself. So even as your older messages are deleted from the server, all your messages are stored on your computer. It's important to retain those messages even after your transaction is closed in case there are questions or disputes later. If you don't want to keep them all in your e-mail programs (they do eat up hard drive space), consider printing out all the messages and adding them to your paper files, then you can delete them from your computer.

Any message you send from an e-mail program is stored only on the computer you sent it from, not on all the computers you might use to access e-mail. Similarly, any messages you send from the Web are not saved on your computer. In both cases, you might want to blind-copy yourself so the e-mail is sent to all your computers and thus stored on them.

Also, consider creating folders in your e-mail programs for each client, so it's easy to find messages. To make messages even more manageable, you might create a folder called Past Clients in which you move client folders as transactions are complete—this way, they remain available but don't clutter up the list of folders you use every day.

In addition, if you use multiple computers, consider creating a folder on each where you store client and other files, so you can quickly check the counterpart folders on your other computers to make sure they contain the most recent versions of the same files. Be careful as you move files, so you don't accidentally overwrite a newer version with an older one. Fortunately, Windows and Mac OS will flag such overwrites and give you the chance to cancel the move.

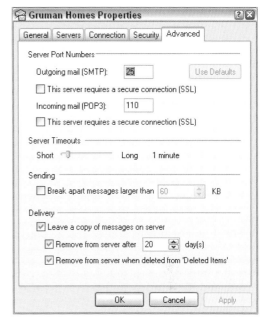

If you access e-mail from multiple computers using e-mail clients such as Microsoft Outlook, be sure to set them all to leave messages on the server. Here's what the settings look like for Outlook and Outlook Express.

CHAPTER 3

Working with Electronic Media

ISSUES COVERED

- How does digital photography work—and differ from film?
- How can I create electronic versions of papers and other documents?
- How do I work with layout and other tools for flyers and other materials?
- How do I work with Web pages?

A big part of being a real estate agent is producing and working with documents: flyers, postcards, disclosure packages, tour sheets, inspection reports, and so on. In some cases, you're creating the documents, while in others you're a conduit between the seller and buyer.

In both cases, you can use technology to ease the process. In later chapters of this book, I'll help you apply this technology to specific business issues and show you how you can apply these technologies to specific business processes. This chapter is more of a primer on the common tools, leading you through the functions and features you will likely use for a variety of business tasks. Obviously, there's no way one chapter can be a thorough tutorial on several tools, but I'll give you pointers on which ones to use and how to use them.

After you decide which tools you want to use, you can refer to the many good books available that can give you deeper insight into these tools. Chapters 1 and 2 list many of the popular technology tools available. (The CD that comes with this book includes links to several recommended how-to books as well as to software vendors' Web sites.)

Working with Digital Photography

Digital photography has transformed a real estate agent's ability to present clients and would-be buyers with immediate visuals on properties that might be of interest to them. You no longer need to wait for film to be developed. And it's easy to take digital images and share them with clients, as well as use them in Web pages, print advertisements, flyers, and so forth.

What to Know When Taking Pictures

But while very convenient, digital photography has its own issues to consider. If you're experienced with traditional 35mm photography, you'll quickly discover that a digital camera doesn't take the same pictures you're used to—the physics that make film cameras work is different than the physics that make digital cameras work, so many of the expectations you've formed from using film cameras simply don't apply when using digital cameras. For example, digital cameras usually have a slight pause between the time you press the button to take a picture and when the picture is actually snapped, so you need to relearn your timing. As another example, the boundaries of a picture as viewed through a digital camera's LCD screen aren't the same as what you see through a film camera lens's viewfinder, so you may take digital photos whose edges are not where you expected them to be. Some of these differences are reflected in what you look for when shopping for a camera:

A digital SLR camera typically has the best image quality and greatest range of photographic controls. And many have optical viewfinders to make it easy to see what you're shooting even in bright light. But they are larger and heavier than many agents prefer.

- **Size:** Generally speaking, the smaller the digital camera, the lower the image quality even if the megapixel rating is identical. That's because the camera sensor is smaller in smaller cameras, making individual pixels smaller and thus less detailed. It's like the difference between 110 and 35mm film cameras—small size means less quality. So, an SLR-format digital camera is pretty much equivalent to an SLR-format 35mm film camera, while a small pocket digital camera is more like a 110 film camera.

- **Picture enlargement:** Also generally speaking, digital images don't enlarge as well as film images, because the pixels become more quickly apparent. If you're taking full-page photos, you'll want a professional-level camera with 8 megapixels and an SLR format set at maximum resolution.

- **Views:** If your digital camera has both a viewfinder and an LCD preview screen, the LCD screen more accurately reflects what will be photographed. Viewfinders typically show a wider canvas, so objects toward the edge are often cut off.

- **Resolution:** You can usually set the image resolution on a digital camera. Higher resolution means more detail but also larger files. Film doesn't let you adjust the quality before you shoot.

- **Zoom:** Many digital cameras use digital zoom beyond a certain point of image enlargement. These digital zooms use an electronic "cheat" to enlarge the object you're shooting. This "cheat" degrades image quality, so try not to exceed the digital camera's *optical* zoom limit—the maximum enlargement as determined by the camera's lens—rather than use the higher digital zoom percentage. You'll find the optical and digital zoom maximums in the camera's manual.

- **Color:** Colors tend to be flatter in digital photography, so images can often look washed out. This is particularly true outdoors, where the sky and background sunlight can make the whole image too bright, losing details. You might need to take outdoor photos in the morning when the outdoor brightness is less. You might also need to enhance your photos in an image-editing program such as Adobe's Photoshop Elements or Corel's Paint Shop Pro to increase the contrast.

- **Lighting:** Digital cameras have more difficulty taking accurate pictures in low light—detail is usually obscured. If possible, use a flash or push up the ISO setting to get a more accurate image. A photo taken with a flash can end up looking washed out because there's too much brightness in the image, while a photo taken with a pushed-up ISO setting will likely be on the dark side, but you can usually fix an image by adjusting the brightness using image-editing software.

A pocket digital camera typically has lower image quality and just a modest range of photographic controls, but it is easy to carry around or leave in the glove compartment because of its small size and low weight. However, few pocket cameras have an optical viewfinder and rely instead solely on an LCD preview screen that can be hard to see in bright daylight.

I recommend testing any digital camera before relying on it for real work. Take pictures of your home, for example, to get a sense of the image quality, image size, and lighting issues so when you shoot a client's home, you'll get the results you need. Likewise, experiment with the images in an image-editing program and in sample flyers and other documents that you print out to see how they look. You'll typically find, for example, that digital photos work best when printed on an inkjet printer at no more than 4 inches in width. For commercial printing, the images might need to be smaller.

And remember: It's not worth spending lots of money for a fancy, super-high-quality camera, since the kinds of pictures most real estate agents need to take don't need that level of quality. Your photos are typically used on the Web and in fairly small sizes in printed ads and brochures. If you need full-page glossy photos for one of the slick real estate magazines, for example, you'll likely want to hire a professional photographer.

How to Deal with Image Files and Formats

Digital photographs are almost always stored by the camera in the JPEG format. If you're buying a camera that uses a different format, be sure that it comes with software that lets you convert the images to at least one of the three widely used image formats on a computer: JPEG, GIF, or TIFF. Image-editing software can usually read all three formats, plus a bunch of others, and even save from one to the other, letting you convert to different formats.

Typically, you use the TIFF format for images that are printed, and either JPEG or GIF for images that are placed on the Web or displayed on a computer (such as on a hard drive, a CD, a DVD, or some other storage device).

You can use JPEG and GIF images for printed material. Just know that they might not look as good as an original TIFF file. Note the word *original*: a JPEG or GIF file won't be any higher in image quality after it's converted to the TIFF format. But if the original image is a TIFF file—and that's extremely unlikely if the source was a digital camera—converting it to JPEG or GIF could degrade the quality.

The reasons for this quality difference come down to the fact that TIFF files were designed for print output, and thus typically are set at a resolution of 300 dots per inch (dpi)—called pixels per inch (ppi) by some programs—which means there are 300 tiny dots in every inch of the image that the human eye combines into a single image. (If you take a magnifying glass to a newspaper or magazine photo, you'll see those dots. The finer the dots, the better the image quality.) But computer monitors display typically 72 dpi, and the GIF and JPEG formats are typically set at 72 dpi, meaning they are coarser and less exact when printed.

Common Image Sizes Revealed

Image Size (pixels)	Max. Print size (inches)	Max. Web size (inches)
1600 × 1200	5 $\frac{1}{3}$ × 4	22 $\frac{1}{4}$ × 16 $\frac{2}{3}$
1280 × 960	4 $\frac{1}{4}$ × 3 $\frac{1}{5}$	17 $\frac{3}{4}$ × 13 $\frac{1}{3}$
1024 × 768	3 $\frac{3}{5}$ × 2 $\frac{1}{2}$	14 $\frac{1}{5}$ × 10 $\frac{2}{3}$
800 × 600	2 $\frac{2}{3}$ × 2	11 $\frac{1}{9}$ × 8 $\frac{1}{3}$
640 × 480	2 $\frac{1}{8}$ × 1 $\frac{3}{5}$	8 $\frac{8}{9}$ × 6 $\frac{2}{3}$

Of course, by resizing an image, you can change the dpi—shrinking a 72 dpi image to a quarter of its size results in a 288 dpi (72 × 4) image, for example—so the original dpi might not mean that much. What does matter is the dpi when you print the image, and that's why enlarging digital images much past 150 percent usually results in a ragged, low-quality image.

So how do digital photos get their dpi? It comes down to the image size the camera creates when you shoot the photo. Most cameras let you choose an image size, so you have some control over size. Let's say your camera takes images that are 1600 pixels wide by 1200 pixels high. On a monitor set at 72 dpi, that comes to about 22$\frac{1}{4}$ by 16$\frac{2}{3}$ inches—way too large for a typical Web page, which is about 800 to 1000 pixels wide. But when printed at 300 dpi, that same image comes to about 5$\frac{1}{3}$ by 4 inches—even though it's the same file.

THE BIGGER PICTURE

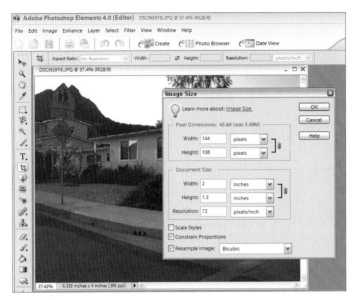

The bottom line: Use high-resolution settings for files you print, but don't bother doing so for Web images, since the extra size just makes the file bigger and takes longer to download or display.

CD RESOURCE:

For calculating photo size based on original image resolution, intended output size, and destination medium, a Microsoft Excel-based calculator called "Zango ImageCalc" is included.

Using Adobe Photoshop Elements, I'm resizing this 1600×1200-pixel photo to 144×108 pixels and also resampling it to 72 dpi (from the printing standard of 300 dpi) for use on a Web page. Note how the size drops from the original 5.8 MB to a download-friendly 45.6 KB.

How to Adjust Image Attributes

When working with images, you can count on the fact that you'll need to adjust them—their size, their resolution, or something else.

Resizing and Resampling

Perhaps the most common adjustment involves resizing an image. What would you do if your image is larger than the final size needed for your Web page or printed document? Just make it smaller, right? Well, yes, but there's more to it than that: Ideally, you would *resample* the image—which adjusts the image DPI setting to match its new size, essentially throwing away extra detail. Say you have a 300 dpi image that you want to print at half its size, making it a 600 dpi image. Those extra dots per inch won't be useful to the printer, but will increase the printing time and file size. The best thing to do is to resize a copy of the original image in an image editor to 50 percent, then resample it to 300 dpi—this way you get the resolution you need, but no more.

(Be sure to work on a copy so you always have the original intact.) This need to resample after reducing an image's size is particularly true for Web images, because they need much lower resolution (72 dpi) to display properly.

Resizing and resampling are just two types of adjustment you're likely to make to your images. The others are cropping, brightness and contrast adjustments, and color balancing.

Cropping

Cropping means to remove unwanted portions of an image by clipping one, several, or all sides. Some programs let you draw a rectangle around the area you want to keep, then select a Crop tool or menu item to eliminate everything outside that rectangle. Other programs show a frame around the image whose corners or sides you can move to crop the image, much like resizing a folder window in Windows.

Brightness and Contrast

You'll often need to adjust an image's brightness or contrast. Typically, digital photos are darker than expected, but you can increase the brightness to fix that. Sometimes, you will also need to adjust the contrast so details are more apparent. Note that you can typically increase brightness considerably—50 or even 70 percent—without distorting the image, but adjusting contrast much past 15 percent often makes the image look fake. Most image-editing programs let you adjust the brightness and contrast using sliders in a dialog box. You simply select the brightness and contrast controls either from a menu option or from a toolbar to access the dialog box.

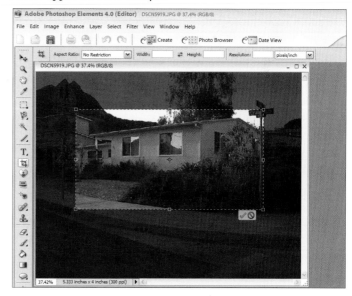

Here, I'm cropping the photo so that the focus is just on the house.

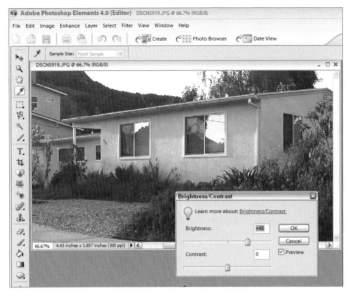

I'm brightening the image, because the original photo was too dark—a common issue when shooting digital photographs outdoors in bright daylight. Even a setting of +45 percent doesn't distort the image's appearance.

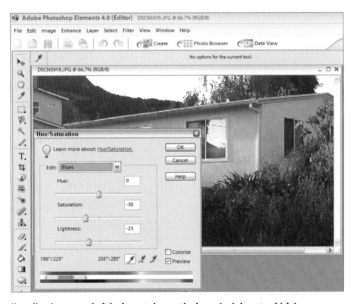

I'm adjusting several of the hues to lessen the house's pink cast, which is exaggerated in the photograph. These kinds of adjustments aren't an exact science, so just play with the sliders for one or more of the colors (hues) until it looks right to you.

Color Balance

A tricky feature is color-balance adjustment. The human eye is wonderful at balancing colors in all sorts of lighting conditions, more so than a camera. So often the photo you take doesn't look like the real thing. That's why most image-editing software comes with tools to adjust the individual colors (also called hues) so you can rebalance the colors to produce a more realistic image. There are limits, of course—cameras, computers, and printers can't reproduce all the colors the human eye can see, so you'll never get an exact match. And there's only so much color information in a digital image, so it's easy to distort the image and make it look unnatural.

But if you do try to rebalance the colors, you'll typically get three controls per color, even if the names differ: hue (the actual color), saturation (the intensity of that color, ranging from 0 [white] to 100 [maximum color]), and lightness (which is brightness but just for the selected colors). Note that some programs use a scale of 0–100, while others use a scale of 0–255. It doesn't really matter what the scale is as long as you can preview the results onscreen.

Working with Electronic Documents

Any real estate transaction involves lots of papers: contracts, disclosures, and marketing materials. In some parts of the country, a disclosure package can run a couple hundred pages. Multiply that by every interested buyer, and you're talking about lots of paper. Add the effort it takes to deliver these documents—by fax, by mail or courier service, or by driving somewhere to personally deliver them—and you're talking about a major investment of agent effort.

The number of pages in contracts and disclosures will not go down—in fact, they'll continue to rise as lawyers add more and more clauses meant to protect clients. But you can reduce the amount of paper you use in a transaction.

How? By using electronic documents when possible. Electronic documents are onscreen versions of paper documents. They can reduce paper usage and increase communications convenience.

Every agent knows that only a small percentage of people who look at a property will make an offer. And for those who ask for a disclosure package, signifying some real interest in the property, less than half typically will actually make an offer in many markets. By making the disclosures available as an electronic document, you can easily distribute the disclosures to all interested parties without the hassle of making and distributing paper copies. Prospective buyers and their agents can go through the disclosures on their computers, printing them out only if they want to make an offer (since at that point they'll need to sign or initial the disclosures). As you can see, the use of PDF files helps both listing and buyers' agents.

Electronic versions of documents also help in recordkeeping. While you still need paper copies in your files in case of later dispute, you can save electronic copies on a CD that's readily accessible in case you later need to review the documents. Only when you need the archived paper copies do you have to go through the file cabinets in the basement or wherever they are stored.

And electronic documents are a great way to send flyers, MLS information, and so forth to your clients via e-mail or Web links, so they can quickly get the information and review it at their convenience. Electronic documents speed up communication and reduce the time and expense of paper delivery.

CD RESOURCE: For real estate contract forms, links to Realforms, TrueForms, and Winforms/Zipforms.

CROSSING THE LINE INTO FAKERY

Do not use color balance or any image-editing technique to fake a photo. That's unethical and could constitute fraud. For example, covering up damage by "repainting" a wall digitally is fakery.

However, some changes fall into a gray zone. For example, cropping out a damaged shed or ugly neighbor's house might be OK for the seller's agent who's showing a few pictures to put the property in its best light. After all, any buyer would be expected to see the property in person and thus see everything.

But if you're the agent for an out-of-area buyer, you should be sure the photos you provide show both good and bad aspects of the property, so the client has a fair sense of the overall condition.

And, along these lines, don't change the color of walls and so forth unless you're specifically showing your client how she might repaint the property to give her ideas—that way it's clear you're not showing the real color.

THE BIGGER PICTURE

Creating Electronic Documents

OK, so how do you get these electronic documents? The answer is a technology called Portable Document Format (PDF) that works on both Windows and Macintosh computers. The software to read these files—called Adobe Reader—is free and easily downloaded, so it's easy for other agents and clients to deal with these files. (Most Web browsers come with a version of Reader already installed so anyone can open PDF files directly from Web pages.)

To create these documents, you'll need one of two things:

Adobe Acrobat Professional lets you create PDF files from scanned-in documents, as well as from the programs you use on your computer.

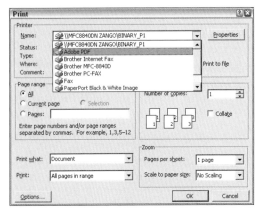

Converting a document on your computer to PDF typically involves "printing" the document to a virtual "printer" with a name like Adobe PDF or PDX-Xchange, which creates a file.

- Software that converts documents—both scanned in and created on your computer—to the PDF format. Examples include Adobe's Acrobat Professional, which lets you create PDF files from other applications and convert scanned-in pages; Docudesk's DeskPDF, which lets you create PDF files from other applications; and ScanSoft's PaperPort, which lets you convert scanned-in pages. To create PDF documents from other programs (such as Microsoft Word or PowerPoint), you typically see a "printer" named something like "PDF" in your printer list. You "print" a document to this "printer" to create a PDF file. If you install a program like Adobe's Acrobat Professional on your computer, you may also see an option in programs like Word to create PDF files directly; in that case, you can use that tool or the virtual-printer method previously described. (Note that Mac OS X has built in the ability to create—but not annotate or edit—PDF files by means of a Save As PDF button in applications' Print dialogs.)

■ An account with a service that converts documents you fax to the service into PDF documents that are then e-mailed back to you. Providers include Data on Call, Innoport, and MongoNet. These services often charge per page in addition to a monthly fee, so they're best used as a backup conversion method.

The MongoFax service lets you fax documents to MongoNet's computers, which convert them to PDF files and e-mail them to whomever you want. This special cover page lets the service know where to send the converted fax.

CD RESOURCE: For PDF creation software, links to Adobe, Docudesk, and ScanSoft. For fax-to-PDF services, links to Data on Call, Innoport, and MongoNet.

Annotating and Editing Electronic Documents

You'll likely also want a program that lets you annotate or do minor editing of your PDF documents, which both Acrobat Professional and DeskPDF allow. For example, you might want to explain certain terms in a contract or disclosure using the electronic equivalent of a sticky note.

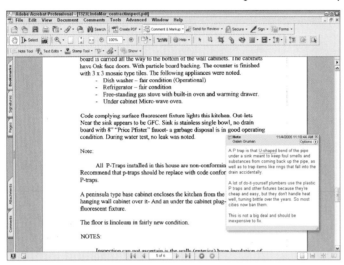

Annotating electronic documents with comments can help clients understand disclosures and contracts more easily. You can also use such annotations to mark where they need to sign or initial pages.

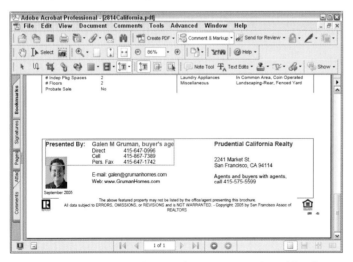

PDF editing tools also let you make minor changes to text, such as adding the phrase "buyer's agent" here.

Or you might want to make slight adjustments to PDF marketing materials—such as fixing typos or removing lockbox codes from an MLS-generated flyer (this typically happens because the other agent entered agent-only information such as lockbox codes in the public marketing section of the listing). I use this ability to add the phrase "buyer's agent" after my name in flyers that I generate from my office's MLS listings and post on my Web site, so there's no confusion as to whether I am the listing agent for those properties.

However, you can't make significant changes to PDF files, such as moving text or images around. And text editing is limited to individual lines, not entire blocks of text. If you need to make major changes to a PDF file, you must make changes to the original document using whatever software created it. Think of PDFs as paper documents with set content for which you can only add comments or make small changes visible to your clients.

While editing is limited, you can insert and delete pages from a PDF file, letting you, for example, merge several documents into one file or delete unnecessary pages.

Distributing Electronic Documents

While it's usually easy to distribute electronic documents via e-mail and Web links, there are some technology issues to keep in mind.

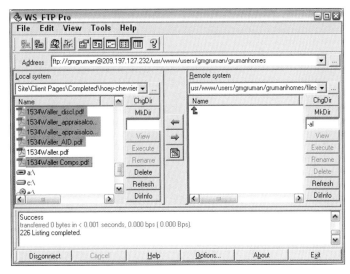

Using a file transfer program, I'm uploading several PDF files to a folder on my Web site so a client can download them at her convenience.

Keeping File Sizes Manageable

The file size of electronic documents—whether PDF files, Word files, PowerPoint files, or anything else that your client or business partners can work with—can easily get big. Large files are slow to send via e-mail, especially if your recipient has dial-up access. And many e-mail servers will not permit messages over a certain size—usually around 6 MB—be transmitted.

As you and others make comments, and add and delete pages, the file size grows. So be sure to use the Reduce File Size option in programs like Adobe Acrobat Professional to minimize the PDF file's size. (Think of each change as a layer that gets added to the file. The Reduce File Size option essentially creates a new PDF file, streamlining the data by merging those layers into one.)

Still, the Reduce File Size option can do only so much. If the files are still too big, try breaking your PDF file into several smaller files by exporting sets of pages to a new document and deleting them from the original. You would then send each smaller file in a separate e-mail, so you don't trigger the e-mail server's message size limit. But that makes more complexity for you and the recipient. Therefore, it might be better to leave a large file intact and make it available on your Web site as a link the recipient can download from a high-speed connection—avoiding the e-mail limits altogether.

Managing Files on the Web Server

To provide links you must have your own Web site and the ability to place files onto the server hosting it. (See Chapter 1, "The Right Office Tools" for more details.) I recommend you create a folder on the Web server to contain these files. You could create one folder called files for all clients or create a folder for each client, depending on how you prefer to manage your files. Be sure to not use spaces in the folder or filenames; names with spaces confuse some Web browsers. Also, avoid capitalizing folder names, since some browsers won't recognize the folder name if the user enters it in lowercase, which most people will do when entering Web addresses. (Of course, if you send the client the link in an e-mail or have it on a Web page, you don't need to worry about how they type it in—since the client won't need to type in the address—and can thus capitalize it as you prefer.)

If you have lots of files and other links for a specific client, you might want to create a private Web page for that client, as explained in Chapter 9, "Communicating Better with Clients." But if you're only posting a file occasionally, you don't need to go to that effort. Just send the client an e-mail that includes the link to the file. That link is your Web site's address followed by a /, followed by the folder name (such as docs), again followed by a /, and finally the filename, for example, www.grumanhomes. com/docss/123Main_discl.pdf. (Note that capitalization is important, so be sure the link is capitalized the same way as the folder and filenames.)

When the client clicks that link from an e-mail (or pastes it into a Web browser), his Web browser will open the file 123Main_discl.pdf from the docs folder on the Web site. (Of course, you have to place that file in the specified folder on your Web server for the link to actually open the file.) The browser will see the filename extension .pdf and know to load the Adobe

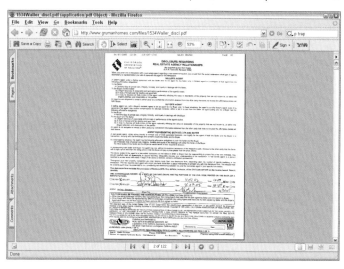

And example of what the client might see when he opens a Web site's PDF link in his browser.

Reader plug-in to display the page. (The Reader plug-in is usually installed along with the browser, but if it wasn't, your client can download it at no cost from www.adobe.com/reader.) At that point, your client can read, save, and/or print the file.

Working with Print Layout Tools

In addition to working with existing documents such as disclosures and contracts, you also spend time creating marketing documents, from listing presentations to open house flyers to market comparison reports.

Chances are you're using Microsoft Word, because it has rudimentary layout capabilities to support multiple columns and can display images. And Word has a pretty easy Table tool that's quite handy for creating lists of comps.

But you can give your marketing documents more oomph and professional character if you use a page layout program like Microsoft Publisher or Adobe InDesign.

The basic difference between using Word and using a page layout program is the level of refinement you can achieve. Layout tools offer finer control over item placement and typographic display, which simply looks better. It's often easy to spot a "homemade" flyer done in Word, which is why a professional-looking flyer produced in a professional-level layout program helps your materials stand out—if you're willing to invest the time and money.

CD RESOURCE: For page layout, links to Adobe and Microsoft, as well as to font sources.

No matter what software you use to create your flyers, open house signs, and so on, if you plan to have them professionally printed, talk to the printer about the kinds of files it can accept and any restrictions it might have on those files. Some printers can work with Word or Publisher files, but many cannot. In some cases, you can create PDF files from Word or Publisher and submit the PDF files instead. But ask first. (Of course, if you're going to print these documents yourself, you don't have to worry about this issue.)

Tips for Using Microsoft Word

Microsoft Word is fine for basic layouts, but as you try to create more sophisticated pages, you'll quickly come across Word's limitations. That's because it was never designed as a layout tool; instead, layout capabilities were added for simpler needs as a bonus.

Placing Items

Microsoft Word does not give you fine control over item placement, but you can still do the basics. Word handles images as objects that are typically anchored to a spot in text so they move with that text as you work on the document. You can control some of the layout attributes—such as whether text overprints the image and where the image aligns—after you find the right controls in Word. The exact location may vary based on your version of Word, but typically you can access the controls by double-clicking an image after you import it. (To import a picture, you typically choose Insert > Picture > From File.)

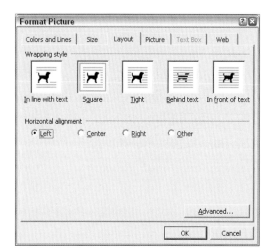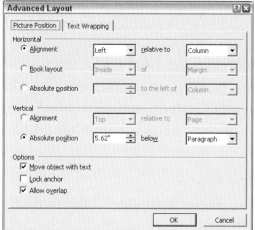

The basic picture controls in Microsoft Word are on the left, and the positioning controls if you click Advanced are on the right.

Note that the more images you have on a page, the harder it is to control their relative placement. Word really isn't designed to let you place several images in specific locations and leave them there, which is something you typically do in a flyer. What you can do easily is place a few images side by side (or separated with a few spaces), such as showing a row of images for a home.

Using Multiple Columns

The other key area to pay attention to in Word is the use of multiple columns. You first need to create a new section in your document—even if you want the columns to start in the middle of a page—by first choosing Insert > Break and then selecting the Continuous section break option before clicking OK. You'll need another continuous section break where you want the multiple columns to end. After you've created the breaks, your next step is to format the columns within the new section. Make sure you click the text pointer inside the section, and then choose Format > Columns. In the resulting dialog box, you can set the number of columns, their widths, and the spacing between the columns.

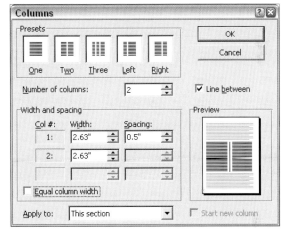

To have multiple columns in Word, first create a new continuous section (left), then apply the desired column settings to that new section (right).

Applying Styles

Don't forget to use styles to maintain consistent formatting of your text. A style saves all the formatting—font, size, alignment, and so on—so you can apply that style repeatedly to ensure consistent formatting. To define styles, choose Format > Style, then click New. Now adjust the settings in the dialog, using the Format button to select different formatting options. Click OK when done with the style, and then click Close. To apply styles to text, make sure your text is selected, choose the style from the Formatting bar or by choosing Format Style, and select the desired style from the list on the left. Then click Apply.

Tips for Using Microsoft Publisher

Microsoft Publisher is a popular layout tool in Windows for people who aren't professional designers. It uses lots of templates and wizards—step-by-step guidance for various actions—to help make good-looking materials easily.

Working with Frames

One thing that really distinguishes professional layout tools from word processors is the concept of frames—independent objects that can hold text or graphics, letting you place and format those objects independently. Publisher uses frames to hold text and graphics. For graphics, these frames are created automatically when you import an image (choose Insert > Picture > From File). But for text frames, you must first draw the frame before you can import the text (Import > Text File) or type in new text. To draw a frame, select the text frame icon (the letter A in the vertical button bar), then click and drag the rectangle shape, which will become the frame, where you want it on your page. (You can move and resize it later.)

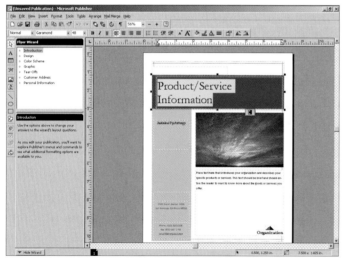

Microsoft Publisher relies heavily on templates and step-by-step wizards to help you create your materials.

Applying Styles

Don't forget to use styles to maintain consistent formatting of your text. A style lets you save all the formatting—font, size, alignment, and so on— and lets you easily apply that style over and over. To define styles, choose Format > Text Styles, then select Create a New Style from the dialog box. Now specify the various settings in the dialog box, and click OK when done. To apply styles to text, be sure your text is selected, and then click the desired style from the list in the Formatting bar (as you would in Microsoft Word).

Applying Colors

One area where Publisher is a bit weak is in its ability to create and apply colors. It works like Word in that you can select any color for fills, text, and lines (there are icons for each in the Formatting bar) by clicking Custom rather than choosing one of the colors initially shown. But you can't create what's called a palette—a set of colors you select to apply over and over again, much like how text styles work for text formatting. Therefore, it's harder to ensure consistent color use in Publisher.

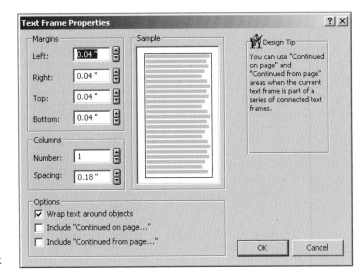

Like professional layout tools, Publisher uses the concept of text frames to hold independent text blocks. These frames can have multiple columns and their own margins.

Tips for Using Adobe InDesign

To create truly professional-quality layouts, you need a professional tool such as Adobe's InDesign. Although this tool lets you do a lot more with your layout than Word or Publisher, it's correspondingly more complex to use. So, if you're a novice InDesign user, start small by creating basic layouts and then experiment with the program's capabilities gradually so you don't get overwhelmed and give up.

Working with Columns and Page Dimensions

When you first create an InDesign layout, you set the basic specifications such as page size and number of columns. These aren't hard-and-fast settings, though: You can change the settings later by choosing Layout > Margins and Columns (for margins and columns) and File > Document Setup (for page dimensions). What can often confuse new users is that the columns you set for InDesign aren't forced on you—they're just guidelines that appear on every page. As you add text (by creating a text frame or by importing text), you can adjust InDesign's settings, including number of columns, independently of what is set in the general document settings. In other words, think of each text frame as its own mini-page that you can format as you want, and then arrange with the other text frames and pictures as you want.

Using the Control Palette

InDesign has a very complex interface with way too many options scattered about. To keep things under control, use the Control palette (the rectangular palette at the top of the window) instead. Its options change based on whatever you currently have selected, helping you narrow down the relevant options. While not everything you want is displayed in the Control palette, most common actions are, so it's very handy. (Note that when you select text, the Control palette has two modes: If you click the A icon, you see character settings, but if you click the ¶ icon, you see paragraph settings.)

InDesign's Control palette gives you quick access to most common functions for whatever is selected. Note that some of the functions reside in the palette menu, the triangle icon in the upper-right corner.

Working with Frames

InDesign uses frames to hold text and graphics. For both text and graphics, frames are created automatically when you import a text file or an image (choose File > Place). You can also draw frames before importing text or graphics (or before typing in your own text) by selecting either of the rectangle-shaped tools from the vertical button bar and then clicking and dragging the rectangle shape that will become the frame. You can place the frame anywhere on the page. (You can move and resize it later.)

One often-used tool not displayed in the Control palette is the Text Wrap pane, which lets you set how text margins adjust when text frames overlap other objects. (Making text surround other objects is called text wrap.)

Because InDesign uses independent text frames, sometimes it can be frustrating trying to get text to flow from one frame to another, whether on the same page or across pages.

Importing Text and Graphics

The method InDesign uses to import text and graphics is confusing. In InDesign, that action is called placing, so you use the Place dialog box to select text or graphics to bring into the layout (one at a time, of course). Choose File > Place to access that dialog box.

KEYS TO GOOD DESIGN

If you're not experienced with marketing or publications design, chances are you'll make at least a few rookie mistakes. Here are the most common ones. As you can see, they typically relate to trying to do too much at once:

- **Limit fonts:** Keep the use of fonts to no more than two. Note that this limit does *not* count italics or boldface variants of a font, nor fonts in your logo.

- **Pick readable fonts:** Avoid the decorative ones. Your goal is to communicate your message, so don't make the reader work at deciphering the letters. There are many elegant or classic fonts that add style to your text without also adding confusion.

- **Limit colors:** Minimize the use of colors or shading in the background as attention getters. You should use color to call attention to just a few key items, such as photos, a logo, or a headline.

- **Don't clutter the page:** Tiny type, lack of margins, lots of objects crammed together, and so forth are big turn-offs. Instead, say and show just what you need.

- **Focus the reader:** Have one main visual element—typically a block formed by the title and the main photo—and make sure everything else is secondary. That way, the reader's focus stays on the key message.

- **Limit separators:** Avoid lines between objects, boxes around objects, and so forth—they clutter a page fast. One or two of these elements is usually enough.

- **Limit columns:** Avoid using too many columns—narrow columns are hard to read. Similarly, avoid using staggered columns, because they make it hard for the reader to know where to read next.

Applying Styles

Don't forget to use styles to maintain consistent formatting of your text. You can apply a style repeatedly for consistent professional documents. To define styles, choose Type > Paragraph Styles, then select New Paragraph Style from the palette menu (the little arrow that appears in a palette's upper-right or upper-left corner, depending on the specific palette), then specify the desired settings in the dialog box, clicking OK when done. To apply styles to text, select your text, and then click the desired style from the list in the Paragraph Styles pane.

You'll also see something called character styles, which lets you create styles for sections of text within a paragraph, affecting only highlighted text. A paragraph style affects the entire paragraph.

InDesign's Paragraph Styles pane lets you apply consistent formatting to text easily, as well as define and modify the styles.

CD RESOURCE: Template files in Word, Publisher, and InDesign formats for you to use to create your own materials.

Working with Web Creation Tools

The other type of electronic document you might work with is a Web page, which is created using Hypertext Markup Language (HTML). Whether you create your Web site or hire someone to do it for you, it's very likely that you'll want to make changes to the site's pages—updating your listings, for example, or updating neighborhood information—and thus will need to at least edit the pages' HTML code occasionally.

You can do a lot of that editing in a Web creation program's design view, which hides the actual HTML code from you—just like working in a word processor or page layout program hides the code used to create and format pages. But unlike word processors and page layout programs, Web creation programs let you work with the underlying HTML code, and in some cases it's actually easier to edit the code directly—if you know what you are doing—than using the program's design view to apply the desired formatting. That's why most designers switch back and forth between their Web creation program's design view and code view.

HTML is not a flexible language, so creating a sophisticated site with lots of interactivity and custom formatting is difficult. If you're creating your own site and aren't experienced in HTML, focus instead on a pleasing, informative but straightforward design. As your pages get more complex, the more likely it is that you'll need work directly with the underlying HTML code.

Most Web creation tools offer both a design view and a code view, so you can switch between working on the layout visually and tweaking the underlying HTML code. Some programs, like Macromedia Dreamweaver, offer a split view so you can see both. Another common option is a formatting palette (shown at the bottom) to let you apply HTML settings without learning how to write code.

When you create Web pages, keep these tips in mind:

■ **Page width:** Keep the width of Web site pages to about 850 pixels. The common monitor setting is 1024×768-pixel resolution and 850 pixels leaves room for the Favorites or Bookmarks sidebar that many browsers offer.

■ **New window:** Any links to Web pages or documents outside your site should open a new window, so your site remains accessible to the user at all times. When you're creating Web links, there's usually an option named Target: Make sure it is set to _blank for a new window to open when the link is clicked. (No option should be selected for Target if you want to have the link open in the existing window, such as a link to another page within your site.)

■ **Standard fonts:** You can't depend on your site's visitors having the same browser preferences or fonts you do, so always test your pages on a variety of browsers and never use fonts other than standard ones like Arial, Times New Roman, Verdana, Georgia, and Tahoma.

■ **Cascading style sheets:** Use the cascading style sheets (CSS) feature if available to format text. The equivalent of a layout program's style sheets, CSSs help ensure fairly consistent display among browsers. Typically, the CSS is stored in a separate file, so be sure to transfer that file to your Web server along with your HTML pages. (The CSS file's filename extension is typically .css—as you might expect.)

■ **Tables:** The only way to position elements in a Web page is by using tables. The table acts as a layout grid, with its cells determining the relative position of objects based on what you put in each cell. Think of table cells as the equivalent to frames in a layout program. Merge and split cells as needed, and note that you can have tables inside tables. Then place your text and graphics into the appropriate cells.

■ **Cell format:** By default, tables have borders around all cells, but you can change borders by adjusting the Border setting to 0. You can also set how much space appears between cells by adjusting the CellSpacing setting. (To leave a margin inside a cell between its content and the cell border, adjust the CellPadding setting.)

- **Highlighted text:** To highlight text by placing a color behind it, you have to create a one-cell table, put that text in the cell, and then apply a background color. Another way to highlight text is to apply a color to the text itself and/or to apply formatting such as boldface and a different font. You can combine any or all of these techniques.

- **Image size:** Pictures always import at 100 percent of their size, so it's best to save your Web images to the desired size (as described earlier in this chapter). You can change their size in the browser by setting width and height settings, but the result is usually less appealing than if the image is resized first in an image editor.

- **Spelling:** Read your text carefully—you usually won't find a spelling checker in Web creation software, so it's very easy for mistakes to be published on your site.

- **Keywords:** Be sure you insert keywords to help search engines find your site. In your HTML code, these keywords are enclosed in an HTML tag called META, but usually there's a menu option that lets you type these in without having to worry about the code. If you must code these manually, insert the appropriately edited version of the following tag in between the `<title>` and `</title>` tags: `<metaname="keywords"content="real estate, realtor, buy, sell, home, house, condo, your city, your name, your company">`. (Chapter 5, "Online Marketing Techniques," covers keyword techniques in more depth.)

If Web-page creation seems scary from what I've described, don't panic. You can always hire someone to create your Web site, or use a fill-in-the-blank service that generates a site for you, as described in Chapter 1, "The Right Office Tools." If someone else creates your Web site, chances are that you can update the contents yourself (which saves you time and money). That's because it's typically easier to editing Web pages than to create them, since you typically just need basic operations like adding and removing text or adding and removing pictures when editing and thus need to know less about HTML and Web design.

CD RESOURCE: Template HTML files for you to use to create your own Web pages.

Marketing Yourself More Effectively

PART 2

CHAPTER 4

Effective Web Sites

ISSUES COVERED

- Should you build your own Web site or use a service?
- What do you need to set up a Web site?
- What should the Web site contain?
- Where do you find content for your site?

Chances are that you shop online, so you understand the convenience of the Web for checking out products and shopping resources. You're not alone; many people use the Web to shop for homes as well as for electronics, apparel, and other goods. In fact, the National Association of Realtors estimates that about two-thirds of home buyers start their research on the Web. That's a powerful argument for you to use the Web to market yourself and your listings.

The Web has many positives: It's a fast, inexpensive way to deliver information to lots of people as well as target specific information to individuals. The Web is also a convenient way for clients and prospective clients to communicate with you.

But there are some negatives: Notifying potential clients that your site exists is difficult, adding content to your site requires technology expertise most agents don't have, and meeting customers' expectations of quick responses and always-current information seven days a week, 24 hours a day, is also hard.

Still, a real estate Web site is a must-have today. The real questions are: How do you set one up? And how do you determine what information you should place on it?

Setting Up a Web Presence

You can hang your shingle on the Web in several ways. Each requires different amounts of effort, cost, and expertise—and each provides different levels of customer experience and service—so think through what makes sense for your business. If your customers aren't frequent Internet users, there's no need to invest in an elaborate Web presence. But if they tend to be routine computer users, chances are they'll expect you to be Web-savvy as well.

One great thing about the Web is that it's easy to change things, so if you're not sure how much of a Web presence to have, you can start small and then expand if the demand is there. And if you overdo your initial Web site, you can always scale it back.

Getting Your Own Site

Your Web presence can be simple or rich. For example, many brokers give their agents a single page on their sites, often with standard categories agents use to highlight their strengths, list any properties for sale, and provide other information. Some agents create their own sites that have multiple pages, such as pages for community resources, mortgage information, MLS searches, current listings, and tips.

Some agents have their own Web address (such as www.grumanhomes.com), while others use an address belonging to a Web portal such as Yahoo or AT&T WorldNet (such as www.geocities.com/galengruman for Yahoo and home.att.net/~galengruman for AT&T), or to their brokerage (such as www.prurealty.com/gruman).

What's the difference? A big one. Most real estate agents are self-employed contractors affiliated with a brokerage. As such, you're running your own business. You should use a Web address that will stay with you, even if you change brokerages. Also, using Web sites

THE BIGGER PICTURE

HOW THE WEB WORKS

A Web site is essentially a set of files stored in a folder on a server that is connected to the Internet. This folder has a unique Web address.

Technically, the folder has two addresses: an IP address, which is a series of numbers; and a domain name or Uniform Resource Locator (URL), which is a word or phrase that is a shortcut to, or alias for, the IP address.

For example, www.grumanhomes.com is the URL for the IP address 209.197.127.232. Entering either one into a Web browser opens up my Web site. When a user enters www.grumanhomes.com, directory servers on the Internet look it up, find out the corresponding IP address (209.197.127.232), and look up which server hosts that IP address, directing the request to that specific server. The server then figures out which folder contains the Web site's files based on its own internal directory, and then lets the user's browser open up the appropriate page.

Why does this matter? Because it explains why you need two separate services to have your own Web site: a Web host for the files and a domain registrar for the domain name. (These typically are separate companies.) Once you have the domain name, you tell the Web host what the IP address is so the Web host can make the connection to its folders. You'll also need to tell the domain registrar the Web host's nameserver address, so the registrar can update its directory. The two companies will each provide the instructions for its portions of this step.

hosted by a service such as Yahoo's Geocities or AT&T WorldNet raises two problems: First, the complex Web addresses that these services provide are hard for your clients to type in to their Web browsers—that discourages use of your Web site. Second, they show a lack of professionalism—real businesses have their own domains and don't use pages on consumer sites usually used for family photos and other personal pages. Remember, you're a real business and should present yourself as such.

So get your own domain name. In fact, you might want to get several. For example, I use www.grumanhomes.com, but I also have www.galengruman.com, which I have set to automatically forward to www.grumanhomes.com. With two domain names, if potential clients remember my personal name but not my business name, they'll still find me.

Using Your Brokerage's Site

If your brokerage gives you space on its Web site, take it. More presence is a good thing. In some cases, you can set up your agent page on the brokerage site to automatically move any users to your actual site. Even if your brokerage doesn't give you an option to do so on the setup page it provides for you on its Web site, you can often force a redirect from that page to your Web site by adding a snippet of code anywhere on that personal Web page:

```
<meta http-equiv="refresh"
content="0;URL=http://www.yourdomain.com">
```

Just be sure to replace the www.yourdomain.com URL in that code with your site's actual URL! And note that the 0 character in content="0 is a zero, not the letter O.

In some cases, the brokerage's Web site will prevent this code from working, or worse, will simply have the code display as if it were text. In that case, delete the code and consider adding a line in your page's text that tells users what your URL is and to go there for more details. This way, visitors will at least have the opportunity to type it in themselves.

CD RESOURCE: For the redirection code, the snippet is included on the CD.

A CONSISTENT IDENTITY

One consideration when you set up your Web site is the domain name you choose. In any marketing endeavor, it's critical to have a consistent identity.

For example, my Web site is www.grumanhomes.com and my e-mail address is galen@grumanhomes.com. By contrast, if I had my Web site on Yahoo's Geocities service, my Web address might be www.geocities.com/galengruman, but my e-mail address might be galengruman@yahoo.com. (I don't mean to single out Yahoo; you will have similar issues with other providers.)

Achieving a consistent identity goes beyond having a Web address and e-mail addresses reinforce each other. You also want your domain name to match your business name. I've known agents who use e-mail addresses like bestsfagent@yahoo.com; such addresses are not only hard to remember but don't remind you of the actual agent's personal or business name.

Most agents should incorporate their name in their domain name. You could use your own name, such as www. galengruman.com, if no one is already using it, or you could combine it with a real estate-related term, such as www.grumanhomes.com or www.grumansfproperties.com.

If you are a broker, you'll want your domain name to match your company name if at all possible, because customers typically type the company name into their browser (or their search engine) when they can't remember the actual URL.

How to Set Up Your Site

Setting up a Web site involves several steps, including getting the domain name for your site, choosing a company to host your Web site, uploading the site's pages, and configuring your e-mail access.

Remember that you will still need a local Internet service provider such as your cable or phone company or a national provider such as EarthLink for the high-speed or dial-up Internet access at your home. (A Web host makes your Web site available to the world, but it doesn't connect your computer to the Internet.)

Getting the Domain and Web Host

Domains are cheap: You can lease one through a domain registrar for about $10 per year if you reserve it for several years at a time. At most, it should cost you about $20 per year if you reserve the domain for just one year at a time. There are lots of places to register domain names: Web hosting companies and portal providers (like Yahoo) often offer a link to one on their sites. All of these companies provide pretty much the same service, so what distinguishes one from the other usually comes down to price. Another factor to consider is the user-friendliness of their tools to search for available names and the tools to set up the account after you find a domain name you want. I like NTT Verio and GoDaddy, but there are many good services out there.

Web hosting is pretty cheap, too. Although there are many companies that promise hosting service for $10 or less per month, my experience is that their reliability and customer service gets iffy over time. But for not much more money—just $15 to $20 per month—you can get a good local, regional, or national provider. Ask around to see which company your friends and colleagues like. One I recommend is Pair Networks, but there are many good providers doing business, so if you get a recommendation from someone you know, start there. And consider a local provider when possible, because they often provide more personal service.

If you happen to get a company that provides poor service—meaning the Web site and e-mail service go down several times a month, access is really slow, or you have difficulty contacting the company—you can transfer your domain to another Web host.

All it takes is to start your service with a new Web host company, giving it your site's IP address, *plus* updating the domain registrar with your new Web host's nameserver information (which ties your IP address to the server that hosts your site). You need to provide the new nameserver information so that when users type in your URL, the request gets directed to the new location.

Do note that transferring a Web site takes about a week, because there are thousands of directory servers on the Internet that direct Web traffic, and it takes a while for them all to get your new address.

CD RESOURCE: *For domain registration, links to GoDaddy and NTT Verio. For Web hosting, a link to Pair Networks.*

Setting Up E-Mail and Pages

Note that almost all Web hosts include e-mail service, letting you access your e-mail through mail clients such as Microsoft's Outlook as well as by going to a Web page where you can log in to check your mail (handy when you are accessing the Internet with someone else's computer). You'll need to set up your e-mail client

SITE SERVICE OPTIONS

Setting up and maintaining your own Web site can seem very daunting. However, there's a whole industry of providers who can manage your Web site for you. They promise to provide an easy interface that will let you update your content by filling in templates, at a cost of $20 to $200 per month. Examples include Agent123, ListingDomains.com, RapidListings.com, and RealtyDrive.com.

Hiring one of these companies might work very well for you if you really don't want to hire your own designer or do your own design, or if you are not comfortable with the idea of working with Web pages, Web hosts, file uploading, and so forth.

You'll pay more for this option and have less flexibility about what your site can contain, but you gain convenience so you can focus on finding and serving your clients.

THE BIGGER PICTURE

A typical agent Web site includes the following pages:

- **Home page:** This page—usually named index.htm or index.html—identifies your key benefits and provide a clear navigation to the rest of your site. This page often includes a few brief customer testimonials.

- **Listings:** A page of your and/or your brokerage's current listings.

- **Resources:** One or more pages of resources (such as financing, first-time buyers, local information, and professional referrals).

- **Sign-up page:** A page where visitors can register for a newsletter, market analysis, and/or current property list.

You might also consider adding these pages:

- **MLS search:** A page that connects your site's visitors to your local MLS's public search system (often called an IDX).

- **Sales trends:** A summary of recent sales trends (such as average price by area or property type).

software so it knows how to check your mail; your Web host will provide the instructions for popular e-mail clients such as Outlook. For other programs, you might need to hunt around to find the equivalent fields.

After your domain is active and your Web host has activated your server space and account, you need to load your Web pages onto the server. The Web host will provide the connection information to do so. Typically, there are two ways to transfer files to the Web host from your computer: One is to use file transfer protocol (FTP) software, the other is to use the interface provided on the Web host's Web site (this interface is usually called the control panel). FTP software is typically faster at transferring your information, so if you foresee updating your site frequently, get a good FTP program such as Ipswitch's WS_FTP Pro for Windows or Fetch Softworks's Fetch for Mac OS X. (If you use Microsoft's FrontPage Web-creation software, the FTP function is built in. Just be sure to have your Web host enable FrontPage extensions for your account so FrontPage can do its thing.)

If you create your own Web site, you'll need an HTML authoring or editing program. While there are dozens of such programs available, three command the lion's share of users: Microsoft's Windows-only FrontPage, which is designed for nontechnical users, and Adobe's Macromedia Dreamweaver and GoLive programs, both available for Windows and Mac OS X. Both Adobe programs are designed for more professional users but also use a visual interface that let you do much of the work without ever working directly with code. FrontPage is easier for many novices, but its Web pages tend to look a bit canned because they rely so heavily on templates.

CD RESOURCE: For file transfer, links to Fetch and Ipswitch. For Web creation and editing software, links to Adobe and Microsoft. Web templates and code snippets (samples) are also included on the CD.

Elements of a Good Site

However you host, update, and create your Web site, you need to make sure it is an effective Web site. Creating an effective site involves having a solid sense of design and identity as well as a clear understanding of what you want the site to accomplish. That's easy to say, but hard to accomplish.

Design and identity require creative abilities that not all of us have, and if you don't, hire a professional designer. (That's what they're for!) An ugly, unfocused, or hard-to-navigate site will harm you, not help. If you design the site yourself, look at as many agent sites as you can to get a sense of what works visually and what doesn't. Also consider hiring a professional editor to edit your text, both for obviously unprofessional issues such as typos but also for the overall effectiveness of its presentation.

And remember, you can still maintain and modify the site yourself even if you don't design it.

Keep the Goal in Mind

Remember, the basic purpose of a Web site is to drive potential clients to do business with you. Everything you do on your site should reinforce that goal, so keep the following principles in mind:

- **Make it easy to contact you.** Contact information should be easily found and easily read, and it should exist on every page. Include your primary phone number and e-mail address. Be sure the e-mail address is a clickable link that automatically opens the user's e-mail client (something any Web creation program can do; it's called a mailto link). You also might include your cell phone number if it's not your primary number, but don't include your office's main number, your fax number, or your separate voicemail number (if you have one)—too many numbers can confuse people.

When linking to outside content, such as these Google maps for recommended restaurants, be sure that a new window opens so it's clear what is your original content and what comes from some other source.

■ **Lead users to action.** Include information about when you'll be hosting open houses or when your office or floor-duty hours are, so users can easily drop by to meet you in person. Offer forms they can fill out for a market analysis or listings within their criteria. Provide links to flyers of your listings. If you don't have listings consistently, consider providing links (if your broker gives permission, of course) to your brokerage's listings that include you as the contact for buyers seeking an agent. These flyers can be individual Web pages or PDF flyers that users can download and print, with your contact information prominently provided.

Below are two examples of good agent Web sites. Both sites make the contact information prominent and make it easy to see what the agent's site offers. Each page focuses on specific benefits for customers.

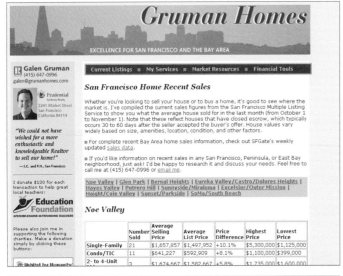

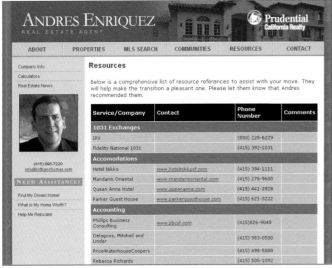

■ **Focus on the benefits of working with you.** Your descriptive text, resources offered, and so forth should reinforce why you are the best listing or buyer's agent. That doesn't mean you should list all your wonderful traits—that quickly becomes annoying braggadocio—but it does mean you should emphasize your specific skills, background, and experience. For example, if you "farm" (focus your marketing on) a specific town or neighborhood, show your intimate knowledge of that area with local recommendations and resources. This information reinforces your expertise more than any mere claims can. And be sure to include customer testimonials—a few words each from several recent clients is all you need.

- **Reinforce your professional network.** Real estate agents are problem solvers, helping clients navigate not just the sale or purchase of a property but also the issues surrounding financing, escrow, and repairs. Provide referrals to mortgage brokers and others you trust who are likely to promote you to their clients as well, creating a network of self-reinforcing contacts that show you're well connected and that other good people trust you.

Many brokers provide their agents with a Web page within the brokerage site. Take advantage of it, but if possible, have the page redirect users to your site, either automatically or by including a prominent link to your site.

- **Don't give away your core services.** It's perfectly good to provide some basic services on your Web site, such as mortgage calculators and public MLS searches, to help prospective clients get a feel for your offerings and give them the ability to perform some of the basic research that you want them to do before they engage your time (such as knowing what they can really afford and what's really available). But remember that most Web users are accustomed to thinking of the Web as a place for free stuff, and you can't stay in business working for free. So don't try to serve the freeloaders. Instead, focus on offering services that save you time, help customers become better educated, and demonstrate your professional approach.

- **Don't include too much.** Don't try to cram everything onto a Web page or Web site—you'll confuse and overwhelm your audience, and they'll move on. Each page should have a specific focus, so stick to that focal point. The site also should be about your real estate services, not about other businesses or personal issues. If you run multiple businesses, maintain separate Web sites for each. If they're related, provide links among them. For example, perhaps you sell real estate as well as manage properties. In that case, have a real estate Web site and a property management Web site, and then be sure that each site links to the other. But if you sell real estate and also fix trucks or sell gift baskets, don't link these unrelated businesses.

Sources for Content

Most of what appears on your Web site will come from three sources:

- Your own original content, such as your listing information and your personal guide to neighborhoods

- Professional content such as MLS sales data, office listings, and loan calculators that come from real estate-oriented providers

- Public content such as school information from public sources such as the school district or a government agency

In most cases, you need permission to use content other than what you personally create. Although it's usually legal to cite other sources for brief snippets of data, there's no hard-and-fast rule as to how much information you can use without permission before it becomes copyright infringement. So get in the habit of asking for permission or of using links to the material instead.

Using Property Information

A real estate agent's Web site should include information on properties—after all, that's what most buyers are looking for when they go to an agent's site. Most agents don't have listings available all the time, so you can't count on just showing your own listings to satisfy visitors' interest in current listings.

I recommend that when you do have property listings that you showcase them on your home page. If you have lots of listings, maybe showcase one or two on the home page and then provide a link to a listings page that details all your listings.

But you should also let visitors see other agents' listings. That gives them a reason to come to your site and see why you'd be a great buyer's agent for them. You have two good ways to offer such listings to your site's visitors:

- Showcase your office's listings (those listed by other agents in your brokerage)

- Provide access to the public portion of your local MLS

Presenting Office Listings

To publish information about your office listings, you'll first need permission to publish the listings, either from your broker or from the individual agents, based on your broker's policy. Assuming you have permission, a great way to know what listings your office has is to set up an automatic search on your MLS so it sends you an e-mail every time a new listing from your office appears. (Many MLS systems let you set up such automatic notification for clients, as Chapter 9, "Communicating Better with Clients," explains, so you just add yourself as a client and set the search criteria to be all listings where the listing office is your brokerage.) Not all MLS systems let you send automatic notifications based on saved searches; if your MLS doesn't, you'll need to rely instead on internal documents such as sales sheets to get this information.

With that information in hand, you can update a page on your Web site devoted to office listings. I arrange mine in a table by property types (single-family homes, condominiums, and multifamily dwellings). I then sort the listings within those property types by price. This arrangement is simple for me to maintain and provides an easy way for potential buyers to scan what's available. But you could arrange these listings as a list or use another layout of your choice. (Your knowledge of Web creation software, covered in Chapter 3, "Working with Electronic Media," might lead you to choose a certain presentation approach because you are comfortable using the software to accomplish that type of layout.)

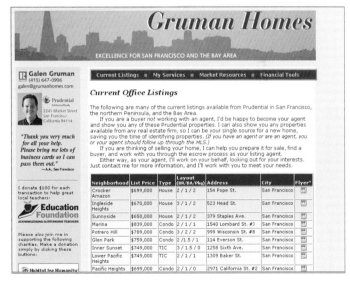

Presenting office listings can be a good way to give potential buyers reason to return to your site often.

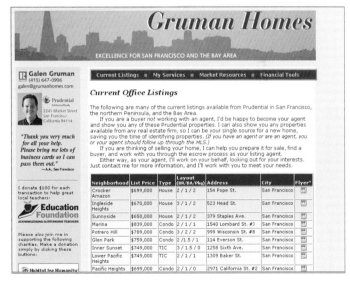

When you show office listings, be sure to do two things:

- Make it clear you are not the listing agent. After all, you're not, and you don't want buyers with agents or other agents to call you about these listings. If you're not clear that you're seeking to represent buyers interested in these or other properties, you could be accused of interfering with the listing agent's efforts.

- Make it clear that you can help potential buyers who don't already have agents. Remember, a major reason to have a Web site is to get new clients, so make a brief sales pitch on your behalf on this page. (In fact, every page should have a brief sales pitch, even if it's just "Call me for more information.")

Making the MLS Accessible to Visitors

Another way to get potential buyers to your site is by offering MLS search capabilities. Make sure your local MLS allows such public searching. Two terms are used for this public search capability: Internet Data Exchange (IDX) and virtual office Web site (VOW). Whatever it's called, potential buyers, potential sellers who want to assess the market, and current clients who want to privately explore properties outside the criteria they've discussed with you all like being able to see what properties are available.

Some agents are nervous about providing MLS search capabilities to the public, thinking that buyers will have no need to use them. I disagree: After all, getting lists of potential properties is just a small fraction of the service a real estate agent provides to buyers. But seeing what's available helps buyers become educated about the market, so they're more realistic when they do contact an agent. I also find that many buyer clients use the public search feature of the MLS to double-check me, especially in the early stages of our relationship. I welcome this, because they invariably find

Offering public MLS search capabilities can also keep visitors coming back. I "framed" the public MLS inside my site, so visitors stay within my environment.

DON'T STEAL CONTENT

When putting together a real estate Web site, it's tempting to copy information from other sources to present a unified package of information in one place. But that can easily make you a thief of copyrighted material. Get permission to include material that you did not create, even if you give the source credit on your site. That means:

- Ask your broker if it's OK to include office listings (those listings where other agents in your office are representing the seller). The brokerage may give you blanket permission do so, or it may require you to get permission from each agent separately.

- Don't post listings, pictures, and so on from other brokerages without getting the individual agents' permission first, and understand they will likely need their brokers' permission as well.

- Never excerpt or republish content or tools from other Web sites, newsletters, or publications without first getting permission to do so. If you work for a large brokerage, it likely has free content for agents to use in their sites and newsletters. Still, unless the material is clearly labeled as something agents may use in their marketing, always check before using it.

- Find out what content your local MLS, Realtors association, and brokerage let you use as part of your membership in those organizations—most give agents blanket permission to republish some data, such as recent sales data, as long as it is properly credited. Just don't assume what you can use—always verify.

- If you can't get permission, consider linking to the source material if it is available on the Web, but never use techniques such as framing to make that content appear within a window on your site. Instead, use hyperlinks to such content. I recommend that any links outside your site open a new window, so it's clear the content is not on your site. (When you're creating Web links, there's usually an option named Target; make sure it is set to `_blank` for a new window to open when the link is clicked. To have the link open in the existing window, such as a link to another page in your site, no Target option should be selected.)

inappropriate properties I've screened out, giving me an opportunity to show them that I'm actively engaged and not wasting their time with properties that don't match their needs or goals. Those results help clients quickly see the value I bring.

Many MLS systems have a public search function, so many people won't think of going to your site to look up properties. That's why you need other reasons for them to come to your site. But after they're at your site, having MLS search capability in addition to your other content is a convenience that provides incentive for them to want to come back: It's easier to go to one place than to hop around a bunch of different sites.

Typically, one major advantage to you of including an IDX or VOW search is that the results all identify you as the contact for more information, not the listing agent—this lets your clients explore options without you having to worry about the other agents poaching them. (By contrast, when people use the search feature at a public MLS site or at a multi-MLS site like www.Realtor.com, they're given the listing agent's information.)

To implement an IDX or VOW on your site, you typically have to use a special URL from the MLS that ensures that all listings found provide your contact information. You can use that URL on your site in one of two ways:

THE DARK SIDE OF OUTREACH

While you're publicizing yourself on the Web and in other media to attract customers, these same outreach efforts will draw salespeople to you like flies to honey.

Companies selling everything from training programs to Web-site creation services will start e-mailing and calling you, culling your information from Web-site searches and sometimes even by buying your contact information from government agencies and your brokerage. Even if you have registered your phone number on the national Do Not Call registry, that list is just for residential lines, so your publishing that number for business purposes gives phone-based salespeople the right to call you anyhow. Just ask them not to call you again.

You'll also get a lot of e-mail solicitations from mortgage brokers, training companies, Web-service providers, and vendors of tschotchkes. I recommend that you "unsubscribe" to all unwanted e-mail pitches to help keep the volume down. (Also consider using some of the antispam tools mentioned in Chapter 1, "The Right Office Tools.")

I recommend that you do *not* publish your fax number on your Web site or in public databases, since doing so increases the chances of getting spam faxes. While new laws prohibit unsolicited faxes, many unscrupulous companies send them out anyhow, even if you call to have your number removed.

- **Provide a link:** You can just use the MLS link in your menus or elsewhere on your site. When visitors click it, they will be taken from your site to a page that looks nothing like your site (instead, it will be a variation of the public MLS site), which can confuse visitors to your site.

- **Frame the search:** You can "frame" the MLS search inside your site. This technique keeps your visitors in a familiar environment: yours. Framing is an HTML technique that's pretty easy to implement. All you need to do is add the following code where you want the MLS search "window" to appear in your Web page: `<iframe width="`*xxx*`" height="`*yyy*`" src="`*url*`"></iframe>`. Be sure to replace *xxx* with the desired window width (in pixels), *yyy* with the desired window depth, and *url* with the actual URL for the MLS search page. You'll probably need to experiment with different height and width values until it looks right. Remember that this is code, so you must enter it into the code view of your Web creation software, not in the design view.

CD RESOURCE: For the framing code, the snippet is included on the CD.

Providing Mortgage Tools

One area that many buyers need help on is figuring out what they can afford. In many real estate markets, buyers need to be preapproved for their offers to be taken seriously. But even if that's not the case where you work, you want your buyer clients to really know their budget upfront, so you and they don't waste time on homes they can't actually afford.

However, many people don't like to talk about money with strangers, and they fear being ripped off by mortgage salespeople. You can help them on both counts by providing some basic mortgage tools, so they can privately explore their financial options before they're ready to open up to a stranger.

Buyers can find mortgage calculators online in hundreds of places. All they have to do is search for *mortgage calculator* in a search tool like Google. But for agents looking for a mortgage calculator to include on their Web site, the choices are more limited. Zango Group offers a trio of mortgage calculators—to calculate how much a buyer qualifies for, to calculate mortgage payments, and to compare loan options—as well as a separate calculator to estimate the financials of rental property investments. Other Web site calculator providers include HSH Associates and TimeValue Software.

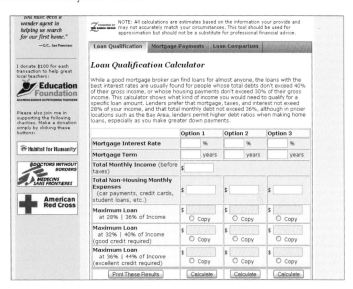

Mortgage calculators give potential buyers a reason to visit your Web site: private exploration of financial options before they're ready to talk to a person.

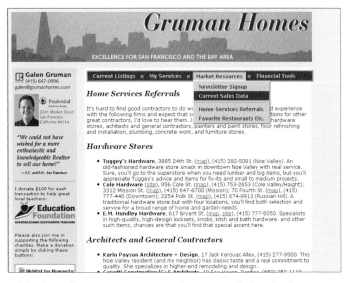

Helping buyers keep current on mortgage interest rates is also a handy way to encourage repeat visits.

You'll also want to give your visitors context about current mortgage rates, so they can budget accordingly. One good source for this information is HSH Associates, which offers several versions of its interest-rate charts that you can include on your site easily. Best of all, after you've added the code to your site, the rate information updates automatically, so you don't have to regularly update the page yourself.

THE BIGGER PICTURE

CD RESOURCE: *For mortgage calculators for use in agent sites, links to HSH Associates, TimeValue Software, and the Zango Group.*

Providing Other Information

You might provide lots of kinds of information on your Web site, but keep the following in mind:

■ **Limit free information:** You're not in the business of providing free information. You should include information that shows off your abilities to potential clients, so stay focused on a few key areas and always be sure to (gracefully) tell your visitors why they should talk to you directly to get great service.

■ **Maintain the site:** The more information you provide, the more you need to maintain. Nothing is worse for a Web site than being out of date: It shows laziness, sloppiness, or disengagement, none of which help sell you.

Most often, a real estate Web site should include information about the local market—such as neighborhoods, schools, and activities—as well as information about your services. Agents often provide this information through sign-up forms for newsletter subscriptions, how-to documents, or local general disclosures. This material typically comes from your broker, Realtors association, or government and community sources.

In many cases, though, you can create the content. For example, you could provide a page on local resources, listing contact information for the gas company, water company, cable TV providers, phone companies, and so forth—everything someone who's moving will need to have handy. I provide links to my favorite neighborhood restaurants and to a few trusted sources for plumbing, hardware, and so forth. You might choose to keep those recommendations to yourself and instead provide information on local schools or parks.

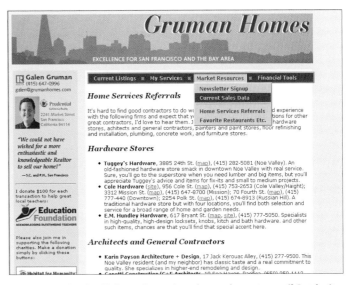

Provide some free local information to show that you know your stuff. But don't give away everything; you want to have some exclusives for your paying clients.

Pick what makes sense for your market and for your expertise, but pick just a few such areas for which to give away information on your Web site. For the other topics you know well, create checklists or other printed documents that you give your clients during a transaction as part of your enhanced service package. That'll help word spread about the extra mile you go for your clients. Remember, the goal of putting some of this content on your Web site is to show your knowledge of your area, so potential clients know that you know your stuff.

In addition to this local market expertise, be sure to provide FAQs—frequently asked questions—for sellers and buyers. Most people do not know how real estate works, and they have lots of misunderstandings about agency, commissions, and so on. One I hear all the time is a belief that an agent can sell only the properties listed in her office—like salespeople at the shoe store who can sell only that store's stock. By offering FAQs for sellers and buyers, you can answer the common questions and debunk the common myths. (I recommend offering separate FAQs for buyers and sellers, so each page focuses on its specific audience.)

Having FAQs provides several benefits: It shows you know how the business works; it presents you as a client-oriented, helpful agent; and it helps your Web site (and thus you) look more impressive. Another advantage: It gives you a great follow-up for potential clients you meet at open houses or on floor duty. If they seem new to real estate, you can answer a few questions live, and then give them a card that has your Web site address on it and tell them there's a page on your site that'll answer a lot of their other questions at their convenience. (Of course, let them know that you're also happy to talk about any of those issues by phone or in person.) Now they have another reason to learn more about you.

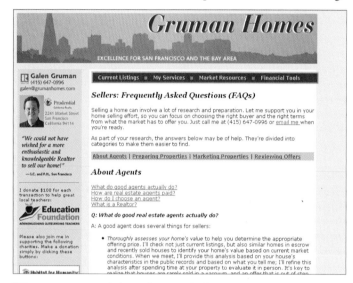

FAQs are a great way to help new buyers and sellers understand how real estate really works, and also give them another reason to see your stuff.

CHAPTER 5

Online Marketing Techniques

ISSUES COVERED

- How do you get people to come to your site?
- How should you advertise over the Web?
- How can you use newsletters and other electronic outreach methods?
- What legal and privacy issues exist in electronic outreach?

From the breezy stories you see on the local news to the pitches you get from various providers, you'd think simply having a Web site would make you the center of the real estate universe. Just hang your shingle and clients will beat down your door. Please don't believe that rosy scenario for one minute.

Don't get me wrong, having a Web site is very important. People don't like being "sold," so a Web site provides a safe place for them to explore you before they're ready for direct communication. Many clients, especially buyers, start their research for properties and agents on the Web, so having a site is a critical facet of your marketing strategy. Today's clients also want to check you out after meeting you or being referred to you, and a Web site provides a way for them to do that.

But the Web is awash in sites that no one knows about. There are millions of Web sites, and no easy way for people to find you.

That Web site you learned to create in Chapter 4, "Effective Web Sites," is a tool to show off your stuff to potential clients who do find you, but in and of itself, it does not bring you business.

Leading People to Your Site

Because the Web is a vast sea of sites spanning the entire globe, the most difficult step is getting people to your site. Fortunately, there are a few things you can do, some high-tech and others decidedly not.

List Your Site Everywhere

You should include your Web address, along with your phone number and e-mail address, in everything you distribute to people: in flyers, on your business cards, in any Realtors association profiles and member directories, in your MLS profile, in ads, and in your broker's printed and online agent directories. If you send out postcards, calendars, refrigerator magnets, or other marketing tschotchkes, make sure your Web address is on them. Basically, anything you distribute should include your Web address.

You're probably listed in more places than you think. Your broker likely has its own Web site with a list of agents. Your local Realtors association likely has a site listing all agents; so do the local, state, and national Realtors associations. Your local MLS will almost always have an agent search feature. You might be listed in business associations, service groups like the Kiwanis Club or Elks Lodge, and alumni groups. Review your profile in all such lists and be sure to add your Web address where that's an option.

It's particularly important to list your Web site in every online directory you are included in. (The reason is that search engines typically give more prominent placement in their search results to Web sites that are linked to by other sites.)

Be Sure That Search Engines Find You

Because the Web is so vast, one of the most common ways for people to find information is to use a search engine like Google (www.google.com) or one of the search engines included in portals such as Yahoo, MSN, and AOL.

There are two basic ways to help a search engine find your site and know what its content is, so it can present it in response to user searches:

- **Keywords:** Search engines use Web crawlers—tools that read through the top of each page to collect information for indexing that page. These Web crawlers look for keywords embedded in your Web site.

■ **Indexes:** Many search engines let you add details about your site to their indexes, and a whole bunch of companies will take your money to improve the odds the search engines will display your site in response to a query.

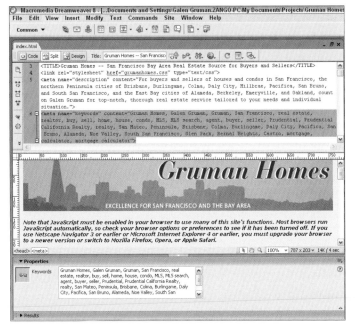

I've highlighted the keywords in my Web site's home page. In the top window is the actual HTML code, while the bottom window shows the keywords in a friendlier dialog box. Most Web editing programs let you work directly in your choice of HTML code or friendlier dialog boxes.

Adding Keywords

To ensure that Web crawlers get the information they need about your Web site, you need to enter keywords into your Web pages—at least into the home page (the one named *index.html* or *index.htm*). There are four places to enter this information, and you should enter this information in all four places.

First, in your Web page's HTML code, you should include a tag like `<meta name="keywords" content="real estate">` somewhere between the `<head>` and `</head>` tags. (A tag is a specific piece of HTML code, usually enclosed in `<` and `>` characters.) The list of terms inside the quotation marks after `content=` should of course include all relevant terms, such as your name, cities and areas served, and words that people will likely search by such as *real estate*, *realtor*, *house*, *buy*, and *sell*. Note that capitalization doesn't matter.

You will probably use the same basic keywords on every page, although you might want to add or customize keywords on specific pages. For example, if your site has a page about mortgages, you should add keywords such as *mortgage*, *finance*, *loan*, *rate*, and *interest* to that page's meta tag.

Second, also in the HTML code, you should include a tag like `<meta name="description" content="Specializing in San Francisco real estate for buyers and sellers">`, also somewhere between the `<head>` and `</head>` tags. Include as many of your keywords as possible in the description, but the keywords should be written as sentences, because it might be the text that displays in search results as the description of your site.

Third, also in the HTML code, you should include a tag like `<title>San Francisco real estate for buyers and sellers</title>`, somewhere between the `<head>` and `</head>` tags. This tag should be a phrase or short sentence that succinctly describes your site, using your most critical keywords. This text often appears in search results as well.

Fourth, the text of your pages (if you're working in the actual HTML code, that's anything between the `<body>` and `</body>` tags) should include as many of the keywords as possible, because search engines compare the actual content of a site's pages with the keywords to make sure the site actually is about what the `meta` tags claim it to be. Obviously, not every keyword is relevant on any page, but be sure to include all the keywords that are relevant. One way to accomplish this is to include a succinct sales pitch of your services on every page as a repeating element.

You might not see these `meta` tags directly in your HTML editing software—tags might be accessed through a dialog box.

For example, in Adobe's Macromedia Dreamweaver 8, you can add new tags by choosing Insert > HTML > Head Tags, and you can edit existing tags by choosing View > Head Content and then selecting from the row of tag icons at the top to have the current tag data display in the Properties palette at the bottom.

In Microsoft's FrontPage 2003, you can add new tags by choosing File > Properties and going to the Custom tab. Then click the Add button in the User Variables section to get a dialog box where you enter the tag name (such as `description`) and the tag contents. Click OK when you're done. To edit head content in FrontPage, follow the same steps for creating a meta tag but instead of clicking Add, select the desired tag and click Modify, then edit the text.

The complexity of adding meta tags without using actual HTML code in these two programs shows that sometimes it's better to bite the bullet and just deal with the code directly.

The most effective way to enter this keyword information is to create a list of all the terms you want the search engines to associate with your site—to help your site appear in a user's search results—*before* you create your Web pages. Create a blank

As you can see from these results, search engines like Google rarely show individual real estate agents' pages anywhere near the top of its search results, because agent pages typically get small volumes of visitors, lowering the score used to determine their position in the search result lists.

Web page with these tags already added for use as a template, and then use a copy of that template as you create each new page for your site (that way the meta tags are also in each page). If your Web site already exists, add this information to the home page and then copy its code to all other pages rather than reenter it from scratch on each page. I've included a sample of all these tags on the CD that accompanies this book to help get you started.

CD RESOURCES: For helping search engines find your site, a code snippet containing example meta *tags.*

Updating Search Engines Directly

You can supplement these embedded keywords by entering terms directly into many search engines. This can speed up your entries into the search engines, since it can take a few months before the Web crawlers find your site on their own. Some domain registries and Web hosts offer a free or low-cost service to do this for you; you can also pay sites such as NetMechanic to submit your site information on your behalf. I would try their free service first, to see if it gets any results before agreeing to pay money for "premium" services. It's impossible to guarantee the effectiveness of these services, since the search engines have their own secret index methods these site-submission services can't control. Paying for "optimized" search-engine placement is one of those areas where the lure of technology can cause real estate agents to waste money. Don't be lured.

I *do* recommend you take the time to list your site yourself on key search engines such as Google, HotBot/Lycos, and Yahoo Search, as well as the Open Directory Project that is compiling local directories of businesses and other resources for the Web. (Note that several popular sites such as AltaVista, AOL, and Netscape use one of these search engines instead of having one of their own.) Even though you're not likely to get at the top of their lists, you do increase your chances of being in the first dozen or so pages—and even higher if users enter detailed search queries.

As you can see, search optimization isn't a high-impact use of your time or money. But it is worth an hour or two implementing the keywords in your site and submitting your site to search engines.

CD RESOURCES: *For search engine submissions, links to Google, HotBot/Lycos, NetMechanic, the Open Directory Project, and Yahoo.*

Participate in Local Sites

We all know that real estate is a local business, but sometimes we forget that the Web is really a global resource, so 99.999 percent of the people using it will never be prospective clients of yours. But the Web is also home to many local sites, online directories, and communities that use the easy access of the Web to serve small geographic areas. That's a perfect venue for real estate agents.

The trick is to find those local sites that might be a good place for you to participate in. Do Web searches, check local newspapers, ask your fellow agents, and of course ask your friends and colleagues if they know of any local business directories or community sites. Then check out the sites to see if there's a possible fit.

One popular community site is Craigslist (named after founder Craig Newmark), which provides classified ads (free in most areas) and community discussion boards in dozens of cities. So it's a great example to use to show you the pros and cons of using local sites. But keep in mind that these pros and cons apply to all such sites, not just Craigslist.

Classified Ad Sites

Craigslist can be a good place to advertise your property listings. But note that in many areas of the country, Craigslist classified ads (called *posts*) are littered with out-of-area properties, mortgage lenders advertising their rates, and a variety of likely scams such as "80 percent off repossessed homes." That garbage quotient is particularly high in its urban listings, burying legitimate listings and turning off prospective buyers.

Despite the high garbage quotient in many of its sections, I still recommend using Craigslist to post your listings, but you need to delete and repost your listing every few days, so it doesn't get swept out of sight by all the garbage listings. (Listings expire automatically after 10 days in most areas, but in many areas, a single day's posts can fill two pages, so your ad still gets buried quickly.) If you're in one of the Craigslist cities that require payment for real estate classifieds, you'll of course see less junk and therefore won't need to repost as frequently.

CD RESOURCES: *For local community sites, a link to Craigslist.*

Community Forums

The other half of Craigslist is its group of community forums, which in most areas include real estate forums. These forums seem like a good place to show your expertise by offering advice on posted problems, but many times they just waste your time. Because it has local sections for dozens of cities and is often profiled in business magazines, Craigslist is a popular example of both the good and bad of community forums. But make no mistake: The pros and cons of forums are likely to exist in any community forum, especially those that promote free speech and don't charge membership or posting fees.

THE BIGGER PICTURE

CREATING YOUR OWN COMMUNITY SITE

If there's not a good local business or community site in your locality, you might consider starting your own local directory or site. While you might consider undertaking this effort yourself, it usually makes more sense to partner with a local business association or with other agents and/or mortgage brokerage and title company colleagues. Such an effort would bring in local businesses, volunteer groups, and so on, all of whom would help in the promotion through their own marketing, advertising, and communication efforts.

If you do create a local site, be careful that it is truly a local site, not just a big ad for you (and your partners). Visitors will quickly know if a site is what it claims to be; if you mislead them, you'll lose their trust. If you help create a real local site, keep it neutral. Use ads and links to get its visitors to your marketing-oriented personal site. Otherwise, you'd be better served to add community resources to your personal site, as I described in Chapter 4.

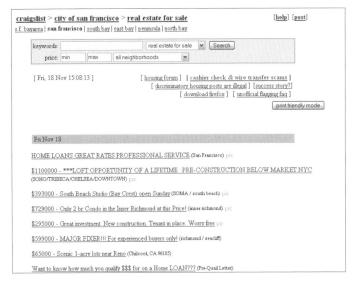

craigslist > city of san francisco > **real estate for sale**   [help] [post]
s.f. bayarea | san francisco | south bay | east bay | peninsula | north bay

keywords: [   ] [real estate for sale ⌄] [Search]
price: [min] [max] [all neighborhoods ⌄]

[Fri, 18 Nov 15:08:13]   [housing forum] | [cashier check & wire transfer scams]
[discriminatory housing posts are illegal] [success story?]
[download firefox] [unofficial flagging faq]
[print friendly mode]

Fri Nov 18

HOME LOANS GREAT RATES PROFESSIONAL SERVICE (San Francisco) pic

$1100000 - ***LOFT OPPORTUNITY OF A LIFETIME : PRE-CONSTRUCTION BELOW MARKET NYC (SOHO/TRIBECA/CHELSEA/DOWNTOWN) pic

$393000 - South Beach Studio (Bay Crest) open Sunday (SOMA / south beach) pic

$729000 - Only 2 br Condo in the Inner Richmond at this Price! (inner richmond) pic

$295000 - Great investment. New construction. Tenant in place. Worry free pic

$599000 - MAJOR FIXER!!! For experienced buyers only! (richmond / seacliff)

$65000 - Scenic 1-acre lots near Reno (Chilcoot, CA 96105)

Want to know how much you qualify $$$ for on a Home LOAN??? (Pre-Qual Letter)

Craigslist can be a good place to advertise specific property listings. But, as you can see, its listings are polluted with out-of-area properties and other unrelated offerings, forcing would-be buyers to wade through a lot of junk to see your legitimate listings.

First, if you're just posting marketing materials about yourself, you'll quickly get blacklisted, because the forums are not meant to be used as advertising vehicles. Therefore, never include your phone number or e-mail address in your posts, and never recommend that people contact you for advice. If someone does want to contact you, she can usually click your user name in your posts to get your e-mail address.

Second, these forums tend to attract a lot of negative people with lots of time on their hands. (They're called *flamers.*) Flamers pollute the forums with hateful comments, particularly against landlords, mortgage brokers, and real estate agents, and they flood a forum with inane arguments. For flamers, a true discussion is not the point; participation is an opportunity to anonymously be cruel to others or to feel self-important. Because there are no moderators, these flamers get free rein to stomp over everyone else.

Unfortunately, flamers are a common outcome in community forums that aren't moderated (or policed, according to some). Unfortunately, chances are that participating in a Craigslist real estate forum will just set you up for attack, not let you offer legitimate advice that also (and subtly) helps market you.

So before you decide to spend time posting on a community forum, read through a week's worth of traffic and see if it's really a positive venue where reason rules and you can actually communicate with people other than flamers.

CD RESOURCES: For blog providers, links to Blogger.com and TypePad.

Consider Web Advertising

It's an old adage that you have to spend money to make money. But we real estate agents also know that there are hundreds of organizations hoping we'll spend money on their services, which can quickly eradicate any money we do make selling real estate.

Advertising is a natural area in which to spend money, but you have to be careful. It's worth trying a multifaceted ad strategy, such as running ads in local community or neighborhood newspapers, sending out postcards to target neighborhoods, and even buying ad space in more exotic venues such as on bus benches and shopping carts. But test these venues carefully and make sure you track the number of responses you get to see if they're effective. And always talk to others who have used these advertising venues to see if they really work.

When you hear from someone new, just ask how he heard about you. If someone contacts you via e-mail, consider asking her how she heard about you when you reply. (Chapter 7, "Managing Marketing Campaigns," shows you how to track your efforts methodically.)

An increasingly popular form of advertising is Web advertising, because people who use the Web are often in active research mode, looking for properties or agents. So the theory is that they're more ready to contact you than someone who's looking at the newspaper or walking by a billboard.

Tracking Results

It's also easier to track the performance of Web ads than other media. A common technique is to provide a unique link in each ad. You then use the tracking logs—if your Web host provides these—to see how many times each unique page was clicked. If you use this technique, it's wise not to create separate pages for every ad, because each page will include a lot of duplication and maintenance effort. (You'd end up, say, with a copy of your home page for every ad you run to track how many people clicked from each ad.)

THE BIGGER PICTURE

WHAT ABOUT BLOGS?

There's been much ado recently about Web logs, known as blogs. Blogs are Web pages where an individual posts his thinking on a topic or two, perhaps daily, perhaps less often, and then has a space where readers can post their own comments. Often heralded as citizen journalism, the medium is just as often an outlet for egotists and marketers. Like everything else on the Web, the quality varies.

You might consider establishing your own blog to assert your real estate savvy and attract potential clients. That's great, but understand that you'll need to devote time regularly for both creating your content and moderating the responses. And of course, you need to find a way to make your blog known to your potential audience, so you're not your only audience.

I believe that, for most agents, blogs take more time than you can really afford to spend, but that's a decision only you can make. To reduce the time investment, you could use the same basic material from a weekly or biweekly e-mail newsletter as your blog content, making the blog effort a small addition to the work you're already doing. (A blog that is updated less frequently than biweekly doesn't usually gain as much of a following, given the high value Web users place on current content.)

If you do decide you want a blog, some Web hosts offer blog tools to use in your Web site. Or you can use blog sites like Blogger.com and TypePad.

THE e-PRO LABEL

Recognizing the importance of technology in how people today buy and sell real estate, the National Association of Realtors (NAR) is promoting its new e-Pro certification for real estate agents. e-Pro–certified agents take a course that teaches them about Web and e-mail marketing, using technology to serve clients, and other techniques that you're learning in this book. (Just to be clear, this book and the e-Pro certification are unrelated, and the content of each was developed separately.)

The idea is that real estate agents can use the e-Pro label in their marketing to let potential clients know they are tech-savvy. However, as is true for all the certifications offered by NAR and other organizations, clients have no idea what the certificates mean.

Perhaps NAR will extensively advertise the e-Pro label as it does the Realtor label, and clients will begin demanding agents who have the e-Pro certification. But until then, consider e-Pro certification as simply a training class on potentially useful techniques for using online technologies to sell real estate. Clients won't know or care about the label; they'll simply judge you on what you actually do.

Instead, each of these unique pages should redirect users to your home page (or whatever page you want the visitor to see). At a minimum, a redirect page contains the following HTML code (you'll also find the code on the CD that accompanies this book):

```
<html>
<head>
<meta http-equiv="Content-Type"
content="text/html; charset=iso-8859-1">
<meta http-equiv="refresh" content=
"0;URL=yourURLhere">
</head>
<body>
</body>
</html>
```

Replace the *yourURLhere* with the actual URL to your site, such as http://www.grumanhomes.com to go to the home page or http://www.grumanhomes/mlssearch.html to go to a specific page. Ideally, you'd also have some text in between the <body> and </body> tags that provides instructions of where to go if the redirect does not work for some reason. For example, for my site, I have the following code, which tells the visitor what the destination page is and provides a clickable link to it:

```
<p><b>If this page does not automatically jump
to the Gruman Homes page, please click here:
<a href="http://www.grumanhomes.com">
http://www.grumanhomes.com</a>.</b>
```

Paying by the Click

An increasingly common type of Web advertising charges you only when visitors click the links in them (these visitor actions are called *clickthroughs*), so you know exactly what the ad's performance is. Google is a good example of a site that charges for clickthroughs: You tell Google the search phrases you want your ad to appear with, and you pay whenever a user clicks your ad after conducting the search.

Obvious terms like *Akron real estate* or *Tampa homes* in these search-phrase-based ads tend to be expensive, since many other agents use them as well. That creates competition for which ads will be placed more prominently, which raises their prices. Your ad is also presented along with competitors' ads, diluting your message. So consider buying more specific search phrases to reduce the competition. For example, a Los Angeles agent who specializes in western Los Angeles might buy neighborhood-specific terms such as *Los Angeles Mar Vista Real Estate* and *Los Angeles Palms real estate*.

Also, you might consider—either instead of or in addition to the obvious terms—buying search terms that reflect the interests or characteristics of your audience instead of buying real estate market terms. For example, you might choose *Detroit machinists credit union* or *Denver kennel club* so your ad appears to Detroit-area union members looking for a credit union or to people in Denver looking for pet-oriented organizations. The downside to this approach is that the people seeing your ad may not be currently interested in buying or selling real estate, but the upside is reaching an audience without significant competition from other real estate agents.

At a fee of a few cents to a few dollars per clickthrough, depending on the desirability of your ad placement, you can quickly go through hundreds of dollars with clickthrough-based ads. Fortunately, most sites that sell ads based on clickthroughs let you cap your total spending, removing your ad when that cap is reached. I strongly encourage you to set a fairly low cap when first buying Web ads, so you can test the effectiveness of your ads based on actual contacts with prospective clients rather than on raw clickthrough counts. After all, it's not how many people go to your site that counts but how many people follow up and contact you by phone or e-mail.

Outreach via E-Mail

It's common for agents to mail postcards or letters to a neighborhood "farm" on a regular basis to establish a presence and try to solicit new clients. But at about $1 per recipient, including postage and printing, these mailings can be very expensive. In the Internet Age, there's a new spin on the concept: e-mail newsletters. E-mail newsletters have several advantages over printed mailings beyond their very low cost:

- **Immediacy:** E-mails can be more immediate, because they can be sent at any time and are available to the recipient within minutes of being sent.

- **More content:** An e-mail can include more information, since you're not restricted by page size.

- **Interactivity:** An e-mail can include actionable items, such as links to your site and your e-mail address, making it a bit more interactive for the recipient.

E-Mail Marketing Issues

To send out an e-mail, you must have an e-mail address, and addresses are hard to get. There are online sources where you can buy thousands of e-mail addresses, but it's very hard to get a list targeted to just one or two neighborhoods. (In smaller towns, check with your local Chamber of Commerce: It may rent you e-mail address lists of people who have inquired about relocating to the area.) And we all know how annoying unsolicited e-mail is, so even if you were able to get addresses for many people in your target area, you're more likely to annoy them than to attract them with unrequested e-mails.

That means any e-mail newsletter or other messages you decide to send will be to people who have provided you with their e-mail addresses in the first place: people you met at open houses or at the office, or people who signed up on your Web site. These are the people you want to have reading your e-mails, because they have already indicated an interest in real estate in general and your services in particular. E-mail is also a great way to stay in touch with former clients and gives you a chance to communicate periodically so they will think of you when their friends and colleagues ask for agent referrals.

RESPECT RECIPIENTS' PRIVACY

One really annoying thing about the Web and e-mail is all the spam—unwanted e-mails and pop-up ads—that get in the way of what you really care about. It's easy to become a spammer yourself, sending people messages they don't want. Unwanted e-mail can become annoying; almost guaranteeing recipients won't ever do business with you.

Federal law—the CAN-SPAM Act—requires that you honor privacy requests and stop sending e-mail to anyone who doesn't want it. While you might send an e-mail to someone who didn't request commercial e-mails from you, you must stop sending messages when asked. For more details on the CAN-SPAM Act requirements, see the link in the Web Resources: Services section on the accompanying CD.

At a minimum, your commercial e-mails must include your name, your company name, your e-mail address, your postal address, an accurate message title, and a "clear and conspicuous" way for recipients to get off your list (to unsubscribe). The unsubscribe method can be as simple as a note in each e-mail saying, "Reply with 'Unsubscribe' in the message title to stop receiving further e-mails," or it can be a more elaborate database system that your Web designer creates. However the requests are processed, be sure to honor the requests before your next e-mail goes out—by law, you have 10 days to remove their e-mails.

There's a wrinkle for e-mails sent—knowingly or not—to mobile devices such as cell phones, BlackBerries, and Treos, where the customer pays to receive the e-mails: You must get the recipients' permission *before* you send them an e-mail. Thus, you should include a statement in your sign-up forms (electronic and printed) along the lines of "Note that some e-mail services charge recipients for messages received. You agree to pay any such charges for the e-mail address you provide." For unrequested mailings, such as from mailing lists you rent, you can check an FCC database of such mobile e-mail addresses before sending.

Additionally, there are now laws that forbid sending unsolicited faxes and making unsolicited phone calls to people on the Do Not Call registry (see the link in the Web Resources: Services section on the accompanying CD). The bottom line—no matter what the medium—is to not send materials to people who didn't ask for them. The sole exception: regular postal mail.

When you do send out e-mail newsletters and other marketing materials, make them as useful as possible—that will make the recipients more likely to read them. Current market information, useful tips for selling or buying a home, and so forth are helpful types of content to include. It's great to offer your own personal commentary as well, but make sure you don't stray into giving advice outside your agent role. For example, you should not provide accounting or legal advice unless you are an attorney or certified accountant—ditto for interpreting code or construction requirements. When you include content of this type, be sure to cite the sources or provide links to appropriate materials. (As covered earlier in this chapter, do not use other people's content without permission.)

WHAT ABOUT RSS?

A new way of distributing newsletter-type content has gained popularity in the last year, 2005. It's called Real Simple Syndication (RSS). With RSS, users click a button on your site that essentially causes your site to send them new content either when you post it or on a regular schedule. Users love this because they no longer have to go from site to site to see what's new—it all comes to them in one RSS reader program, sort of like how a newspaper brings news from several sources into one place.

But using RSS today to distribute content requires some pretty technical knowledge. (To help you explore RSS, the accompanying CD includes some sample RSS code and links to RSS software.)

Although RSS is just a few years old and its tools are fairly primitive, you can expect that most Web creation, Web browser, and even e-mail client software will be RSS-savvy by 2008, if not sooner. Because RSS looks to be the wave of the future, you might want to start getting familiar with RSS so you can make your e-mail newsletter and/or Web content available via RSS when the time is right.

But you may not want to jump in right now and make your newsletters and Web site available via RSS. That's because users typically don't have to sign up for the service and provide you contact information such as their e-mail addresses. So you won't know who's reading your newsletters or be able to contact those readers directly. Is that a problem for you? The answer depends on the strategy behind your newsletter: to get information on potential clients (then RSS is not a good idea) or to provide general marketing of you (then RSS can be a good idea).

THE BIGGER PICTURE

Tips for Creating E-Mails

After you have your e-mail list and know what kind of content you want to produce, you have to actually produce it. There are two basic ways to do this:

- Use an e-mail campaign system to create and distribute your newsletter.

- Create your newsletter in a Web creation program or word processor and paste it into an e-mail client or e-mail bulk-distribution program.

Most e-mail today is actually in the same format as Web pages: HTML. That means you can create the e-mail content using pretty much the same techniques you use for a Web page, even if you use e-mail–specific tools rather than Web-specific tools to create the content. (I covered the tools and techniques in depth in Chapters 1 and 4.)

Although both can be based on HTML code, there is a big difference between the content of an e-mail message and a Web page: the level of complexity. The more features you add to an e-mail message—lots of images, for example—the larger the e-mail file becomes, which will slow delivery and increase the time it takes for recipients to display the message, thus annoying your recipients. And you should never send attachments, because any attachment raises suspicions that there might be a virus lurking within. Attachments also increase the e-mail size. Also, *don't* use fancy Web features like cascading style sheets and JavaScripts in your e-mails, because your recipients' e-mail clients usually ignore these fancy features and often make the e-mails unreadable.

Also, avoid pasting images into your e-mails. Instead, include a link in the e-mail using HTML code that will call up the image when the recipient clicks the link. Specify the URL for the image in a dialog box or other interface element (typically accessed through a command such as Insert > Image, Insert > Picture, or File > Import Picture). Or, if you're working directly in the HTML code, use the tag <IMG SRC="filename"> (be sure to replace filename with the actual URL for the image).

Remember that an HTML-formatted e-mail can trigger spam filters and thus be blocked. Because so many of the unsolicited ads sent via e-mail are formatted in HTML, Web hosts or anti-spam programs installed by users block all messages that use HTML format unless the recipient has certified the sender's e-mail address as safe.

You can, of course, use your e-mail software to send a plain (often called *text-only* or *unformatted*) e-mail. Unfortunately, this means your formatting options are fewer than those offered on a typewriter.

Many bulk e-mail programs send their messages in both HTML and text-only formats to get around the antispam software, but the best solution is to encourage your newsletter subscribers to add you to their antispam software's list of safe e-mail addresses. You can do so on your sign-up forms.

An e-mail newsletter can be an effective way to stay in touch with former and prospective clients. I send out HTML newsletters using campaign management software, but you can also use regular e-mail clients to send them for you.

Tools for Creating HTML E-Mails

I recommend creating your newsletter content in a dedicated bulk e-mail campaign manager like G-Lock Software's EasyMail Pro. This way you'll have a consistent environment for working on your e-mails, whether they are full-fledged newsletters or quick postcard-type e-mails you send people regularly.

Some people, however, prefer to create their HTML e-mails in a Web creation program like Adobe's Macromedia Dreamweaver, so they create both their Web pages and e-mails using the same tool. That's fine. Just copy the HTML page into a program like EasyMail Pro, or copy it into a blank message in a standard e-mail client like Microsoft Outlook. Do note that some elements in your HTML page might not copy the way you expect, so review your e-mail and make adjustments to text size, colors, and so on. And *always* send yourself a test message to make sure everything is OK before you send your newsletter to your recipients.

 CD RESOURCES:
For bulk e-mail software, links to AtomPark, G-Lock, and LmhSoft. For Web creation and editing software, links to Adobe and Microsoft. For RSS readers and creation software, links to NotePage, Pluck, RNSoft, and Tristana.

DEALING WITH SPAM FILTERS

Because of the huge volume of junk e-mail—spam—that clogs the Internet, many Web hosts and individual users install antispam software. This software can block legitimate e-mails as well. Worse, you as the sender might never know which e-mails are blocked, so the reality is that you might never know if your intended recipients ever see your e-mail newsletters and other mailings.

Therefore, you might want to reconfirm your sub-scriptions every six months or every year to reduce the number of unread messages you send out.

Spam filters do look for several things when deter-mining what is spam: for example, certain words like "Free" and "Mortgage" or the use of $ and ! symbols. Using the HTML format, as well as including image files, can increase the chance your message might be filtered out. And messages sent to lots of recipients in the To, Cc, or Bcc lines of your e-mail program can also cause your message to be flagged as spam. (Bulk e-mail programs reduce this possibility by sending each recipient a separate copy of the message. If your mailing list is small and you have the time, you can manually send each recipient an individual message from your e-mail program. Otherwise, invest in a bulk e-mail program.)

Spam filters are constantly being updated to filter out the latest scams, and there are several filters in use, so there's no hard-and-fast rule as to what you should exclude from your e-mails to get past the filters. But the more your e-mail looks and sounds like an ad, the greater the chance it will be blocked.

Working with Code and Design Views

Most Web creation programs and most bulk e-mail programs let you switch between a "design" mode where you can see how the page looks as you work on it and a "code" mode where you can see the underlying HTML code. When copying HTML code from a Web cre-ation program into an e-mail program, be sure to copy from the source program's "code" mode into the destination program's "code" mode. The "code" mode could be labeled "Code," "HTML," or something similar.

If neither program or only one program has a "code" mode, be sure to copy the formatted content using the "design" modes—which could be labeled "Design," "Preview," "Layout" or some-thing similar—in both programs. In some cases, there is only one mode—the "design" mode—so you just copy from or paste using the program's regular window. But whenever possible, I rec-ommend copying the actual HTML code if you want to cut and paste content from one program to another rather than using the formatted con-tent; you'll reduce the chances of formatting glitches caused by the copy and paste actions.

Don't Limit Yourself to Newsletters

Whatever tools or format you use to create your newsletter files, be sure the information is useful and reflects your marketing mission and skills. After all, technology is only the delivery mechanism. What sets you apart is what you deliver.

And don't limit yourself to newsletters: Other handy content you can deliver via e-mail (in addition to or instead of regular postal mail) include holiday cards and useful short notes (such as a note to consider refinancing two mortgages into one after a client has owned the home for a year or a notice of your office's annual Toys for Tots drive). Just be sure to pace your e-mails' delivery schedule so you're not bugging your recipients.

CHAPTER 6

High-Tech Marketing Collaterals

ISSUES COVERED

- What are the various electronic options for high-tech marketing materials?
- How do you create virtual tours?
- How do you create CD tours?
- How do you create property Web sites?
- How do you create electronic seller presentations?
- What other electronic collaterals should you consider using?

Creating a Web site and using e-mail newsletters to market yourself, as described in Chapter 4, "Effective Web Sites," and Chapter 5, "Online Marketing Techniques," are good ways to promote your services, but don't stop there. Your marketing efforts should also include materials for selling specific properties, and you can use several high-tech methods to do that.

Keep in mind that the majority of your marketing materials will be printed documents, such as flyers distributed to other real estate brokerages, left in for-sale signs' document boxes, and distributed at open houses. Most people like having something tangible to examine at their convenience, as well as something that is easily portable and annotated. Plus it requires no special equipment. That's why printed documents are so widely used.

But electronic marketing collaterals are a great supplement to these printed materials, especially to serious buyers who want to explore the property more deeply than often can be done with a printed flyer or at a quick open-house visit. Agents who use electronic marketing collaterals also stand out from other agents, making them more memorable to both prospective clients and their existing clients.

A Range of High-Tech Options

You have a wide range of choices for high-tech marketing collaterals, including:

- **Virtual tours**, which are video or slide show presentations, to help potential buyers see a property in depth without actually having to go there. Virtual tours often have audio narration and are usually provided on a CD or viewed via the Internet.

- **Audio tours**, which combine images (individual photos and/or videos), documents, and even audio provided on a CD or DVD for potential buyers to review on their computer.

- **Individual Web sites or pages** providing flyers, photos, and perhaps virtual tours and disclosure documents for specific properties you are listing.

- **Electronic seller presentations**, such as PowerPoint slide shows or animated presentations, that you customize for the property you are hoping to list.

- **PDF presentations**, which combine information and photos of the property into one electronic document that can be e-mailed or downloaded from a Web site and provide more details than available via the local MLS.

- **Talking houses**, which use a low-power radio at the home to transmit a recorded description of a property to car radios when people drive near the property.

Producing electronic materials can require more skills and technology tools than the printed materials you're already creating. And providing all these high-tech materials for every property would be overkill. So you first need to decide what high-tech materials would be most effective for the properties you are listing and for the target market. Then choose one or two types of materials.

As you decide which technologies you want to use to create these materials, also keep in mind what your recipient must do to access them. When possible, offer two or three choices of access, such as HTML file, PDF file, or a QuickTime movie. Be sure to stick with document formats that are available for both Macintosh and Windows users—such as HTML, PDF, QuickTime, and Flash, as well as common cross-platform application formats such as Microsoft Word, Excel, and PowerPoint.

CHECKLIST

VIRTUAL TOUR PROS AND CONS

The pros of virtual tours include:

- The use of video or extensive photo slide shows to "walk" the viewer through each room of a home and the surrounding grounds is very compelling.

- Virtual tours help out-of-area buyers evaluate potential properties more easily.

- In some cases, you can provide the virtual tour over the Internet (site visitors would simply download a browser plug-in to view it).

The cons of virtual tours include:

- The tools used to create the tours are complex and expensive. You need a video camera, software to convert the video into a computer-displayable format, software to edit the video into a presentation, and a microphone and software to add the audio presentation to the video.

- The recipients often need specific computer hardware to view the virtual tour, and they may need specific software to view it as well. (Many video-editing tools include free viewing software that you provide the recipients along with the virtual tour, although most of this viewing software works only on Windows PCs.)

(That means you should *not* use Microsoft's Windows-only formats such as AVI video.)

Working with Virtual Tours

Many agents reserve video virtual tours for high-end properties and hire a service firm to create them because of the technical requirements. But slide show-type tours are much easier to put together, so you can make these available fairly easily.

Note that there are services in many cities that will create virtual tours for you—from slide shows to videos—at a typical cost of a few hundred dollars. Because the term "virtual tour" can mean many things—collections of photos, slide shows, panoramic images that users can pan, and videos—be sure you understand what kind of tour these companies actually create and what formats the tours will be in. I don't consider a collection of photos to be a virtual tour, but some people do.

THE BIGGER PICTURE

CD RESOURCES: For free viewer programs for PDF, Flash, and QuickTime files, the CD includes code snippets with which you can add to your Web pages' buttons with links to the free viewers.

Creating Slide Show Tours

To create slide show virtual tours, you have several choices:

- **Use a presentation program like Microsoft's PowerPoint.** This program is usually installed as part of the Microsoft Office suite, so PowerPoint is often a no-cost option for creating slide shows. Plus most agents are usually familiar with the software. You can deliver the slide shows in PowerPoint format or as a Web page.

- **Use an image-editing program like Adobe's Photoshop.** This program is used by professional artists and Web designers, so it's easy for them to create slide shows that are displayed through a Web browser.

- **On the Mac, use the built-in iPhoto software.** It can organize your photos and export a slide show in your choice of Web or QuickTime movie formats.

- **Use consumer-level, image-editing software that also includes image-management functionality.** Examples of such software are Google's Picasa, Nero's Nero, and Roxio's Easy Media Creator. Most of these programs provide their own viewer programs to display their photo collections. That means they're not well suited for use by real estate agents, since they introduce possible compatibility issues in what you distribute. (Picasa lets you create a Web page of your photos that you can upload to your Web server, so no special viewing software is required.) You could also use professional-level, image-management programs such as Extensis's Portfolio that let you publish your images to the Web, but they typically require that you manage your own Web server, not one managed by a Web host so they are best suited for larger brokerages.

You'll also need a digital camera to take the photos (or a film camera whose pictures were loaded on a CD at the photo finisher or whose prints you scanned in). You also may want software to add an audio presentation, as covered later in this chapter, although in slide shows it's easy to add textual descriptions instead in the presentation software.

No matter which program you use to create the slide shows, be sure that your virtual tour is logically arranged. For example, consider starting with an exterior front photo, then follow with a photo of the entry way, the kitchen, the family or living room, the bedrooms, the bathrooms, the basement and/or attic, the garage, and finally the front yard, backyard, and side yards. This order is one that many prospective buyers use when they go to open houses. Whichever order you pick, be sure to keep related photos together—all kitchen photographs should be on the same slide or on consecutive slides, not interrupted by photos of other areas.

Microsoft's PowerPoint lets you package a slide show on a CD by copying all the required files including a free viewer. For maximum compatibility and the ability to deliver your presentation on the Web and on CDs, PowerPoint also has an option to save the slide show as a set of Web pages.

Using Microsoft PowerPoint

In Microsoft PowerPoint, you insert photos into a slide by choosing Insert > Picture > From File—the same sequence that most Microsoft Office programs use. For a virtual tour presentation, you should have one or two photos per slide and descriptive text in the Notes section (choose View > Notes Page to see the slide and its notes together).

When you're finished, you have three ways to distribute the slide show: on a disc, on the Web as a link on a Web page, or on both:

- Provide just the PowerPoint file, under the assumption that many people have the software to open files in this format.

- Provide the PowerPoint file "packaged" with the fonts and a viewer program, so people who don't have the PowerPoint software can view the slide show. PowerPoint lets you do this by choosing File > Pack and Go or by choosing File > Package for CD, depending on the PowerPoint version you have. (These packages work equally well on a CD or a DVD.) The drawback is that PowerPoint only provides a viewer for the platform on which you created the file; for example, if you use Windows, you can only provide recipients the Windows viewer, leaving Mac-based recipients out in the cold. (Also, only recent Mac versions of PowerPoint offer this packaging feature.)

- Only with the Mac version of PowerPoint can you create a QuickTime movie based on your presentation. Many Web browsers can display QuickTime movies, and Apple's QuickTime viewing software is a free download for both Windows and Mac users.

- Convert the presentation to the Web's HTML format, which can be opened by any browser. Choose File > Save as Web Page to have PowerPoint convert the presentation into a set of Web pages. All the files will be stored in one folder, which you can then put on a disc or on a Web server.

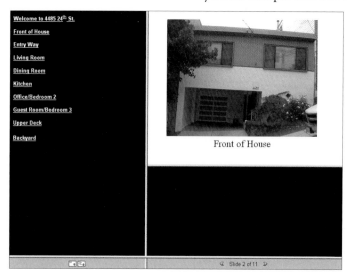

Microsoft's PowerPoint can save a slide show as a set of Web pages, as shown here, so anyone can view the virtual tour from a Web site or a CD.

If you use PowerPoint, I recommend providing HTML and either PowerPoint or QuickTime versions of your slide show virtual tours. Users can then use either the universal Web interface or the single-file PowerPoint or QuickTime. Single-file formats like PowerPoint and QuickTime are easy for users to download for repeat viewings on their computer.

Using Adobe Photoshop

Another method is to create an animated slide show graphic, using an image-editing program like Adobe's Photoshop. The process is a bit tricky, so I don't recommend it for beginning users. In Photoshop, you create a layer for each photo in your Photoshop document—this is easy, since each image you copy into a Photoshop document is automatically placed on its own layer. (Be sure that all your images have the same dimensions. You can use Photoshop's Crop feature to make them all the same size simultaneously, or you can individually resize each layer's contents.) Essentially, you'll end up with a virtual stack of photos in the same file.

After you've created this virtual stack of photos in Photoshop, you then switch to the companion ImageReady application (File > Edit in ImageReady). In ImageReady, open the Animation and Layers panes (using the Window menu). You should have a separate frame for each photo, which you create by choosing New Frame in the Animation pane's palette menu. (The palette menu is the triangle icon in the upper-right corner of the pane.) For each frame, go to the Layers pane and make sure that only one layer is visible (only that layer should have the eye icon visible in the leftmost column).

After you've created all the frames for your photos, select all the frames by clicking the first frame and Shift-clicking on the last one. Now click any of the small arrow characters under the frames to open a menu that lets you set how long each image will display. (This is also a good time to save your file.)

You can now create two kinds of animation files for use on the Web: an animated GIF file and a Macromedia Flash file.

■ To create an animated GIF file from ImageReady, choose File > Save Optimized As, then provide a filename and make sure the Images Only option is selected in the Save as Type menu. The resulting GIF file can be used in a Web page or opened directly in a Web browser—no special software is required to view the file.

■ To create a Flash file from ImageReady, choose File > Export > Macromedia Flash (SWF). In the dialog box that appears, keep the default options by clicking OK. Choose a filename in the next dialog box and select Save to create your Flash file. Note that recipients need Macromedia Flash Player to see the animation; most browsers will ask the user to install this software if it's not already installed.

Note that you can place a Flash file inside a PDF file created by Adobe InDesign, so anyone who opens the PDF file will see the animation. InDesign will convert the Flash file to the QuickTime movie format when it creates the PDF file. Your recipients need the free QuickTime Player, which their Web browser usually offers to download if they don't already have it.

No matter which program you use to create animation files, I recommend you use the animated GIF format in files accessed through a Web browser, whether from a Web site or a CD. That provides the broadest level of compatibility.

Adobe's Photoshop lets you create animated GIF files, which play a set of images in a recipient's Web browser. You can also export these as Flash animation files for use in a PDF file, as stand-alone files on a CD, or on the Web.

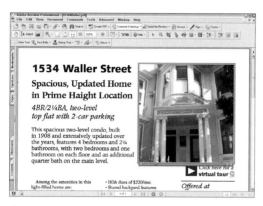

If you decide to offer an animation in another format, I strongly recommend that you include a link to the required player software from the PDF file or Web page that contains the animation. This provides a safety valve in case the user's computer doesn't have the required software and her browser doesn't ask to install it automatically. The CD accompanying this book includes code snippets that provide the necessary links for Adobe's Macromedia Flash Player and Apple's QuickTime Move Player.

This PDF flyer includes an embedded QuickTime slide show movie that readers can play. (The slider bar below the image shows the movie's progress.)

Using Google Picasa

In Windows, a simple way to create slide show virtual tours for both Mac and Windows users is by using the free Picasa program that is available from Google. After you import your files and move the ones you want to display into their own folder within the Picasa software, just choose Folder > Export as Web Page to open the Export as Web Page dialog box in which you choose the size for each photo. Then click Next> to open the Select a Web Page Template, where you have a choice of a half-dozen layouts for your Web presentation. After selecting a template, click Finish. Picasa will then generate the Web page and convert the photos to a Web format, for use on the Web or on a disc.

Picasa also has an option called Create a Gift CD in its View menu that will write the folder's images to a disc (if you have a burner drive on your computer) and include the necessary software for recipients to play back the photos on their PC. Note that this playback software works only on Windows PCs.

The free Google Picasa software lets you export a folder of photos as a Web page for access by both Windows and Mac users.

Using Apple iPhoto

On the Mac, a really simple way to create slide show virtual tours for both Mac and Windows users is by using the iPhoto program that comes with Mac OS X. After you import your files and move them to an album within the iPhoto software, just choose File > Export to open a dialog box in which you choose whether to save the slide show as a Web page or as a QuickTime movie. You can even choose to include a music file to play as part of the QuickTime presentation.

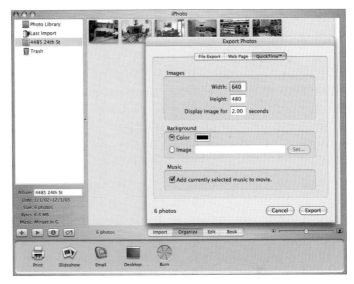

The iPhoto software that comes with Mac OS X lets you export a set of photos as a QuickTime movie or as a Web page for access by both Windows and Mac users.

Using Panoramic-Image Software

If you really want to get fancy, you can create panoramic presentations. You can take several photos from the center of a room, providing a set of overlapping images that you stitch together into one file using special software. You can then export either Flash or QuickTime files that a recipient can pan through, as if they were in the room turning around.

Typically, you need a fish-eye lens on your camera to create the rounded effect that lets the stitched-together images maintain perspective as your recipient pans through them. There are several programs you can use including Easypano's Panoweaver and Tourweaver, IPIX's Real Estate Wizard, 3DVista's Real Estate, and 360 Degrees of Freedom's virtual marketing suites. But you need a knack for working with photography to use them effectively. (Of these, only Panoweaver is Mac-compatible.)

The less technically inclined you are, the less capable you'll be at producing good tours with these programs. But you never know until you try, so I recommend that you take advantage of the 30-day trial versions that most of these companies offer so you can see how much you can accomplish with them. You may surprise yourself!

CD RESOURCES:

For image-management tools, links to Extensis, Google, Nero, and Roxio. For presentation tools, links to Adobe, Apple, and Microsoft. For panoramic tour software, a trial version of 3DVista's Real Estate on the CD plus links to Easypano, IPIX, 3DVista, and 360 Degrees of Freedom. The CD also includes code snippets so you can add download buttons in HTML files so users can quickly get Adobe Reader, Macromedia Flash Player, and Apple QuickTime Player.

Creating Video Tours

A more sophisticated form of virtual tours uses video shot at the property, like you see in those "houses of the stars" TV shows. These virtual tours require skills in video photography, video editing, and video production—beyond the abilities of most real estate agents. If you decide to offer such video virtual tours, I strongly encourage you to hire a professional videographer to create the tour for you. Since the cost can easily surpass $1,000, I'd reserve this option for exclusive, high-end properties that need the extra marketing effort, such as because of a slow market.

But, if you're a savvy auteur of home movies, you might try to make your own video virtual tours. Ideally, you have a digital video camera, so you can download the movie files directly to your computer in a format such as MPEG. And you'll need video-editing tools like Adobe's Premiere or Apple's Final Cut Pro (for professionals), or Adobe's Windows-only Premiere Elements (for home-based auteurs). While you may be tempted to use the built-in Windows Movie Maker software for Windows, it saves its files to a proprietary format that requires the Windows-only Windows Media Player program to play.

Be sure to save your movies in either the QuickTime or MPEG formats so anyone can play them. Both formats can be played using Apple's QuickTime Player and Real's RealPlayer, which are both available for Mac OS and Windows. Macs come with QuickTime already installed. Windows PCs come with Windows Media Player already installed; Media Player can play MPEG files as well as its own proprietary format. Most Web browsers offer to download the required software to display QuickTime and MPEG videos on the Web if the recipients' computers don't have the necessary software installed.

CD RESOURCES: For video-editing tools, links to Adobe and Apple. For video playback, link to Apple and Real.

Working with Disc Tours

Most real estate agents are used to marketing with paper: newspaper ads, flyers and handouts, market comp worksheets, disclosure packages, and so on. After all, paper requires no special equipment for the recipient, and the tools to create paper documents—particularly, a word processor—are available and understood by most agents.

The volume of paper can be overwhelming. Plus, today's younger buyers and sellers have been weaned on videogames, the Internet, iPods, and other multimedia gadgets. So why not provide potential buyers with your marketing materials in a richer visual medium?

The disc tour is a great way to deliver those materials. Recordable CDs (called CD-Rs) cost less than a dollar each—often even cheaper when on sale or bought in bulk—so providing a CD is inexpensive. They also hold a lot of information, so you can include a dozen photos, a complete disclosure package, market comps, and a flyer, and still have plenty of room for fancy materials such as narrated virtual tours and community resource Web pages.

You could also use DVD-Rs, which hold about four times as much as a CD, since most new computers now come with DVD drives. Just be sure the recipients know they're getting a DVD rather than a CD—they look alike—and that they know it won't play on the DVD player connected to their TV.

In other words, a disc tour is simply a disc containing whatever combination of marketing materials you want to provide.

Content Options for Disc Tours

In some cases, you can provide your paper documents in electronic form as a set of PDF files. With PDF files, you won't kill as many trees giving prospective buyers the data they need to make a preliminary decision on whether to make an offer. They'll have to print—or you will—the final documents that need all the initials and signatures if they do want to make an offer, but you won't have to make copies of the multiple-hundred-page materials to give to all the other people who decided not to make an offer. If you're paying for the photocopy expenses, a CD is actually a cheaper way to distribute these materials. (DVDs are more expensive, about a dollar each, even on sale.)

THE iLIFE OPTION

For creating virtual tours—both slide show and video—Macintosh users can use Apple's iLife 06, which lets you create slide shows and movies from digital photos and movies. iLife is powerful yet easy to use, but it has one major issue: It's not compatible with the vast world of Windows computers.

You need a Mac to use iLife. And its slide shows are viewable only on other Macs and Apple iPod Photo handhelds. So chances are iLife isn't a tool you can rely on to develop virtual tours for the public at large.

But you can create DVDs with iLife that work with most DVD players, so recipients can see your virtual tour on their TV sets or on their DVD-equipped computers. They won't be able to open disclosure packages and other files, but if you don't want to include those files on the disc anyhow, that's not a problem.

THE BIGGER PICTURE

Often you'll want the disc to contain more than just a set of documents. After all, why not take advantage of the multimedia capabilities of today's computers? If you offer a disc tour that has several kinds of elements in it, your recipients will appreciate having all the pieces clearly organized. They'll also want some way to know all the items that the CD contains. There are two basic ways to satisfy this need:

- Treat the disc as a virtual Web site, with all the files on the disc rather than on (or in addition to) your actual Web server.

- Treat the disc as a collection of files organized by folder, such as a Virtual Tour folder, a Photos folder, and a Disclosures folder.

In practice, you should do both so a recipient who opens the disc's HTML files will see a familiar interface, while recipients who treat the disc like a hard drive can open the organized set of folders and easily identify the content. (You might also put a text file on the disc that simply lists the contents of each folder.)

Think of interesting materials to include beyond the basic marketing and disclosure materials. For example, you might include an audio narration that would play in a car stereo, or a virtual tour converted to a movie playable on a TV through a DVD player.

You can create discs that work in multiple environments: such as on a computer and in a car stereo, or on a computer and in a DVD player connected to a TV. But be careful: The process for creating such multipurpose discs can be involved, and every program does it differently. So be prepared to spend some time figuring out the software the first time you make an audio CD or video DVD. And always test the disc in all the devices your recipients might use—CD player, DVD player, Windows PC, and/or Macintosh—before distributing it.

Creating Audio Narrations

To create an audio narration for a CD, use the audio recording features that come with your computer. Or you can use the audio recording features in a CD-burning program like the SoundTrax program included with Nero's Nero or the Sound Editor program included with Roxio's Easy Media Creator in Windows, or the CD Spin Doctor software included with Roxio's Toast on the Mac.

You'll need a microphone connected to the microphone connector on your computer, of course. (It's best to use a headset microphone to maintain a consistent audio level. With a headset microphone the distance between your mouth and the recording part doesn't move even if you move your head, ensuring a steady volume.) And be sure your recording software is set to receive audio from the microphone rather than from the computer's CD drive.

Record the audio file and edit or adjust anything you want to change in your software. (Be sure to write a script first, rehearse it several times, and speak in a clear, enunciated voice with a

MAINTAINING PLATFORM COMPATIBILITY

About 90 percent of all computer users have Windows PCs. So it's tempting to forget about the other 10 percent that use Apple Macintosh systems. Most electronic materials can be produced for both sets of users, so why exclude anyone?

CDs created for PCs—these use a format called ISO 9660—are readable by Macs. DVDs are also readable on both platforms, because they share a common standard (UDF).

Common file formats can be opened by programs on both Windows and Mac OS X. For example, PDF, Flash, QuickTime, and Web (HTML) files can all be opened on both platforms. And Word, Excel, and PowerPoint are widely used on both systems, so most recipients can open these files on either platform as well.

But avoid using proprietary formats for photo collections, virtual tours, and other materials—unless you're confident that the recipients all have Windows PCs or all have Macs. If you're making a disc for just one client, you can ask her if she uses a Mac, but if you're making a stack of discs to give out at an open house, you don't have that chance.

If you do use proprietary formats, even for all-Windows or all-Macintosh recipients, remember that they might not have the right software to open these special formats. So make sure you include the appropriate viewer programs on any discs you hand out. And try to stick with viewer programs that have both Windows and Mac versions.

Additionally, if you provide both Mac and Windows versions of software on a disc, you should create a hybrid disc that both platforms can read. Although Macs can read PC-formatted discs, Mac applications written to a PC disc often don't run on a Mac. (Test this first, because you might luck out.) So, when you create hybrid discs, you usually need to create the disc on a Mac and choose the hybrid disc option in a program like Roxio Toast. (You might want to invest in a low-cost Mac Mini for such disc creation.) You need to copy the PC recipients' files to one *partition*—the portion of the disc for one platform—and the Mac recipients' files to another partition.

When you're finished with your cross-platform disc, be sure to test the disc to make sure it works on both platforms.

THE BIGGER PICTURE

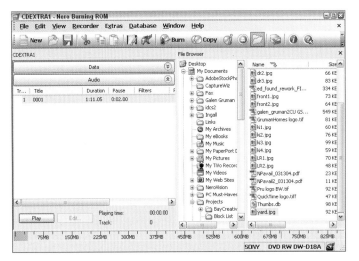

You can create discs that hold multiple kinds of data—such as CD audio to play on a stereo and various files that open on a computer—in programs such as Nero's Nero (shown here) and Roxio's Easy Media Creator and Toast. Each set of data is kept on a separate "partition," as shown on the left.

smile, steady volume, and clear tone.) In Windows, you'd record the audio typically as a WAV file, then convert it to the CD audio format using programs like Nero and Easy Media Creator; on a Mac you'd record it as an AIFF file and then convert it to CD audio using programs like Toast. Often, the conversion is automatic as part of burning the disc.

Be sure to save the final audio file in audio CD format, *not* in a computer format like MP3 or WAV. When you create your CD, place the audio file in its own partition, formatted as CD audio, so a standard CD player will be able to play it. Note that a CD player requires the CD audio partition to be the first partition on the disk; most modern CD burning programs handle that partition order automatically.

CD RESOURCES: For audio CD creation, links to Apple, Nero, and Roxio.

Creating DVDs for TV Display

To create a DVD video that plays on a standard DVD player, you can also use software such as Nero's Nero or Roxio's Easy Media Creator. You can use this software to open the source video files, edit them, and then save them in the DVD format—complete with a DVD menu, if you want.

As with audio files on an audio CD, you need to place the DVD files in a separate partition on the disc (the partition is formatted as UDF, which the software might simply label as "DVD").

Whether you are creating a CD with a separate CD audio partition or a DVD with a separate DVD video partition, your data files will be in a separate partition (or in two, one for Windows and one for Mac). When you *burn* the disc, be sure that all partitions are burned onto it—the partitions should appear in the software's list of items to burn.

CD RESOURCES: For DVD creation, links to Nero and Roxio.

Working with Property Web Sites

In Chapter 4 you learned how to create Web sites that market your services as an agent. So it's natural to use the Web to help market specific properties that you are listing.

Present Web Sites or Web Pages?

There are two schools of thought on how to deliver property-specific information on the Web:

- Create a unique Web *site* for each listing, using its address as the domain name (such as www.123main.com). Proponents argue that it's easier to remember and shows the sellers how you're marketing their property specifically rather than yourself.

- Create a unique Web *page* for each listing, with links from your Web site's home page. Proponents argue that this method increases the chances of people seeing the page because both those interested in the specific property and those who visit your site for other reasons can see the page.

I tend to agree with the second approach, but the flexibility of the Web lets you have it both ways if you want.

One option for having your cake and eating it too is to set up a virtual domain for each listing (such as www.123main.com) and have that domain redirect the visitor to a page on your Web site (such as www.grumanhomes.com/123main.html). You would set up this virtual domain—sometimes called a parked domain—and then redirect in the control panel or other interface provided by your Web host.

WHAT'S A PARTITION?

A partition is a virtual disk on a disc—think of it as a folder that only specific equipment can open. Creating partitions is a way of making a disc work in multiple devices. A car CD player, for example, will "see" just the audio CD partition on a CD, while a Windows PC will see the ISO 9660 partition (as will a Mac, unless there is a separate Mac partition on the disc as well).

On a DVD, you could similarly have a UDF partition for a DVD video that a DVD player would see and separate partitions for computer data.

Because most computers can play both CDs and DVDs, computer users will likely see most, or even all, the partitions on the disc: Each partition will appear as a separate disc within Windows's My Computer or the Mac OS X's Desktop.

THE BIGGER PICTURE

CREATING A WEB PHOTO GALLERY

If you decide to deliver a series of pictures as a photo gallery rather than as a slide show, one good way to do this is to show a series of small GIF or JPEG images, called *thumbnails*, on your Web page (whether it is accessed on the Web or from a disc). Each thumbnail, when clicked, opens a new window with a larger, higher-resolution GIF or JPEG image. This approach lets you put all the photos in one convenient place on your property page and still make the details available to whomever wants them.

First, save copies of your photos as smaller images, resizing them to maybe 75×50 pixels or 100×67 pixels. Use the inverse dimensions—50×75 or 67×100—for vertical (portrait) images. (Also, be sure to resample all the images to 72 dpi if they're not already at that resolution.) It's best if all the images are the same size. (Chapter 3, "Working with Electronic Media," explains these techniques.)

Second, save copies of your photos (with real names) as large images, resizing them to perhaps 600×400 pixels (400×600 pixels for vertical images), also at 72 dpi. Again, it's best if all your images are the same size.

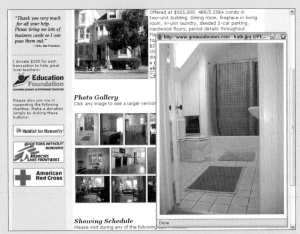

A photo gallery displays larger images of files in separate windows when clicked.

Third, add the thumbnail photos to your Web page.

Fourth, create links from the thumbnails to the large photos. Here's a helpful trick: Rather than add a link to the actual photos, use a simple JavaScript in the link so that a window opens the exact size of the photo. (Otherwise, each link will open a new, full-size browser window that obscures your property page.) You'll need to edit the link in your Web creation software's code view to do this, but the code is simple:

```
<a href="#" onClick="javascript:window.open('photoname.jpg','',
'width=600,height=400');">
```

Replace *photoname.jpg* with the actual name of the large photo file, and change the width and height as appropriate to match the image's actual dimensions (in pixels). Keep in mind that this code is only the first part of the link. The entire code, including the thumbnail image (the `<img src>` tag) and the `</a>` tag that closes the link, would look something like this:

```
<a href="#" onClick="javascript:window.open('photoname.jpg','',
'width=600,height=400');"><img src="photoname-thumb.jpg" width="100" height="67"
border="1"></a>
```

Another way is to simply create an index.htm file for the property's Web site that contains nothing but redirect code, which sends a visitor to the property page on your site:

```
<meta http-equiv="refresh"
content="0;URL=http://www.grumanhomes.com/123main.html">
```

Just be sure to replace the URL above (`www.grumanhomes.com/123main.html`) with the URL for your actual property page.

If you create a separate site for each listing or as pages on your site, you should always have links to those listings from your Web site. The Web doesn't care whether links are to pages on your site or to another site—it's still a link—so take advantage of this link flexibility and always make the links to your listings available to your site's visitors.

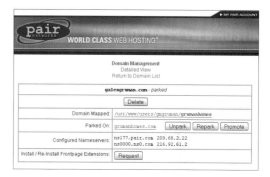

CD RESOURCES: *For redirecting a Web page to another and opening a new window from thumbnail images, see example HTML code in the Web Site Code Snippet folder.*

Your Web host usually provides a control panel in which you redirect one domain to another. Here, I've redirected, or parked, www.galengruman.com to www.grumanhomes.com. Anyone who enters www.galengruman.com will automatically be sent to www.grumanhomes.com.

Recommended Property Site Contents

Whether you create separate Web sites for your listed properties or separate Web pages, be sure to include the following information:

- A photo gallery, an animated GIF or QuickTime slide show, or a video virtual tour

- A description of the property—essentially the key points listed on the MLS and included on your flyers

- Scheduled open house dates

- Your contact information

I would *not* put a link to a PDF disclosure package on the site. Instead, I would note the availability of the disclosure information and ask buyers' agents to contact you for the complete package, so you know who've you've given it out to and can report to your sellers how many people seem seriously interested based on those requests.

As you can see, a property Web site (or page) is essentially a type of flyer delivered via the Web that takes advantage of the fact that you can display more information than available on a printed page and that you can offer multimedia content as well. You can also get really fancy and offer links to local resources, history of the area, and anything beyond the basics you think might be of interest to your clients.

Just be sure that you don't lose focus on the property you're trying to sell. On a property Web page, I recommend that you include only items directly related to the property, such as its history. (Don't include a general resource such as links to community schools, for example. Contextual material should instead be on your main Web site.) If you create a separate site for each property, you might include links to community resources pages and/or other listings to provide more context about the property. But link to these pages on your main site rather than separate copies that you have to maintain on each of your property sites. (This link also helps drive people to your main site to learn more about *you*.)

Working with Seller Presentations

The seller presentation can be a very effective weapon in getting a listing. Or it can be totally useless. Much of the effectiveness of a presentation depends on the seller's expectations.

Many times, sellers decided to work with you because they got a strong referral from a friend or colleague. In that case, the "presentation" is often a conversation about price, strategy, and marketing recommendations followed up with current comps and other materials to reinforce the points made in that initial discussion.

But when you're competing with multiple agents to get a listing, you want to show your best face. Certainly, after examining their property, you'll prepare comps, recommendations, and so forth in written form for your meeting with the owners. And, you'll refer to individual pages in the package as you give your presentation. The actual presentation may be informal, or formal—based on your intuition as to what will cinch the deal.

When it's time to give a formal presentation, you might want more than a printed package for the prospective client to use to follow as you give your verbal presentation. You could use a visual presentation delivered on your laptop's screen. If you have a marketing or sales background, you could use a PowerPoint presentation, with slides containing photos, sales and other financial data, and bulleted recommendations. (If you're not a PowerPoint whiz, you can buy templates from companies such as RealtyStar.)

If you want to get really fancy, you could deliver a complete animated presentation with audio, video, fancy dissolve effects, and so on using tools such as Adobe's Macromedia Flash Player or Apple's QuickTime Player to display your video. You'll also need fancy video and animation tools, like Apple's Final Cut Pro and Adobe's Macromedia Flash Professional. This level of investment—of both time and money—probably doesn't make sense for most residential properties, however.

I suggest being careful when using computer-based presentations, because technology can get in your way rather than help you. Most people want an agent they trust and feel comfortable with, something that an interactive conversation can demonstrate more than a canned spiel with computer graphics.

Because a polished presentation does show you in a professional light, having one could help separate you from other agents. My recommendation is that you create a presentation template and prepare a canned presentation for your potential client, so it's ready to go if you think that's what the client wants when you actually meet. (You could also offer the presentation after you've had a getting-to-know-you conversation, following the conversational "soft sell" with the "hard sell" presentation.) Whether or not you use an onscreen presentation, leave a printed version behind as part of any package of documents you create to show market comps, showcase your marketing techniques, and so on. And if you choose not to show the onscreen presentation, you can always point out specific slides from the printed version to show the potential client how detailed your preparations were.

CD RESOURCES: For the presentation software, links to Adobe, Apple, Microsoft, and RealtyStar. For links to viewer software, links to Adobe and Apple.

Working with Other Options

As technologies evolve, people figure out new ways to apply them to sales and marketing, so expect to discover additional ways to use technology in delivering your marketing materials. (Chapters 4 and 5 cover general marketing techniques to help you get your name out.) Here are examples of some new and emerging technologies to pay attention to:

- **Talking houses:** For a few hundred dollars, you place a low-power, battery-operated radio transmitter near the house that contains an audio narration you recorded about the property. (Often, the radio is enclosed in a small box that you attach to the for-sale sign, fence, or railing.) People can tune in to that radio frequency on their AM radio and listen to your presentation. Talking houses can make sense in rural and suburban markets where people drive to each property rather than park nearby and walk to them. If it's raining or your flyer box is empty, the narration can help satisfy a prospective buyer's interest. However, I would always provide a traditional flyer in addition to the audio: People can't take home a radio presentation for later review or write notes on it, as they can a printed flyer.

- **Mobile messaging:** Text messages on cell phones and handhelds like the BlackBerry and Treo are increasingly popular communication mechanisms, especially for young people, executives, and traveling salespeople. So we can expect to see ads, spam, and other marketing techniques appear in this medium as we have seen happen on the Web and in e-mail. I recommend being careful, however, and not use this medium for anything but short status messages to existing clients. First, long messages or messages with attachments often don't get fully delivered. Second, users of these services pay to receive messages, so ads and unwanted messages cost them money. Both of these factors make recipients very touchy about what they get. A recent federal law in fact requires that you get permission before sending messages to any of these services' users (see Chapter 5 for details).

CHAPTER 7

Managing Marketing Campaigns

ISSUES COVERED

- How do you build and maintain marketing lists?
- How do you deliver marketing campaigns?
- How do you track a campaign's success?

You know which technology-based outreach methods to use, and you have the marketing collaterals ready to go. (If not, check out Chapter 5, "Online Marketing Techniques," and Chapter 6, "High-Tech Marketing Collaterals.") That's a big part of the battle. But a major task remains: the logistics of managing your campaign.

Sending out flyers, postcards, e-mails, and so forth can be a futile exercise, with no results to show for the time and money. How do you know what's effective and what's not? The answer is to have a plan, called a campaign, for your marketing materials.

If you're like most agents, you don't spend a lot of effort managing your campaigns. If you have enough business coming in, you probably don't have a pressing reason—nor the time—to worry about the campaign details. Many agents "manage" the campaigns in their head, tracking roughly which marketing venues seem to be effective and thus concentrating their efforts in those areas. That's fine—if your business is working well, you can leave it that way. But if you think you're not spending your resources wisely or want to try to increase your business through more stringent marketing efforts, read on.

Where Technology Can Help

CHECKLIST

CLIENT DATA

When you build contact lists, collect as much of the following information as you can. And remember you should accumulate all these details over time rather than try to squeeze them out of everyone the first time you talk.

- [ ] Name
- [ ] E-mail address
- [ ] Phone number (home and work)
- [ ] Mailing address
- [ ] Client category (active seller, previous buyer, etc.)
- [ ] Personal data: birthday, names of family members, etc.
- [ ] Source of contact (how they found you: ad, Web site, referral, etc.)
- [ ] Notes (such as what they're seeking or bought, when they bought or sold) that will help you keep in touch appropriately

Where Technology Can Help

Technology can greatly help you manage your campaigns in several ways. It can help you:

- Develop and maintain lists of contacts, such as previous clients, potential clients, and so on. Databases or contact managers let you manage your contact lists.

- Deliver the campaign materials. Bulk e-mail software or Web-based services can handle the delivery of your campaign materials. (Chapter 1, "The Right Office Tools," lists several such tools, and the accompanying CD has links to all of them.)

- Track the results of your campaigns. A simple spreadsheet can help track the effectiveness of various marketing efforts, including nontechnology efforts such as sign-up lists at open houses.

Building Contact Lists

At the heart of any marketing effort is the contact list: the people you're sending the marketing materials to. There are usually several such lists in real estate: your previous clients, your current clients, prospective clients you met at open houses or who contacted you via your Web site, and lists of people whose information you get from other sources (such as title company–provided mailing lists for neighborhood postcards or e-mail lists obtained from a commercial list company). These lists might include e-mail addresses, phone numbers, or postal addresses.

Then there's the marketing you do through ads, where you don't know exactly who is seeing your materials, but you have (you hope) targeted the ads to a reasonable set of potential customers, such as by placing a print ad in a community newspaper or buying an online ad that appears for a specific search such as *San Francisco real estate agent* or *Las Vegas relocation*. There are no contact lists to manage for such ads, but you should keep track of who responds, as I cover later in this chapter.

As you acquire contacts, be sure to gather consistent information for them. For example, if you send out e-mail newsletters, gather e-mail addresses for everyone in your contact lists if possible, so you can distribute that newsletter broadly. If you send out postcards through regular mail, collect mailing addresses. If you call people to promote yourself, collect phone numbers.

Another way to build your contact list is to acquire lists from other people. For example, to get new mailing addresses (beyond the people I already know, such as past clients, and those who respond to my marketing), I use a service from a local title company that gives me a Web-based interface to my state's title records. Then I can get a list of homeowners, their mailing addresses, and their phone numbers for a specific area and even refine that list by excluding, for example, non-owner-occupied addresses or properties that were purchased in the last three years.

One idea if you use such a title records–based list: Find out how long the typical homeowners in your area stay in their home, so you can search for properties that have been owned for that length of time. Nationally, people tend to move every five years, so you might search for addresses of homeowners who bought four to six years ago, since they're statistically more likely to sell (and buy) in the near term than other owners.

Some title companies will give you this data if you ask a title officer for it. The information is usually sent as an e-mail attachment or mailed to you on a floppy disk or CD rather than provided through a self-service Web interface. (Typically, title companies that provide access to such data limit it to agents who've brought them business. But it never hurts to ask.)

Of course, these title-records lists won't have e-mail addresses, or names of renters for rented properties, so they're mostly useful for printed mailings, door-knocking visits, and telephone solicitations.

Main Menu

Farm Search

Search Criteria
Complete the following search fields to generate a Farm candidate list for the location you specified.

Output option:	☐ Include Subject
Search By:	○ Zip Code ● Radius 1/4 mile ▼

☐ All Properties
☑ Same As Subject
☑ All Residential Properties
    ☐ Single Family Residence Only ☐ Condominium
    ☐ 2-4 Units (MFD) ☐ Vacant Land

Select Land Use Code:
☐ All Commercial Properties
    ☐ Commercial Office ☐ Recreational/Entertainment
    ☐ Industrial ☐ Heavy Industrial
    ☐ Transportation & Communications ☐ Agricultural/Rural
    ☐ Vacant Land ☐ Institutional
    ☐ Governmental/Public Use ☐ Historical
    ☐ Apartments
☐ Specify Land Use

Select Phone Number Filter: ● ALL RECORDS ○ Only Records With Phone Numbers
Select Address Filter: ● ALL RECORDS ○ Only Records With Standardized Site Addresses*
    *(Highly recommended for mailing labels)
Select Owner Filter: ● ALL RECORDS ○ Owner Occupied ○ Absentee Owners
Select Sale Type Filter: ● ALL SALES ○ Full Transfer Only ○ Partial Transfer Only

Some title companies provide real estate agents access to public records on property ownerships so they can create contact lists based on various criteria. Ideally, this data is accessible through a Web interface, such as this service from Fidelity National Title, so you can create the lists at your convenience.

Managing Your Contacts

You can manage your contact lists in two basic ways, each of which has its pros and cons:

- You can use a unified database of all contacts, and then export the appropriate subset for a specific marketing effort (such as sending new property listings to buyers who've contacted you in the last three months). This database requires consistent data entry and enough information per contact to be able to create those subset lists when you need them. All this information can lead to complex databases and complex search settings.

- You can have multiple databases (typically in the form of address books or contact managers), one for each type of contact list. For example, you might use a bulk e-mail program's address book to store e-mail addresses and an Excel spreadsheet to store mailing addresses. Multiple databases help you keep each list's purpose clear and each list easier to manage. But it's hard to make sure contacts that belong in several lists are actually in all the lists and that you keep them updated to boot.

As the number of contacts becomes larger, the more you should have a unified database strategy, using a database like FileMaker's FileMaker or Microsoft's Access, or a professional contact manager like Eurekaware's Real Estate Contact Manager (which works as a companion to Microsoft's Outlook e-mail program), Now Software's Now Up-to-Date and Contact, Sage's Act, or Top Producer's Top Producer. For smaller lists, you can use the address book features in Microsoft's Outlook and Entourage e-mail client programs or use a handheld organizer such as a Palm or Hewlett-Packard iPaq.

Even with a unified database, chances are that you'll still have extra lists of contacts floating around, such as client profiles stored on the client management page of your brokerage's and/or MLS's Web site and in your client folders. But these are more for current transactions, so you have, for example, a client's work fax number handy to get a paper signed. The basic contact information for these clients should be in your database or other standard lists, but don't worry about putting every detail about these clients used in a transaction in your databases.

CD RESOURCES: For database and contact management software, a tryout version of Eurekaware, plus links to Eurekaware, FileMaker, Microsoft, Now, Sage Software, and Top Producer Software. For bulk e-mail delivery, links to AtomPark, FNIS, G-Lock Software, LmhSoft, and Top Producer Software. For national do-not-contact information and registries, links to the relevant federal agencies.

Differentiating Active and Passive Contacts

Your contact lists will grow over time, as you meet people at open houses and on floor duty, as people call or e-mail you, and as friends and former clients make recommendations, and so on. I recommend you differentiate active contacts from passive ones, and skew your marketing efforts to the active ones.

An active contact is someone who called you in the last two months about buying a house, or someone you met at an open house. Members of the active group are serious about a real estate transaction, so they're in the process of choosing an agent. These people have the most immediate payoff potential for you.

A passive contact is someone in your "farm" area who's never contacted you or someone who contacted you a while back but hasn't responded to your follow-up inquiries. Members of the passive group may one day be clients, but more often will not be. You essentially are sending ads to these people hoping that when they're interested in real estate, or if asked by other people if they know a good agent, that they'll think of you.

The passive group will likely take the majority of your marketing dollars simply because they will far outnumber the people who are actively interested in real estate at the moment. But if you think of your marketing in terms of cost per contact (both time and money costs), you should spend more per person on the active ones to focus your efforts appropriately.

DON'T BUG PEOPLE

Understand that many people don't want to give you information about themselves, especially contact information, because they don't want to be bothered. Therefore, be sure that you state up front (in your Web forms or on a sign-up sheet, for example) how you will use any contact information you collect.

I find it helpful to tell people that I will not bug them if they give me their phone number and that I will not deluge them with e-mails if they provide their e-mail address. You must also honor all requests to stop contacting people—and do so immediately. After all, if you annoy someone, they're pretty much gone as a possible client.

Federal and state laws also require that you honor "opt out" requests for phone, e-mail, and fax solicitations, as I explained in Chapter 5. There are also requirements for providing notice on how to opt out, as well as rules requiring you to remove phone numbers and some e-mail addresses from your lists if they are in national do-not-contact rolls. But even if these laws didn't exist, it's smart to not annoy someone you hope to gain as a client. And hounding people won't turn them into clients, anyhow.

THE BIGGER PICTURE

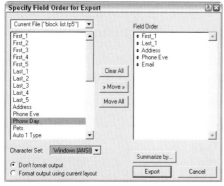

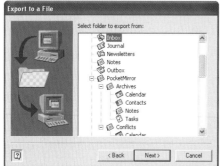

The CSV format is a near-universal standard for exchanging contact information among programs, but each program exports such files in its own, often multiple-step way. Here are screenshots showing part of the process from (top to bottom) FileMaker, Microsoft Outlook, and Sage Act.

Delivering Campaign Materials

Once you have your contacts, you need to get that contact information into the delivery system, whether that's your regular e-mail program, a bulk-email program installed on your computer, or a Web-based e-mail distribution service. If you store the contact information in the delivery tool—such as a bulk e-mail program's built-in address book—the information is already there. If you maintain your own database or contact management system, you'll need to transfer that contact information yourself.

Transferring Contact Lists

The exact method of transferring contact information depends on the program you use, but the data will almost certainly export in comma-separated value (CSV) format, which almost every database and contact-management program can import. (CSV is simply a fancy way of saying each element in the contact information is separated by a comma, so the program reading the file knows, for example, where the first name ends and the last name begins. A similar, widely used format is tab-delimited, which uses tab characters instead of commas to separate the elements.)

Here are the steps for exporting contact information from the most popular programs (note that the exact steps might vary based on the version of the program you have). Be sure to name your exported files using a descriptive name (like "Central Philadelphia Farm Postal") so you'll remember which file to use when you make your mailings.

Apple Mail

Neither this program nor the related Address Book utility exports contact information, so you'll need a different program for storing your contact lists.

FileMaker

If you want to export just selected contacts, choose them in the program's Find or Browse mode. (If no records are selected, all records will be exported.) Follow these steps:

1. Choose File > Export Records.

2. In the resulting Export Records to File dialog box, enter a filename and select Comma-Separated Text Files from the Save as Type pop-up menu, and then click Save.

3. In the resulting Specify Field Order for Export dialog box, choose the fields you want to export by selecting them in the window on the left, and then click »Move».

4. Be sure the Don't Format Radio Button is selected, and then click Export.

Microsoft Access

To export specific records, use the Access tools to filter out the records you don't want, so only the ones you want are displayed. (Access will export all records displayed in the current database table.) Now follow these steps to complete the export:

1. Choose File > Export.

2. In the Export Table dialog box that appears, choose an export format from the Save as Type pop-up menu. (I recommend you choose Text Files for the broadest compatibility with other programs.)

3. Navigate to the disk and folder where you want to save the file, enter a filename in the File Name field.

4. To export the records, click Export All.

5. In the Export Text Wizard dialog box, choose Delimited and click Next.

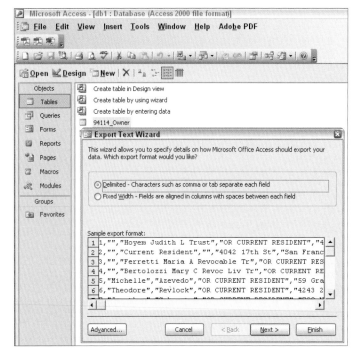

When exporting in Microsoft Access, be sure to use the text format as your file format, and double-check that the commas that separate individual records look to be in the right place in the onscreen preview.

6. Export Text Wizard's options will now change. Choose Comma or Tab, as appropriate for whatever program will open the exported file. (Choosing comma will create a CSV file, while choosing Tab will create a tab-delimited file.)

7. Click Finish.

Microsoft Entourage

Note that Entourage doesn't have an option that lets you select specific addresses, so all your addresses will be exported. Follow these steps:

1. To start the export, choose File > Export Contacts.

2. In the Save dialog box, enter a filename and choose the folder location in which you want to save it.

3. Then click Save.

Microsoft Outlook

Note that Outlook doesn't have an option that lets you select specific addresses, so all your addresses will be exported. Follow these steps to start the export:

1. Choose File > Import and Export, select Export to a File in the Export to a File dialog box, and click Next.

2. Choose Commas Separated Value (Windows)—like all dialog boxes in this sequence of steps, this dialog box is also named Export to a File—and click Next.

3. Choose a file to export and click Next.

The Tech-Savvy Real Estate Agent

4. Enter a filename for the exported data (click Browse if you want to save your exported list to a specific file and/or disk), then click Next.

5. In the dialog box that appears, you can click the Map Custom Fields button to get the Map Custom Fields dialog box in which you select the fields you want to export and specify the field names and order you want to apply to the exported data. Click OK to close the Map Custom Fields dialog box with your new settings.

6. Click Finish.

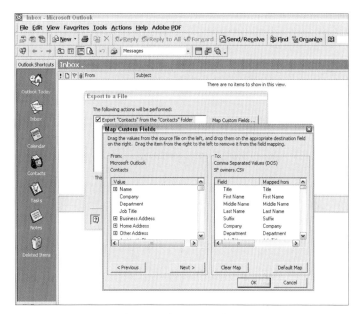

When exporting contact information from Microsoft Outlook, you can specify which fields to export and what field names to give them.

Microsoft Outlook Express

Note that Outlook Express doesn't have an option that lets you select specific addresses, so all your addresses will be exported. To start the export, follow these steps:

1. Choose File > Export > Address Book. Choose the Text File (Commas Separated Value) option in the Address Book Export Tool dialog box that appears, and click Export.

2. In the CSV Export dialog box, enter a filename for the exported data (click Browse if you want to save your exported list to a specific file and/or disk), and click Next.

3. In the dialog box that appears (also named CSV Export), select the check box next to the fields you want to export; uncheck any field you don't want to export.

4. Click Finish. (There is no option to select specific addresses.)

Palm Desktop

Follow these steps:

1. Select the addresses you want to export from the Address list (be sure none are selected if you want to export them all), then choose File > Export.

2. Choose Comma-Separated from the Export As pop-up menu, and enter a filename in the File Name field. Select either All or Currently Selected Records for the Range radio buttons, depending on what you want to export.

3. Click Export.

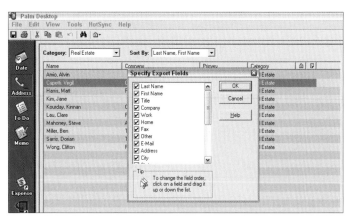

The Palm desktop lets you specify which contact fields to export when creating comma-separated lists from it for import by other software.

Sage Act

To export specific records, use the Lookup menu to retrieve those that meet whatever parameters you want. (If you want to export everything, you'll be able to specify that fact in step 4 below.) Now follow these steps to complete the export:

1. Choose File > Export.

2. Click Next in the resulting Export Wizard (1 of 6) dialog box.

3. In Export Wizard (2 of 6), select Text Delimited in the What Type of File pop-up menu and enter a filename in the Filename and Location field (click Browse to select a different disk and/or folder).

4. Click Next. In Export Wizard (3 of 6), choose the appropriate records to export—Current Lookup (those you selected in the Lookup menu earlier), All Records, or Current Record—and click Next.

5. In Export Wizard (4 of 6), select Comma in the Select Field Separator section, and click Next.

6. In Export Wizard (5 of 6), indicate the fields you *don't* want to export by selecting them and clicking Remove Field. When you're finished, click Next.

7. In Export Wizard (6 of 6), click Finish.

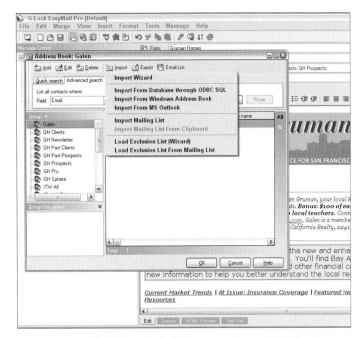

Importing contact list information is similar to exporting such lists: You choose the appropriate format of the file you are importing from a menu with a name like Import. Shown here is G-Lock Software's EasyMail Pro bulk e-mail program, which supports several types of file for importing contact lists into its internal address book.

Importing Contact Files

Just as there are different ways to export CSV files, there are different ways to import them. Typically, the methods for importing are all variations of a basic exporting procedure. For importing, you typically choose an Import option (often in the File menu) and select the file you want to import. Depending on the program, you might be asked for the file format (such as CSV) and will likely be asked which fields you want to import. Often, the program gives you the chance to name each field (such as First Name and E-mail) or lets you match the imported fields against predefined names, so the importing program can label or categorize the data appropriately.

Sending E-Mail Campaigns

After you've composed your e-mail and set up the contact list, sending the campaign usually is a simple process: press the Send button or equivalent. That is assuming you've set up the bulk e-mail software correctly and there are no limitations from your Internet service provider (ISP) on what you can send.

When you do send your e-mails, issues sometimes come up that hinder delivery. Some are based on ISP limits, while others are imposed by the recipients' e-mail servers. Here's a list of some of the possible issues when sending lots of e-mails:

- **E-mail limits:** Many ISPs limit the number of messages you can send in an hour or on a daily basis. ISPs do this to thwart the efforts of spammers that use the ISP's system to send unwanted messages. By restricting the number of messages per hour, they make spammers seek another venue for spewing their spam. But these limits can also get in the way of your legitimate work. If your ISP has such limits, you'll need to break up your campaign into separate "chunks" so that each chunk (set of e-mails) is fewer than the ISP's limit. These limits are often not stated anywhere in your contract, and technical support people might not know about them either until you push them to dig a little deeper and ask for a supervisor or internal e-mail expert. Typically, your first inkling that there may be such limits will come in the form of error messages, such as "mailbox is full" or "quota is exceeded." Some bulk e-mail programs will see these error messages and automatically try to send the unsent messages later. But other programs won't retry automatically; they typically just show in their report logs that only some of your messages were delivered, forcing you to resend the unsent ones.

- **Misplaced addresses:** If you use a standard e-mail client like Microsoft Outlook to send your messages, never include a list of recipients in the To or Cc field (use the Bcc field instead and add your own e-mail address in the To field). When you put all the addresses in the To or Cc fields, each message will include everyone's address, plus if any one of your recipients should select Reply All, everyone in the To or Cc field list will receive the reply—very annoying.

- **Spam filters:** Many e-mail servers block messages sent to *many* people simultaneously (and each filter defines "many" in its own way). It's best not to use a regular e-mail client that sends one e-mail to multiple people in the same To or Cc field. I suppose you could make a separate copy of the e-mail for every recipient, but that's a lot of work! Instead, it's best to use bulk e-mail software that automatically takes your message and sends a separate copy to each recipient as separate e-mails. When you set up this software, be sure to provide your e-mail address and Web domain (usually in a Settings or Delivery dialog box), because many e-mail filters double-check to see if the sender's address is legitimate before accepting any bulk e-mails. Note that some programs call the Web domain the HELO domain. Also, some recipients use e-mail servers, like EarthLink, that won't deliver messages until the sender is approved. In this case, you will receive a message asking you to verify who you are by answering a question, clicking a link, or taking some other action; only if you complete whatever action is required will your message get through. Fortunately, you only have to do this verification once per recipient.

After you send your e-mails, you'll no doubt get a few that bounce back because the e-mail address is incorrect, no longer exists, or is bogus. Of course, you'll only get these messages if you entered a correct reply-to e-mail address in your bulk e-mail program. Typically, this reply-to address is part of the sender account you created in the program (bulk e-mail programs typically let you set up several different senders, such as for sales, marketing, and support staff). Some programs, such as Sage's Act, use your existing e-mail client (such as

Be sure to correctly set up your bulk e-mail software before using it; for example, to specify a correct reply-to address and how many messages to send per hour. I use G-Lock's EasyMail Pro for my e-mail newsletter, and this screenshot shows some of my setup. My ISP limits me to 400 outgoing messages per hour, so I set an hourly limit of 395 (so I can send a few other e-mails in addition the newsletter). I've also made sure my correct domain name (grumanhomes.com) is entered so spam filters can verify I'm who I say I am and let my messages go through.

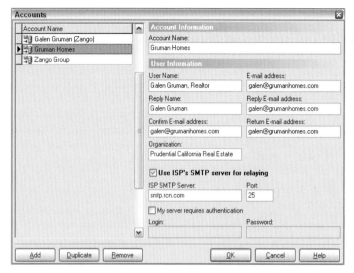

Make sure you correctly set up your sender account information in your bulk e-mail software so you'll receive notices of any invalid e-mail addresses. (Shown here is the setup in G-Lock's EasyMail Pro.) A correct setup also lets spam filters know you're legitimate.

Microsoft Outlook) to send the messages and will pick up settings such as your reply-to address from that program.

When you receive bounced e-mails, be sure to update your contact list, deleting invalid addresses and correcting incorrect ones. (You might also want to resend your e-mail to the corrected addresses.) If you use a Web-based service provider to handle your e-mail distribution rather than a program installed on your computer, the provider typically processes the bounced e-mails and updates the copy of the contact list stored on its servers—so be sure to periodically synchronize the server's lists with any lists stored on your computer.

Easing Print Material Creation and Delivery

Computer technology has long given a major boost to the creation of printed materials The desktop publishing revolution of the 1980s made it easy for almost anyone to create their own quality documents, reducing costs and enhancing creativity especially among small businesses, educators, students, and volunteers who no longer had to spend lots of money for professional design.

Of course, opening the publishing tools to amateurs also led to many ugly, ineffective documents, but I think on the whole people have gotten a lot smarter about producing printed materials in tools as varied as Microsoft Word, Microsoft PowerPoint, Microsoft Publisher, and Adobe InDesign.

Today, Web technology extends that creativity to the Internet, making it easy to forget to take advantage of the power of the (well) printed word. And Web technology now can help you produce and distribute your print documents, not just create them.

Creating Printed Materials

As described in Chapter 3, "Working with Electronic Media," you are likely creating your printed flyers, postcards, business cards, seller presentations, and comp sheets using various software packages—such as Microsoft Office for basic documents and Adobe InDesign or Microsoft Publisher for fancier, more formatted documents.

All these programs come with an attractive selection of fonts and digital images to help you present high-quality materials to your clients and prospective clients. Sometimes real estate materials can look homemade, which is great for pies but not for marketing materials. You can really stand out by creating materials a cut above in quality.

And of course, after you've created your materials, you need to distribute them. Typically, that means taking your files to a local printer or to a chain such as FedEx Kinko's or Office Depot and paying to print the actual materials. Once printed, you typically affix address labels printed on your home computer or perhaps labels received from a title company or list-rental firm, add the postage, and drop them in a mailbox. (To print labels at home, you can use the mail-merge feature in a program like Microsoft Word. Word includes a template document that positions the labels correctly for the type of label sheets you have, or you can use an add-in program for Word such as Avery Label Wizard, which is available as a free download.)

Of course, you have to have the content for these files, such as logos, photos, and the correct fonts—as well as the ability to lay them out correctly.

While you should take full advantage of technology such as layout programs, fonts, and image editors to create top-notch marketing materials, there's more that you can do with technology to enhance and simplify your efforts with printed documents.

CD RESOURCES: For label-making software, a link to Avery.

CHECKLIST
MUST-HAVE SOURCE FILES

If you create your own marketing materials, whether for electronic or print use, you should have the following building-block files available:

- Good-quality photos in digital format (from a digital camera, from a photo CD created by a photo developer, or scanned from a printed photo). Have a 72-dpi JPEG or GIF version of your images for use on the Web and a 300-dpi TIFF version for use in printed materials, as explained in Chapter 3.

- Company and/or personal logo, preferably in EPS format or in 300-dpi TIFF format.

- A scan of your signature in GIF, JPEG, or TIFF format to use in documents you create electronically.

- The fonts used in your brokerage's materials, such as its stationery and business cards.

Using Web Services to Print Materials

For example, you can often save time, hassle, and money by sending a document in PDF or other file format to a Web-based production service and it'll mail the completed document back to you. (Do a Web search for "printing service" to find such a service.) A Web-based printing service is a handy way to produce business cards and postcards—and is often less expensive than ordering them through your brokerage. In some cases, you can even upload a CSV file of your contact list and have the materials mailed directly to your contacts—no more printing labels, affixing labels, and affixing postage!

One technique I often use is mailing postcards to my "farm," past clients, and neighbors where I have a listing. The postcards might promote our Toys for Tots drive during the holidays, announce a new listing, or provide a survey of current prices to potential buyers and sellers.

For my postcards, I use a service from the U.S. Postal Service called NetPost Online that lets me upload a Word file containing my postcard, letter, or other template. I then upload the file of mailing addresses, and one of the post office's suppliers prints and mails my cards for me. Printing and delivery take about a week, but you get a discount on postage. (A full-color, two-sided postcard typically costs about 45 cents to print and mail, a savings of 10 to 15 percent compared to having it separately printed and mailed. Plus you don't have to affix all those stamps!) Some larger brokerages offer a similar service to their agents, often providing high-quality images as well.

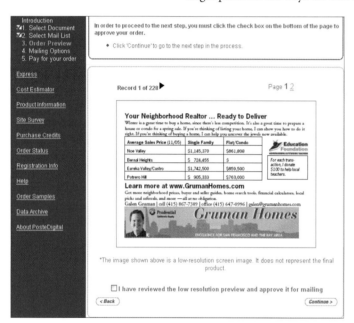

The post office's NetPost Online service lets you send digital files to be printed and mailed to your address list, saving you both time and money.

CD RESOURCES: *For the electronic creation and distribution of printed materials, a link to NetPost Online.*

Evaluating Campaigns' Effectiveness

After you've sent out your marketing materials and paid for your ads, you need to track their success. "Success" means "leads to a contact," such as getting a phone call or e-mail inquiry.

The only way to really know which materials led to contacts is to ask people when they contact you how they heard about you. Sometimes, they'll reply to an e-mail you sent out (or one that was forwarded to them by someone on your list), so you'll know immediately what collateral they're responding to.

I recommend keeping a log of what people respond to. I periodically enter that data into a spreadsheet and can quickly see the effectiveness of each of my campaigns. On the CD that accompanies this book, I've included an Excel spreadsheet you can use to enter this data and see the results. Feel free to modify the spreadsheet; just be sure that you copy entire rows when you add specific campaigns, so the calculations are copied along with the visible fields.

If you're an experienced Excel user, you can create elaborate calculators to assess campaign effectiveness, such as tracking responses over time to see, for example, whether ads in the summer do better than those in the winter. Or you can simply keep logs in a text file or on a sheet of paper to figure out any season-

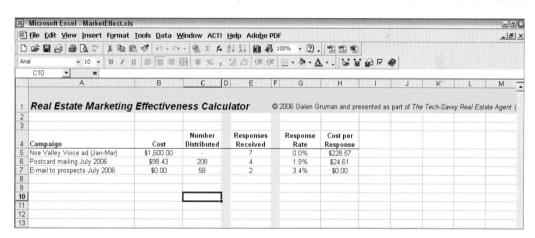

A spreadsheet is a handy way to quickly calculate the effectiveness of various marketing efforts.

ality to your marketing efforts. Using technology tools like Excel can be a great help, but don't spend so much time creating fancy calculators that you lose sight of the goal: getting a basic sense of what works and what does not.

A final note on marketing effectiveness: Sometimes your marketing and advertising is not about getting specific responses. Instead, it's about keeping the potential client base aware of your existence—what the folks on Madison Avenue call image advertising. There's no way to assess whether image advertising is worth the money unless you're willing to hire a firm to survey people in your target market to see if they know who you are—and that's an expensive proposition that only larger brokerages can rationally consider.

I recommend doing periodic image advertising—such as sending postcards to your "farm" area or using local ads—to keep your name visible. But limit these expenses to a specific percentage of your marketing budget—perhaps 25 to 40 percent, so your budget doesn't escalate out of control.

CD RESOURCES: *For assessing marketing campaigns' effectiveness, an Excel calculator.*

Facilitating Your Communications

PART 3

CHAPTER 8

Managing Your Contacts

ISSUES COVERED

- How should you use contact managers?
- How should you manage e-mail, fax, and phone services?
- Should you consider unified messaging centers or services?
- What capabilities do new technologies like VoIP offer for agents?

Real estate is a relationship business, which means it's critical that you manage your relationships and the information about them, systematically. Technology can help you manage your contact information using methods such as address books and contact managers, but that's just part of where technology can help. Technology can also help you make the actual contacts, such as phone calls, fax transmissions, and e-mail messages.

Of course, much of this management isn't based on the use of technology. You need a system in place that works for you, giving you convenient access to contact information as you need it. And that means understanding how you'll use the contact information.

Once you know how you want to use contact information, you can develop that systems—and then choose the right technology to support that system.

But that's just part of where technology can help. Agents have several conduits— phone calls, fax transmissions, and e-mail messages—for connecting to other people. And new technologies now give you choice in how you make phone calls, deliver faxes, and transmit messages. It's no longer as simple as calling the phone company to set up service.

CHECKLIST

CLIENT DATA

When you build contact lists, collect as much of the following information as you can—and remember, you can accumulate all these details over time rather than trying to squeeze them out of everyone the first time you talk.

- Name
- E-mail address
- Phone number (home and work)
- Mailing address
- Category (active seller, previous buyer, etc.)
- Personal data: birthday, names of family members, etc.
- Source of contact (how they found you: ad, Web site, referral, etc.)
- Notes (such as what they're seeking or bought, when they bought or sold) that will help you keep in touch appropriately

CD RESOURCES:

For contact and schedule managers, trial software from Eurekaware on the CD, as well as links to Eurekaware, Microsoft, Now Software, Palm, and Sage. For handheld organizers, links to Hewlett-Packard and Palm.

Using Contact Managers and Databases

Almost everyone has her own system for managing contacts, and there's a huge industry ready to provide tools to manage contacts, for example:

- An address book, a Rolodex, or other paper-based system.

- A handheld device such as a Palm Zire or Treo, or a Windows Mobile-based device such as Hewlett-Packard's iPaq. (Note that Windows Mobile is the newest name for what Microsoft first called Windows CE and then called Pocket PC.)

- A dedicated contact manager on your computer, such as Now Software's Now Up-to-Date and Contact.

- A contact manager built into an e-mail tool such as Microsoft's Outlook.

- A contact manager built into a more complex sales-management tool such as Sage Software's Act.

- A contacts database in a program like Microsoft's Access or FileMaker's FileMaker, or even as a spreadsheet in Microsoft's Excel.

- A contact manager provided by the MLS system or the brokerage, where contacts are stored on a server accessible via the Web.

Which tools you choose are based largely on your personal preferences and experience—if you've worked for a sales organization, you've probably used a program like Act for years and so have no reason to change tools now, for example. And many people who've worked in business have used Outlook for years, and again can keep using the familiar tool. (Such agents might consider using Eurekaware's Real Estate Contact Manager, which is a plug-in module for Outlook that adds real estate–specific contact fields. The accompanying CD includes a trial version.)

Collecting Information Consistently

Whatever tools you use, the key is to be consistent in the information you collect. That doesn't mean you collect the same information for everyone, but it does mean that you should collect the same information for each category of contact, such as prospective buyer, prospective seller, active buyer, previous client, and so on. Beyond name and basic contact information, the class of contact will determine what else you need to collect. For example, it makes perfect sense to collect information on a buyer's preferred neighborhoods and budget range, but this information is not relevant for a seller.

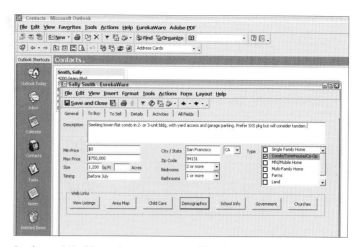

Eurekaware's Real Estate Contact manager adds real estate–specific fields to Microsoft Outlook's contact manager.

Because you can't know what information is pertinent to any individual contact, it's best to always have a notes field where you can enter information like "Prefers lower floors in condos" or "Works at home—street noise an issue" rather than create fields for every possible type of information that might end up being useful.

Keeping Information in Sync

Chances are that you use at least two types of contact-management tools, such as keeping e-mail addresses in your e-mail client and using a contact manager to track all the other information about clients (phone numbers, search parameters, fax numbers, mailing address, and so on). That's typically because programs like e-mail clients include address books that let you type in a person's name and have his e-mail address automatically placed in the e-mail's To field, so you're going to end up with a contact list in your e-mail program's address book even if you use another tool as your primary contact manager. And you probably also carry a paper address book or notepad, or use a handheld organizer, when you're away from your desk to enter new contacts' information and look up information on existing contacts.

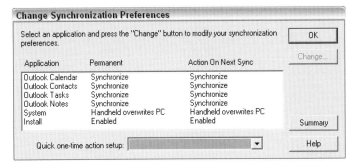

Most synchronization programs let you set up how data is synchronized between a handheld and a contact manager or database. Shown here are sample settings for Chapura's PocketMirror software as applied to a Microsoft Outlook/Palm handheld combination.

Because it's common to use multiple contact managers, you need to be able to synchronize data among them so the information is the same no matter where you look it up. That may require something as rudimentary as reentering or updating information in your paper-based, computer-based, and/or Web-based contact-management systems, or it may mean using technology tools to carry changes in one tool to another.

The tools to synchronize your contact information vary based on which tools you're using, of course. The following are synchronizing options for commonly used programs and commonly used handhelds; the companion CD has links to each. (If you use a Palm OS handheld device, it typically comes with a basic contact manager for your PC or Mac that it can synchronize to. Windows Mobile devices typically synchronize basic data with Microsoft Outlook without needing additional software.)

For Microsoft Outlook

- **With Palm OS handhelds:** Chapura's PocketMirror (included with some Palm OS handhelds' installation CD) and KeySuite, DataViz's Beyond Contacts, Intellisync's Intellisync Handheld Edition, Laplink's PDAsync, LivePIM's SwitchSync, Palm's Outlook conduit (included with some Palm handhelds' installation CD)

- **With Windows Mobile handhelds:** Chapura's PocketMirror, Intellisync's Intellisync Handheld Edition, Laplink's PDAsync, Microsoft's ActiveLink (this software comes with Windows mobile handhelds)

For Microsoft Outlook Express

- **With Palm OS handhelds:** Intellisync's Intellisync Handheld Edition

- **With Windows Mobile handhelds:** Intellisync's Intellisync Handheld Edition

For Microsoft Entourage

- **With Palm OS handhelds:** Microsoft's Entourage Handheld Synchronization (included with some versions of Microsoft Office but must be manually installed from the installation CD)

- **With Windows Mobile handhelds:** Information Appliance Associates' PocketMac

For Apple iCal and Mac OS X Address Book

- **With Palm OS handhelds:** Mark/Space's Missing Link

- **With Windows Mobile handhelds:** Mark/Space's Missing Link

For Sage Act

- **With Palm OS handhelds:** Act Link (included on the installation CD in most Act versions), CompanionLink's CompanionLink for Act, Intellisync's Intellisync Handheld Edition, Laplink's PDAsync

- **With Windows Mobile handhelds:** Act Link (included on the installation CD in most Act versions), CompanionLink's CompanionLink for Act, Intellisync's Intellisync Handheld Edition, Laplink's PDAsync, Pinpoint Tools' TransAct

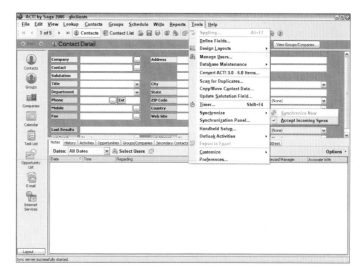

Some programs, such as Sage's Act, let you synchronize databases among multiple users—but only if the databases are installed on a network such as in a brokerage. Agents trying to sync a laptop and a desktop PC typically won't have the sophisticated network setup needed to synchronize this way.

For Now Up-to-Date and Contact

- **With Palm OS handhelds:** Now's Palm Conduit (available if you do a custom installation of Now Up-to-Date and Contact)

- **With Windows Mobile handhelds:** Information Appliance Associates' PocketMac Pro

For Microsoft Access

- **With Palm OS handhelds:** DataViz's SmartList to Go, DDH Software's HanDBase Professional, SmartCell Technology's AccessPlus

- **With Windows Mobile handhelds:** Tiny Pocket Software's DB Anywhere

For FileMaker

- **With Palm OS handhelds:** DataViz's SmartList to Go, DDH Software's HanDBase Professional, FileMaker's FileMaker Mobile

- **With Windows Mobile handhelds:** FileMaker's FileMaker Mobile

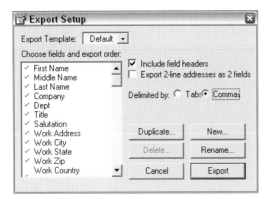

The most common way to exchange information among different contact managers and databases is to export the desired contacts to the CSV format and then import the CSV file into the other applications. Shown here is CSV export in Now Up-to-Date and Contact.

CD RESOURCES: For synchronization software, links to Chapura, CompanionLink, Curosoft, DataViz, DDH Software, FileMaker, Information Appliance Associates, Intellisync, Laplink, LivePIM, Mark/Space, Now Software, Pinpoint Tools, SmartCell Technology, and Tiny Pocket Software.

Synchronizing data among multiple PCs—such as between a desktop PC and a laptop—can be tricky. If you use Microsoft Outlook, Curosoft's OutlookSync can synchronize the address books among multiple PCs. If you use a network– or Web-enabled version of Act or Now Up-to-Date and Contact, you can also synchronize among multiple computers. Otherwise, you'll need to designate one computer as the master and make any changes on that system, then copy the master contact list or database file to the other computers (or in some cases, export the data from the master computer and then import it into the others).

To exchange information among different programs, you'll likely need to export the data to an intermediate format such as CSV and then import that file into the other programs. Chapter 7, "Managing Marketing Campaigns," explains this process for exchanging contact information for sending out e-mails and other marketing materials, but the techniques are the same when exchanging contact information among almost any programs.

The Tech-Savvy Real Estate Agent

Using Communications Services

You hear a lot of talk among techies about computer/communications convergence, where the boundaries between the phone system and the computer networks disappear. There's some truth to that convergence, which can help you better manage your communications systems. In some cases, you can simply take advantage of options built in to your existing phone service, such as using automatic forwarding. In other cases, you can take advantage of these converged systems and, for example, view faxes sent to your voice mail number in your e-mail or via the Web.

Consolidating Communications Conduits

Perhaps the biggest challenge for any agent is to keep track of all the communications channels available. Typically, you have two or three phone numbers (brokerage voice mail, home office, cell phone, and perhaps unified messaging service voice mail) and one or two e-mail accounts (brokerage and personal), one or two fax numbers (brokerage, home office, and perhaps unified messaging service). You could spend all day just checking messages!

The best way to manage this multiplicity of conduits is to rely on just a few and avoid the others. Here's my strategy, which would probably work for you as well:

- I do not give out my brokerage office's main number or the voice mail number it supplies me, so I never have to check that number. (And in case someone does try to leave me a message on it, my greeting requests they call my home office number, and I've disabled the voice mail box so no messages can be left.)

- I use my home office number in all my marketing materials and in all directories I'm listed in.

- I give my cell phone number only to people I'm actively doing business with (brokerage office staff, buyers, sellers, escrow officers, mortgage brokers, etc.). My home office number's answering machine does list my cell phone number, so if someone needs to reach me urgently, she can.

- I give out only my home fax number, so I don't have to check for faxes at the brokerage office.

- I use only my personal business e-mail address in my marketing materials, directory listings, and so on. My brokerage does provide me an e-mail address on its system, but I set that to automatically forward all messages to my personal e-mail.

galen.gruman@prurealty.com   Account Options...   ☑ Languages... ☑

Menu   View Mail   Compose   Search   Calendar   Help   Log Off

This file causes all your mail to be sent to the address specified. This feature is disabled if the text box is empty. Make your changes and press save.

galen@grumanhomes.com

Save

I have my brokerage e-mail account forward automatically to my personal e-mail account, using a setting in my broker's Web-based e-mail console.

You may have different ideas about how to consolidate your communications than I do, and that's great. Here are some variations to my plan you might prefer:

- If your cell phone is your "main" number, give out your cell number instead of your office number. You can probably also have your home office number automatically forward messages to your cell number when you're out. This forwarding capability is often included in phone-service plans or can be added for a monthly fee. And if you work out of the brokerage office most days, perhaps give that out as your "main" number. The point is to steer everyone to just one main number, whatever that might be.

- If you don't want your faxes to sit at your home office, give out your broker's fax number (if that's a more convenient location) or consider using a unified messaging service or fax-to-PDF service that lets you access faxes over an Internet connection on your computer. (See Chapter 3, "Working with Electronic Media.")

- If getting e-mail when you're out of the office is critical, consider subscribing to a cellular service that provides e-mail access from your phone or phone/organizer combo, or to a service like Research in Motion's BlackBerry or Good Technology's GoodLink that sends a copy of your e-mails to a wireless handheld device. These services are great for quick messages, but if you need full e-mail access for attachments for example, consider subscribing to a 3G cellular data service, using a special modem card on your laptop that gives you Internet access almost anywhere. (Chapter 2 explains this technology in more detail.) Note that both types of services can get pricey.

CD RESOURCES: For mobile messaging services, links to Good and Research in Motion. For cellular messaging services, links to Cingular Wireless/AT&T Wireless, Sprint Nextel, T-Mobile, and Verizon Wireless. For unified messaging services, links to IGC, J2 Global Communications, and Telecentrex. For fax-to-PDF services, links to Data on Call, Innoport, and MongoNet.

Increasing Your Reach

In many urban areas, there are many area codes. Being in an area with multiple area codes can impede your business, because potential clients in adjoining area codes may perceive you as not a local agent and thus be less willing to trust you.

Using Toll-Free Numbers

One way around the multiple area code dilemma is to get a personal toll-free number (those with the area codes 800, 866, 877, and 888) from your phone-service provider. (Your cell phone will still have a local area code; toll-free numbers are not available for cell phones.) But using a toll-free area code could peg you as someone completely out of the area, since it's unusual to see toll-free numbers except for regional and national businesses.

PHONE SERVICE OPTIONS

You might think that the new VoIP (Voice over Internet Protocol) service could be handy instead of regular phone service if you already have a high-speed Internet connection at home.

After all, traditional local phone service can get really expensive what with all the taxes and fees, and phone companies have been jacking up the prices by selling local phone service with unlimited long-distance calling plans that, for most people, actually end up costing more money than if they got an inexpensive long-distance provider (such as at www.smartprice.com).

VoIP providers often offer a discount compared to traditional local phone companies, but they too typically add in expensive long-distance plans that make the total cost nearly as high as the local phone company's. (Most people don't make that many out-of-state calls, which is why these unlimited service plans can end up costing you more than they should.)

Note that VoIP service won't work if the power is out or if your Internet connection isn't working. Also, some alarm systems won't work with VoIP phone lines.

So be sure to shop carefully and, if you're not using VoIP to take advantage of its unique virtual-phone capability (as explained in this chapter), consider getting local phone service with your cable company's high-speed Internet service. If available in your area, this is often the cheapest option for local phone service. The only issue: Like VoIP, if the power goes out, this kind of phone line won't work.

THE BIGGER PICTURE

UNIFIED MESSAGING SERVICES

There's an intriguing option for managing all (or at least most) of your incoming communications in one place: unified messaging. Usually delivered as a Web-based service, unified messaging provides a single console for all your messages: voice, fax, and sometimes e-mail. (Sorry, these services don't handle cell phone calls.)

With these services, you get a separate phone number that can take voice messages, receive faxes, and sometimes even forward calls to other phones such as your cell phone. Faxes are converted to image files that you can print or download from the Web console or, sometimes, they're sent automatically to your e-mail. Voice mail messages can be played from that Web console via a computer's speakers, or you can dial an access number to retrieve them via a phone.

Unified messaging systems providers typically charge a monthly fee that varies based on the number of services you subscribe to. In some cases, your brokerage may offer such a service as part of your desk fee. Offerings include IGC's MaxEmail, J2 Global Communications' JConnect, and Telecentrex's RealtyOne800 services.

I personally prefer having a dedicated fax machine at my home office, as well as a phone on whose greeting message I can provide my cell phone number, so my home office becomes my central information hub. But that means I don't see my faxes until I get to my home office.

If you're in your car for the major portion of a day, a unified messaging service can make a lot of sense—as long as you also have a laptop equipped with a cellular modem for Internet access anywhere, as covered in Chapter 2, "The Right Connections." A portable printer is also a good idea so you can print any faxes that require immediate delivery to a client. (I rarely have such an urgent need for faxes or e-mail access while I'm out and about, since clients tend to call, and I can always swing by my home office when the need arises. But I also live in a compact city which means I'm never that far away from the office.)

A sample unified messaging system (here, voice mail and fax) from Accessline Communications, a service my brokerage provides its agents as part of the monthly desk fees.

The Tech-Savvy Real Estate Agent

Using Multiple Cell Phones

You could get several cell phones, one in each area code you want to do business in. To keep costs down, use the pay-as-you-go services. But of course that means you have to carry multiple cell phones, which is a major hassle. I'd consider this option more if I were doing business temporarily in another area, such as selling a relative's home in another part of the state, where you don't want other agents or potential buyers to think you're ignorant of the local market.

Using VoIP Virtual Phones

A new option is to use Voice over Internet Protocol (VoIP) phone service. VoIP uses the Internet to send the audio in phone calls and voice mail messages rather than the traditional phone network. (You'll need a high-speed Internet service such as DSL or cable modem to use VoIP, however.) Because the phone calls travel over a system designed for computer data, the calls and their numbers have much more flexibility than is possible with the traditional phone network.

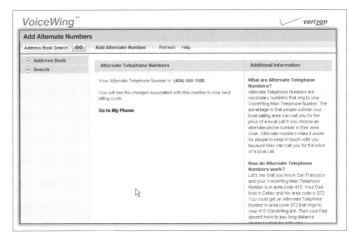

Some VoIP services, such as Verizon's VoiceWing, let you set up virtual phone numbers in your choice of area codes so you can have a "local" number in several area codes that all ring to the same phone line.

For example, in VoIP, a phone number is essentially a mailbox, and it's easy to set up multiple mailboxes that are automatically forwarded to a main mailbox. In the VoIP world, that means you could have local phone numbers in each of the area codes near you that when called ring through to the same phone. With VoIP, you can have one phone but multiple numbers.

Of course, you'll pay a monthly charge for these virtual numbers. Plus, when you call someone, he'll see your main number and it's actual area code if he has caller ID service on his phone—but that's not a big deal, because the goal is to have clients feel comfortable calling you in the first place.

You can't use VoIP with your cell phone to get multiple "local" numbers in different area codes, at least not yet (there are companies working on ways to do so, of course), but you can use VoIP virtual numbers that ring your home office phone, which you then set to automatically forward to your cell phone.

CD RESOURCES: For VoIP services that offer virtual-phone options, links to Lingo, Packet8, Verizon, and Vonage. For help in getting inexpensive phone service, a link to SmartPrice.com.

CHAPTER 9

Communicating Better with Clients

ISSUES COVERED

- How can you use e-mail to stay in closer touch with buyers and sellers?

- How can you use your Web site to better communicate with buyers and sellers?

- How can you use PDF files to more easily inform buyers and sellers?

- How can you keep buyers and sellers abreast of the latest listings?

One of the most common complaints that unhappy clients have about their agents is that they feel out of the loop. Clearly, it's hard to juggle multiple clients at all hours of the day every day of the week. Sometimes they forget we have personal lives to attend to as well. But there's no excuse for not keeping clients informed—even if all you can say at the moment is, "I don't have the answer, but I will let you know as soon as I do. Please be assured that I'm actively working on this."

I'm convinced that a lot of the criticisms about agents keeping clients out of the loop are caused by the fact that clients typically have no idea about all the work you do behind the scenes. But that's your problem, not the clients'. Using technology won't solve the issue of not responding to messages promptly—but keeping clients in the loop with rich details may reduce the number of "urgent" calls you have to answer.

In other words, technology can help you be proactive and provide in-depth information at the same time.

Where Technology Applies

Technology can help you better communicate with your clients in two basic ways.

- You can use e-mail to send the kinds of detailed messages that just clog up voice mail boxes and are hard to follow in a spoken message.

- You can provide your clients several ways to learn about and track the details of their sale or purchase, so they feel informed and see how much you are working on their behalf. For example, you can provide personal Web pages and PDF transaction files delivered via e-mail or the Web.

And even better, you're already using all the tools you need to provide this communication with your clients. (See Chapter 4, "Effective Web Sites," and Chapter 6, "High-Tech Marketing Collaterals.")

Using E-Mail to Stay Close

E-mail is an amazing technology that is easy to take for granted. Messages can be short—perfect for delivering quick information. Or they can be detailed and include attachments—perfect for delivering documents and important details. Unlike voice mail messages, they're easy to read and reread. Unlike faxes, you don't have to wait by the office fax machine to pick up the fax, so no one sees your personal details (after all, most clients do not have fax machines at home).

Here are some examples of how I use e-mail for both quick and lengthy communications:

- **Quick notes:** To e-mail sellers a quick note about how many people came to an open house, if I don't see them immediately afterward. Why keep them in the dark?

- **Required materials:** To e-mail sellers a list of all the materials they should collect before we meet to plan out a listing, such as repair history or required documents (for example, the building reports my city requires or condo agreements). I even e-mail a blank disclosure form so they can fill it out ahead of time. They love getting something they can print out before we meet.

- **Property previews:** To e-mail buyers my thoughts on each property I previewed for them. This lets them know I am in fact looking and also gives them a chance to easily compare properties and react to specific observations—which in turn helps me refine my service to them.

- **Disclosure information:** To e-mail buyers disclosure information, so they can review the documents—which often take hundreds of pages—onscreen before going ahead with an offer. If they decide not to write an offer, we've just saved a tree.

E-mail also lets you summarize the key points made in a phone or in-person conversation, recapping it for the client who may otherwise forget everything that was said. Using e-mail this way also helps you by providing a written record of your conversations with the client, in case there's a question later as to what you told her.

Many people don't like e-mails. They prefer to interact in person or at least on the phone in a "live" way. If you're that kind of person—or your client is—that's just fine. But I still recommend that you use e-mail to recap your verbal conversations so there is a record available in case it's needed in the future.

And even if you and your clients do like to use e-mail as a main way to communicate, you still should talk periodically to reinforce that more human connection that's so critical to a successful business relationship. How often? I'd say at least weekly, but you need to tailor that to what works best for you and your client.

CD RESOURCES: For e-mail clients, links to Microsoft, Mozilla, Netscape, and Opera.

SELF-PROTECTION VIA E-MAIL

I strongly suggest that you print all e-mails related to a transaction if there are any signs of possible problems later, such as when representing a client on a home that has or needs many repairs. You can document your disclosures and any cautions you may have provided on getting inspections or understanding some of the flaws in the property.

Although you can leave the e-mail on your computer's e-mail software until it's needed, that carries a risk: A computer crash or other glitch could wipe out the e-mail. Microsoft's Outlook (and Outlook Express), for example, is notorious for having its e-mail folders get corrupt over time. To minimize that possibility, be sure to save e-mails in folders you create in Outlook rather than in the Inbox and Sent folders that Outlook sets up for you. Putting each client's e-mail messages in separate folders also makes it easier to find the e-mails when needed later. (Be sure to create a Sent and Received subfolder for each client.)

Another key to using e-mail to protect yourself is to watch what you say. Legally, e-mail is considered a written record and can be used as evidence. (Even if you don't keep a copy, your broker's e-mail server may, and you can be sure that a litigious client will keep copies on his computer.) Therefore, write your e-mails carefully, and don't include discriminatory, abusive, or other questionable language. If you stick to the facts, remind clients to consult with experts for things like legal and construction issues, and give honest but calm advice, you should be fine. If you're frustrated, take a deep breath, and write your e-mail when you're calm. (Trust me!)

THE BIGGER PICTURE

Providing Personal Client Web Pages

E-mails are a great way to send information to clients, but they can be hard to manage when you're trying to keep track of a lot of details. That's why I recommend you give each client a personal Web page on your site, so you can post all key information in one place. Your clients can check your Web site at any time and see all the relevant information rather than wade through a bunch of e-mails.

How to Create Client Pages

If you have a Web site that you can modify and update yourself, creating client pages is often easy: Just take your Web template—a blank Web page you were given or that you created when you first set up your site—and use the main section (where each page's unique content goes) to list the appropriate information for each client, with links to any documents mentioned. (See Chapters 3 and 4 for specifics on creating and managing your own Web site.)

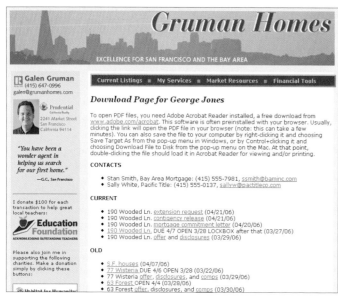

A sample personal client page for a buyer.

If you use a service that generates and updates a Web site for you based on the information you enter into a Web-based interface, you might not be able to create personal client pages. Before you sign up for such a Web service, be sure to ask if creating personal client pages is an option.

To manage these personal pages easily, I recommend creating a separate folder on your Web server for each client, so all content related to that client is kept in one place and is not mixed up with other clients' files. I like to use folder names based on the client's name, such as galeng or ggruman for me.

You can name the client Web page anything you like, but I would either use the client's name (as you did for the folder), such as galeng.html or index.html. Each has its pros and cons:

■ **Using index.html:** The benefit of using index.html is that the user can get to the page by just typing in the URL followed by the folder name, such as www.grumanhomes.com/galeng/. (The browser automatically looks for a file named index.html if no Web page is specified.) But if you use index.html as the file name for each client, you need to be careful not to accidentally overwrite another client's page. Because each client's file has the same name—index.html—it's fairly easy to save client A's file in client B's folder by accident, overwriting client B's file with client A's information.

■ **Using a unique name:** If you use a unique name for each client, the clients would type in a complete URL, such as www.grumanhomes.com/galeng/galeng.html. Using unique filenames makes it all but impossible to accidentally overwrite one client's page with other, but it does make for a longer URL to type.

No matter what the client's Web page URL ends up being, I recommend that you provide it as a link in an e-mail you send the client, so all he has to do is click it. Suggest in the e-mail that the client bookmark the page in his browser, so it's easily available from his list of bookmarks. You can provide these instructions for clients who are not tech-savvy:

1. Open the page by clicking the link in the e-mail.

2. Save the page to your browser's list of saved links, called Bookmarks or Favorites, using the following command, depending on which browser you use:

   ■ In Internet Explorer, choose Favorites > Add to Favorites.

   ■ In Firefox and Netscape Browser, choose Bookmarks > Bookmark This Page.

   ■ In Safari, choose Bookmarks > Add Bookmark.

   ■ In Opera, choose Bookmark > Bookmark Page.

3. The link will now appear in your browser's Favorites or Bookmarks pane.

THE BIGGER PICTURE

USING THE WEB FOR INDIVIDUAL DOCUMENTS

Sometimes, your client doesn't need a personal Web page. For example, you might be working with a potential client who wants a filtered list of possible properties to see how well you know the market. It's too early to invest time in creating a personal Web page, but you don't want to send the file via e-mail because he has an account with a provider like MSN Hotmail or AOL, which often blocks messages with file attachments. You can just transfer the document, such as a PDF file, to your Web server using a file-transfer program, and then send him an e-mail that includes the URL to the file. What's the URL? Easy: it's your Web site address followed by a slash (/) and then the filename, such as www.grumanhomes.com/Jones_homes.pdf.

Be sure not to use spaces in your filenames, because some browsers cannot read the filename correctly if the URL contains a space. Also be sure that the capitalization you use for the URL in your e-mail exactly matches the capitalization of the filename, since some browsers can't recognize a file if the capitalization isn't exactly the same for the link as it is for the file.

What Client Pages Should Include

A personal Web page appeals strongly to buyers, since it can be a venue not only for basic information (like recent comps and handy contact information for the various people involved in the transaction, such as the mortgage broker and escrow officer), but also for details on each property you've asked them to consider and for all the disclosure information you and the seller's agent have provided.

But sellers can also benefit from having their own personal Web page. I recommend including a basic list of the materials they need to get ready to list their home, as well as any forms they need to complete. This in essence lets them use the Web page as a checklist they can access at any time.

Be Discreet in What You Publish

Do *not* post private information on client pages, in case a stranger should come across the personal Web page and see this information. (I'll show you how to minimize this risk a little later in this section, but you can't easily eliminate the possibility.)

For seller pages, I definitely would not post a copy of a listing contract—that's a private matter between you (and your broker) and the seller. I would also not post the disclosures you received from the seller. (I believe disclosures should go only to potential buyers, not to the general public, because they could reveal private information that is only the business of a potential buyer.) A good rule of thumb for a seller's personal Web page is to post only information you want to provide *to* the seller rather than information you receive *from* the seller.

For buyer pages, figuring out what to post is a bit trickier. It's a real convenience for buyers to have all the information about a transaction in one place—including copies of the seller-provided disclosures. As mentioned earlier, these disclosures could contain personal information that should not be made widely available. On the other hand, as soon as a copy is given to anyone—even in the form of paper—the cat's out of the bag.

Therefore, you might discuss the idea of what to post on personal client pages with your broker or attorney, just to be safe.

Protect Personal Information

Here's a list of techniques to help you limit unauthorized access to your client pages:

- **Avoid links from your Web site:** Never link to a client page from your public Web site. Instead, provide the URL to the client via an e-mail. Delivering the link in an e-mail all but eliminates the chance that someone looking at your public pages will stumble across them.

- **Block search engines:** To prevent search engines from listing your client pages, add the following code to your client pages, somewhere between the `<head>` and `</head>` tags: `<meta name="robots" content="none">`. For good measure, also delete the `<meta name="description">` and `<meta name="keywords">` tags that search engines use to figure out when to display your site in response to a user search. (The "Leading People to Your Site" section in Chapter 5, "Online Marketing Techniques," explains how to use meta tags in more detail.)

- **Delete documents:** Remove documents when they are no longer needed, for example, after a transaction has closed. (At the close of a transaction, it's a great idea to give your client a CD with all the relevant files, as explained in Chapter 10, "Managing Transactions More Effectively.")

- **Use passwords:** Require a password to open PDF, Microsoft Word, or other files that contain private information. Ask the client what password she prefers, so she'll have a better chance of remembering it. (And keep a list of these passwords, since you too will need to use a password to open the documents.)

CHECKLIST

A BUYER'S WEB PAGE

A buyer's personal Web page should include the following information, adjusted to your local requirements and market expectations:

- A list of what the buyer needs to have prepared to make an offer (such as loan preapproval, insurance preapproval in some areas, and verifiable and accessible down payment funds).

- Contact information for all parties involved in the transaction, such as mortgage broker and escrow officer.

- Any forms the buyer needs to complete, such as an agency disclosure. I also like to post sample offer contracts so the buyer can familiarize herself with them before the crunch time of writing up an offer happens.

- Details, such as flyers and comps generated from the local MLS system or your own efforts, on homes you think the buyer should consider.

- General disclosures as required or are common in your market, such as for natural hazards or laws affecting rental units.

- Property-specific disclosures for homes the buyer is interested in. (You should take steps to protect these documents, such as requiring a password to open them.)

Here's how to require a password in the commonly used Adobe Acrobat Professional and Microsoft Word programs. Keep the following in mind no matter which program you use:

- The specific steps may vary based on the version of the program you own.

- The document you're password-protecting should be open before following these steps.

- Type the password carefully. If you mistype the password, you won't be able to reopen the file once it has been saved and closed. (If you do mistype it, you can change it before you save and close the file, but once closed, you'll need to know what the mistyped password is to be able to reopen it.)

Adobe Acrobat Professional

In Adobe Acrobat Professional, you can require a password for a specific document by following these steps:

1. Choose File > Document Properties to access the Security pane.

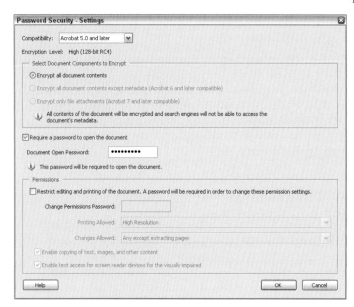

2. Choose Password Security from the Security Methods pop-up menu to open the Password Security Settings dialog box.

3. Check the Require Password to Open the Document option and enter a password in the Document Open Password field.

4. Click OK to close the Password Security Settings dialog box, and then click OK to close the Document Properties dialog box to apply the password requirement.

To help prevent unauthorized access to sensitive or private documents you post to a client Web page, require a password to open the document. Here, I'm requiring a password for a PDF file by using the protection option in Adobe Acrobat Professional (shown in the middle of the screen).

5. Save the document (choose File > Save) so the password requirement is saved with it.

The Tech-Savvy Real Estate Agent

Microsoft Word for Windows

In Microsoft Word for Windows, follow these steps:

1. Choose File > Save As.

2. Look for the Tools menu at the top of the Save As dialog box, and select General Options from the Tools menu. The Save dialog box will open.

3. At the bottom of the Save dialog box, type in a password in both the Password to Open and the Reenter Password to Open fields, and click OK.

4. You'll be returned to the Save As dialog box, where you can click Save to save the file and its new password requirement.

To safeguard private information posted on the Web, I'm requiring a password for a Word file by using the protection option in Microsoft Word (shown at the bottom of the screen).

Microsoft Word for Macintosh

In Microsoft Word for Macintosh, follow these steps:

1. Choose File > Save As to open the Save As dialog box.

2. Click the Options button near the bottom of the Save As dialog box. The Preferences dialog box will open.

3. In the Preferences dialog box, type in a password in both the Password to Open and the Password to Modify fields, and click OK.

4. You'll be returned to the Save As dialog box, where you can click Save to save the file and its new password requirement.

CD RESOURCES: For document editing software, links to Adobe and Microsoft. For file transfer, links to Fetch and Ipswitch.

Using PDF Files to Deliver Information

The PDF file is the third-best technology a real estate agent can use (after the MLS and e-mail). The PDF format lets you take almost any document and deliver it instantly to anyone with a Web browser. Even better, the recipient can print the file even if she doesn't have the software used to create the original. It truly is electronic paper.

How to Create PDF Files

Chapter 3, "Working with Electronic Media," goes into detail on how to create and modify PDF files, so I'll just summarize here:

- **Converting documents to PDF:** You can convert paper documents to PDF files using a scanner and conversion software such as Adobe's Acrobat Professional or ScanSoft's PaperPort. Or you can fax the documents to a service that will convert them for you and send you the PDF file by e-mail.

- **Creating PDF files:** You can create PDF files from any program on your computer, such a Microsoft Word or PowerPoint, by using the program's Print function and selecting the PDF format as your output option. You'll need PDF-creation software installed, such as Adobe's Acrobat Professional or Docudesk's DeskPDF, to use this option. Some programs—mainly Adobe's other programs, such as InDesign—can create PDF files without additional software. The Zipforms/Winforms software that lets you fill in transaction information on your computer is another example of software that can create PDF

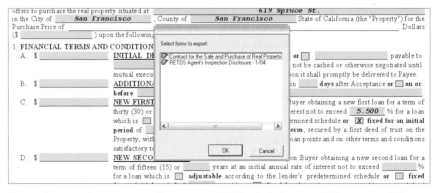

Many real estate software programs let you export PDF files, including many MLS systems and (shown here) the Winforms software for completing real estate transaction forms.

files directly without additional software. (See Chapter 10 for more on RE FormsNet's Zipforms/Winforms.)

- **Exporting from the MLS to PDF files:** You may be able to create PDF files from your MLS system. Many now let you export reports of properties, comps, and market data to the PDF format. These programs typically open a new window in your browser containing the PDF file, which you can then save to your computer. If your MLS doesn't have this feature, you probably can still create PDF files from it. If the MLS can display a printable report on screen (often labeled something like "printer-friendly view"), just "print" it to a file in the PDF format. Again, you'll need PDF creation software on your computer to do this.

How to Add Comments to PDF Files

Creating PDF files for easy document distribution is great, but you can do more. The PDF format was also designed to let people annotate—mark up—documents with notes and even make small edits (such as replacing a few characters on a line to correct an error).

I use Acrobat Professional to add instructions like "Sign Here" and detailed notes (such as to explain what a particular item means) to documents. My clients can quickly see where they need to sign, and I can increase the odds that they read important information buried in the fine print of some huge report.

Annotations in PDF files can help show clients where to sign (as shown at the bottom of this image) or provide bold notes on important pages (as shown in the inset page).

Here's what you can do:

- **Add comments:** Adding comments is easy: Just click the Note Tool button in Acrobat Professional, then click at the location in your document where you want the note to appear. A yellow Post-It Note–like box will appear, in which you can type your comments. You can add as many notes as you like.

- **Highlight text:** You can also use the Highlighter tool (the unlabeled icon that looks like a Magic Marker) to add a yellow highlight over text. Just click the tool, then click and drag the mouse over the text you want to highlight. Release the mouse button to complete the highlighting. If you double-click that highlight, you can add a note as well.

- **Add stamps:** For stamps like "Sign Here," click the triangle to the right of the Stamp Tool button to see a list of stamps. Then select the stamp you want from the list, and click the mouse at the document location where you want it to appear. Again, if you double-click the stamp after inserting it, you can type in a note.

- **Mark up text:** To mark up text, such as to show suggested deletions or corrections, click the Text Edit button, and then select the text you want to mark up. Type in the new text or just press Backspace to show a suggested deletion. To insert text, just click in the text where you want to add text, then start typing. Remember: This won't change the actual text, but it will display your suggested changes in a note.

- **Change text:** To actually change text, choose the Touch-up Text tool (you might need to choose Tools > Advanced Editing > Touch-up Text Tool to see it), and then highlight the text you want to change. Now enter the new text. Note that you can edit text only within a single line, so if you need to make changes across several lines, you need to make the changes to each line separately.

Note that your clients won't be able to add their own comments or do any annotations unless they also have a program like Acrobat Professional. The free Adobe Reader only lets them view pages, print them, and search text in the file. That's fine for most clients, but clients who want to pass notes back to you will have to print out the pages and write their notes by hand, then mail, hand-deliver, or fax the pages to you.

Starting with version 7, both Adobe Reader and Acrobat Professional have a nifty way to show you all the comments in one place, so you don't have to search each page for them: choose

View > Show Comments List, and a list appears at the bottom of the screen. Double-click any entry to see the actual page and location of the comment.

The buttons in Adobe Acrobat Professional provide most of the program's commenting and mark-up features.

CD RESOURCES: For PDF creation software, links to Adobe, Docudesk, and ScanSoft. For fax-to-PDF services, links to Data on Call, Innoport, and MongoNet.

Using MLS and Broker Client-Notification Options

Many clients today are Web-savvy, so they use public resources like Realtor.com or the public access portion of your local MLS (if it provides such public access) to search for listings and see what else is on the market. As I mentioned in Chapter 4, that's a good thing. For buyers, it lets them safely check for properties outside the parameters they gave you, to get a sense of the market before focusing their search, and to compare what they find versus what you find (to double-check on you, which only proves that you're doing a good job, right?). For sellers, it's a way to see what the competition might be as well as to double-check your market analysis.

But you don't need to rely on the client going to a public MLS search. At many MLSs and at some broker systems, you can set up automatic searches for your clients. These clients will get an e-mail with a link to a Web page or PDF file any time a property comes on the market that meets their criteria. (You'll get copied too, so you can check into it quickly and be ready if your client asks about it.)

It's fine to send unfiltered listings automatically to someone exploring the market, but for more focused clients, I recommend that you set up the search so that only you are notified. That way you can screen the properties first, then forward only those properties that you think are worthwhile. That's customer service.

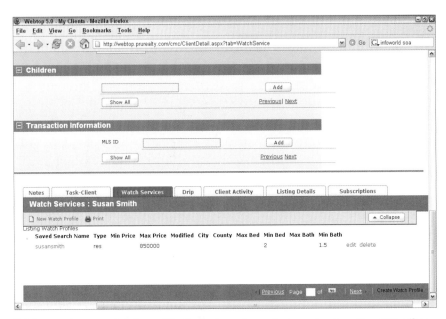

This is a sample automatic listing notification I set up using my brokerage's system. Many MLSs offer a similar capability.

If your client is looking at several options (such as houses in one price range and/or area, and condos in another price range and/or area), you simply set up multiple searches. As the criteria change, you modify them at the MLS or broker site.

The beauty of these systems is that they help you keep in regular contact with your client while offloading some of the initial property-identification work to technology. And that's good for everyone.

Marketing Transactions Effectively

PART 4

Managing Your Tasks and Transactions

CHAPTER 10

ISSUES COVERED

- How can you use technology to help manage your tasks?
- How can you use electronic forms to ease transactions?
- How can (and why should) you create a digital transaction library?
- What online resources are there to support out-of-area transactions?

When you're in the middle of a deal, the number of details to track can be overwhelming. And the number of details only seems to multiply as contractual and legal requirements increase to protect clients. If you have multiple clients, keeping track of all the particulars can be overwhelming—yet a missed appointment or deadline could cost you business or open you up for complaints.

Likewise, missing a key document in a transaction could cause your client to lose out on an offer or unknowingly enter into a bad deal. Not only must you manage your tasks, but you must also manage the information associated with them.

For many agents, the majority of their efforts revolves around getting new clients and keeping track of the available inventory of properties. In your business strategy, it's easy to put off dealing with the transaction details.

But don't let transaction management get short shrift. A well-managed transaction is usually a smooth one that both impresses and protects your client. Take the time to figure out your transaction system and the tools to support it.

Using Tools to Manage Tasks

Keeping track of details is an eternal issue for real estate agents, and there's never been a shortage of "solutions" to the problem in the form of paper and handheld organizers, paper and electronic calendars, and so on. Of course, no tool will keep you organized or on schedule—you ultimately have to use these tools and have a system in place that takes advantage of them.

Having a system is key—and it doesn't really matter whether you use one designed by a time-management expert, one based on a management system such as Franklin Organizer, or one you create yourself. By handling tasks systematically—knowing what they are, when they are due, and when they have been handled—you'll greatly reduce the chance of forgetting a vital step.

But technology can make the process of managing tasks easier. You'll find that different technologies can help make it easier to manage different kinds of tasks.

Appointments, Contacts, and To-Do Items

Electronic calendars—programs like Microsoft's Outlook or Now Software's Up-to-Date and Contact that run on your computer, or functions built in to your handheld organizer or cell phone—are very handy, since they can be set to alert you to deadlines ahead of time. Plus it's often easier to read the appointments, tasks, and reminders onscreen than decipher a note on paper—at least for someone with handwriting like mine.

It's hard to find a calendar program today that doesn't manage contacts and to-do lists. And that's a good thing, because you can use one tool to manage all these details.

Because real estate agents often work away from an office, I recommend that you use a handheld organizer or keep a laptop with you to run these tools. (Chapter 1, "The Right Office Tools," covers the hardware and software tools you might use. Chapter 8, "Managing Your Contacts," covers the process of contact management in more detail.)

CD RESOURCES: For contact and schedule managers, trial software from Eurekaware on the CD, as well as links to Eurekaware, Microsoft, Now Software, Palm, and Sage. For handheld organizers, links to Hewlett-Packard and Palm.

Financial Information

To manage financial information—your income and expenses—you should use a spreadsheet program like Excel or a basic accounting tool like Intuit Quicken or Microsoft Money. If you're savvy about accounting, you'll prefer a professional program like Intuit QuickBooks. I find that the spreadsheet and the professional accounting program are the best tools for me, since the basic accounting applications are really glorified checkbook registers, lacking the categorization options that let you track expenses in various areas and quickly figure out your net profit each quarter.

Yes, I know that no one but me likes to do accounting and taxes. But if you don't manage your finances, you could be hit with big tax penalties for underpaying taxes during the year, miss out on deductions, or get into a bind when your expenses start exceeding your current income—real estate, after all, is *not* a steady business for the vast majority of us.

You don't have to put on green eyeshades and be an accountant to keep a log of your expenses, so at the minimum, keep that log.

CD RESOURCES: For financial management software, trial software from the Zango Group, as well as links to H&R Block, Intuit, Microsoft, Sage Software, and the Zango Group.

CHECKLIST

TOOLS TO MANAGE TASKS

Among the tools that help you stay in control of the tasks and transaction details you must manage are the following:

- **Mileage log:** This log can be a notepad you keep in the car or a spreadsheet you maintain on your computer. Remember: At the end of the year, you must subtract the daily round-trip mileage to your brokerage office from your deducted mileage, even if you don't go every day (just multiply the round-trip distance by 250 to get that figure; this calculation assumes you take two weeks off a year).

- **Expense and income records:** For quarterly taxes, cash flow management, and general awareness of how your business is doing, keep track of your expenses in a paper workbook, in a Microsoft Excel spreadsheet (such as the Zango Group's ZangoTaxCalcQ), or in a basic accounting package such as Intuit's QuickBooks or Microsoft's Money.

- **Transaction tasks and deadlines:** Keep a to-do list and note all deadlines in a paper or electronic calendar. Use a PDA if you're away from the office a lot. It can alert you to deadlines and keep your to-do list handy, and it's easy to carry in a purse, jacket, or car's glove compartment. You might also create a checklist in a program like Microsoft Word of all the documents and tasks required for each specific transaction, so you can tell quickly if any steps or documents are missing. Enclose a printout in your transaction folder, and consider keeping a copy in your car or in a handheld device or laptop for easy access when on the road.

- **Other appointments, tasks, and deadlines:** Use the same system you use for your transactions to manage other tasks, from your marketing schedule to appointments with prospective clients, from accounting deadlines to PTA meetings. You might produce separate pages for short-term tasks, such a list of all open houses to see on a particular broker's tour rather than include the whole list in your current calendar.

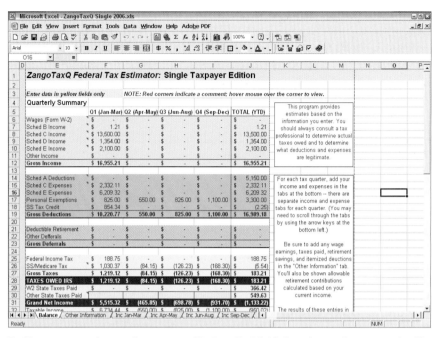

Tracking expenses and taxes using a program like ZangoTaxCalcQ helps reduce unpleasant surprises like tax penalties and cash-flow crunches.

Lists

To manage lists for a specific task—such as a list of homes to visit during a broker's tour or a list of documents to review for a buyer—a word processor remains my favorite tool. Unlike the to-do lists in contact managers and personal organizers, a word processor gives you a lot of room for detail, so your lists can be as long as they need to be. In a business where agents are sued for not dotting all the *i*'s and crossing all the *t*'s in reviewing documents and ensuring the client has all relevant information, I believe it's critical to have complete lists. Using a word processor lets you do that.

And it's amazing how many things you can create lists for that are truly helpful in the real estate business.

If you're listing a property, I strongly recommend you compile a list of all the documents that you have for your disclosures to potential buyers and create a checklist form, so they know what to look for. It helps both you and the buyer's agent ensure that all the documents have been delivered. Because these documents tend to be the same across transactions, you can create a

184   The Tech-Savvy Real Estate Agent

template in a program like Word that you then modify for each listing.

Likewise, you can use a template file to create a personalized checklist for sellers of all the items and tasks they need to handle to prepare their home for sale.

If you're representing a buyer, there are all sorts of lists you can create. Here are a few examples:

- a list of preoffer buyer requirements

- a list of common issues to look for in evaluating a home

- a list of potential providers, such as contractors, inspectors, mortgage brokers and so on

Keep these lists in a folder on your computer so they're all easily accessible if you need to make a copy for each transaction.

Using Transaction Software

According to the National Association of Realtors, about 300,000 agents use electronic forms to fill in details in their offers, disclosures, and other transaction documents. That's less than a third of all agents. Those 700,000 folks still using paper are missing out on something good. Whether you use software on your computer that lets you enter transaction details or use Web-based forms, these tools provide the following benefits:

- **Readability:** Information you enter is readable, so there's less chance of error or misinterpretation.

- **Consistent data:** Information that is used repeatedly in a document, such as a person's name or the property address, needs to be entered just once, saving you a lot of work and ensuring the information is consistent on all forms.

- **Reduction of errors:** Mathematical errors are reduced, since these forms check to make sure that, for example, the down payment amount and financed portion of an offer add up to the offer price.

Prudential California Realty

Gruman Homes

EXCELLENCE FOR SAN FRANCISCO AND THE BAY AREA

2241 Market St., San Francisco, CA 94114 | (415) 647-0996 | cell (415) 867-7389 | galen@grumanhomes.com

Disclosure Receipt Statement
123 City St., San Francisco, CA 94100
Galen Gruman, seller's agent

Before Acceptance:
Please include the following with your offer:
 Mortgage preapproval letter (if financing the purchase)
 Buyer's agency relationships disclosure

Buyer(s) making an offer on this property must also include this statement with their offer acknowledging receipt of the following disclosures. Please initial receipt for each document:

___ Seller's Transfer Disclosure Statement	___ S.F. Report of Residential Building
___ Seller's agent's disclosure	Records (3R)
___ Seller's agency relationships	___ Seller's insurance claim history (CLUE)
disclosure	report
___ Natural hazards disclosure report	___ Condominium (HOA) agreement
___ Pest inspection report	___ Condominium financial disclosure
___ Preliminary title report	statement
___ Water conservation statement	___ Condominium insurance statement
___ Energy conservation statement	___ Condominium financial statement
___ Lead-based paint hazards disclosure	___ HOA minutes disclosure
___ Underground storage tank (UST)	___ Parking and storage disclosure
inspection statement	___ Seller's façade repair and painting
___ Smoke detector statement of	receipts
compliance	___ Previous owner's garage-addition
	records

Within three days of offer acceptance, buyer(s) will furnish signed copies of the actual disclosures and reports above. For copies of reports and records that do not have places indicated for signature and/or initials, please sign and date the first page of each and then initial and date each subsequent page.

Buyer(s) should also include signed copies of the following disclosures provided by their agents or other parties:
 Homeowner's Guide to Earthquake Safety and Environmental Hazards
 Protect Your Family from Lead in Your Home
 General Information for Sellers and Buyers of Residential Property

I have read, acknowledged, and understood the above information,

Buyer's signature   Date

Buyer's signature   Date

Lists generated in a word processor can help both you and your clients ensure that all details are handled in a transaction. Here's one I use for disclosures in my listings.

- **Onscreen preview:** The forms can be exported to PDF format, so your clients can review them onscreen before printing them out for signing. This lets you save paper by correcting mistakes or making changes before you print them for signature.

- **Availability:** Because the forms are stored on your computer or on the Web, you don't have to worry about running out of them, as you do with the paper form.

- **Up-to-date forms:** As the forms are updated by your local Realtors association, you automatically have the most recent version available, ensuring you're using the right forms each time.

RESOURCES FOR OUT-OF-AREA TRANSACTIONS

Occasionally, you'll do business outside your area—such as in another part of your state or, more rarely, in another state. (Remember, you typically need a license in any state in which you sell real estate. The book's companion CD has a link to a National Association of Realtors' Web page where you can check if your state's license is valid in other states.)

Because different regions within a state can have different contracts than you use and because they almost certainly use a different MLS system, it can be hard to conduct business in a "foreign" area. (That's why so many agents refer clients to a local agent in an area for a referral fee of 20 to 30 percent.)

But if you do choose to work out of area, there are a few resources that can help:

- **Realtor.com:** The Realtor.com Web site shows listings across the country, letting you get a sense of what's on the market. Note that the data is often a few days to a few weeks out of date, and you can't look up sales prices, so the information is not complete enough to determine a listing or offer price.

- **MLS systems:** Some MLSs cooperate with other nearby ones, providing a way for agents to search for current and sold properties in those neighboring areas. In the San Francisco Bay Area, for example, four local Realtors associations have set up www.mlslistings.com to provide joint search capability.

- **Brokerages:** Some large brokerages offer their own MLS search capabilities through a Web site available only to their agents. Typically, you can search any MLS system in which the brokerage has offices to see current and sold listings.

- **Title companies:** If the title company you often do business with offers you online access to title records, you can check recent sales prices for specific properties or areas. However, this data is typically 30 to 60 days old, since it comes from public records, and it won't list properties currently for sale or display the offer prices for those that were sold.

- **Other providers:** You can buy paper or electronic real estate forms for other parts of the country from providers such as TrueForms.

Transaction Forms

The most common type of electronic forms is transaction forms—the contracts, addenda, and disclosures used to sell and buy homes. To work with these forms electronically, your local Realtors association, or the company that produces its transaction forms, needs to make them available in a computer format.

Some companies use their own software to provide these interactive forms, such as Realfast's Realfast and RE FormsNet's Winforms/Zipforms; these companies also have a Web-based interface so you can log in from any computer and complete the forms. You typically get access to these forms as part of your Realtor membership or for an extra fee. (RE FormsNet is actually a joint subsidiary of the California Association of Realtors and the National Association of Realtors.) Like the paper forms, they're typically not available to nonmembers.

Some companies provide forms in PDF format that you can complete using the free Adobe Reader or print out and complete by hand. You typically buy these forms individually and are allowed to complete a specific number of transactions for each purchase. An example is TrueForms, which provides PDF forms for 18 regions, as well as a generic form for use anywhere.

PDF forms often are not customized for specific states or regions, as are the forms provided to agents by their Realtors association—in fact, they're typically used by do-it-yourself buyers and sellers looking for a generic, "standard" form. Check with your broker to see if you should be using these generic forms, since they may not meet your errors-and-omissions insurance's requirements.

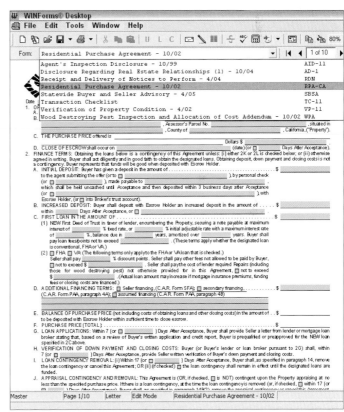

Real estate forms software, such as Winforms shown here, lets you easily enter details in transaction forms.

You'll also find PDF and Word forms for rental property management, such as leases and pay-or-quit notices from a variety of companies, such as Kaktus and Socrates. If you use such forms, be sure they address—or you have an attorney add language to cover—local requirements such as rent control, noise ordinances, and occupancy limits. A good source for localized forms is the Apartment Owners Association, which has local chapters in many areas.

CD RESOURCES: For real estate forms, links to Realfast, RE FormsNet, and TrueForms. For rental property forms, links to the Apartment Owners Association, Kaktus, and Socrates.

Transaction Systems

In late 2005, Real Estate Business Technologies (REBT)—like RE FormsNet, a subsidiary of the California Association of Realtors and of the National Association of Realtors—launched an online transaction management system meant to help automate more than just the data entry of transaction forms.

The Relay Transaction Management system is available for an annual fee and works with Winforms/Zipforms and many MLS systems, so it can exchange data among them. For example, if you have a listing, the online version of Winforms/Zipforms would get the seller information from Relay, as would the local MLS system.

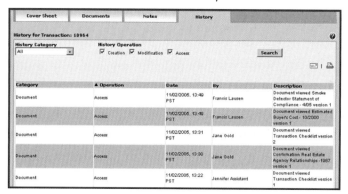

But the Relay system also acts as a communications hub, logging all e-mails between you and your clients, and with other parties. Plus, it provides fax-to-PDF conversion, so any documents faxed to a special number are converted to PDF files and stored along with your other transaction documents in the Relay system. And it can also send automated reminders as deadlines approach.

The new Relay Transaction System provides a central, Web-based service to manage transaction forms, documents, client and agent communications, and even reminders for due dates.

The Tech-Savvy Real Estate Agent

OTHER AGENT RESOURCES

There are certainly many Web-based ways to help clients and to help agents serve their clients. But there are also Web resources to help agents exclusively.

For example, the National Association of Realtors has a Web site specifically for agents: www.realtor.org. Once you sign up, you can access agent–and broker-specific resources such as past issues of *Realtor Magazine*, technology tutorials, Zipforms electronic transaction forms, membership dues payment, and e-mail newsletter subscriptions.

Likewise, your local Realtors association likely also offers Web-based services in addition to MLS access (for those associations that manage their own MLS systems) and agent directories. For example, my local association provides a training calendar and summaries of legal rulings.

Many states offer e-government services that let you renew your real estate license, access rules and regulations, and get links to approved continuing education courses. You can go to your state's Web site by entering www.*xx*.gov in your browser, where *xx* is replaced by your state's two-letter postal code (such as CA for California or ME for Maine). Search for the Department of Real Estate or whatever it's called in your state. Then bookmark the appropriate page in your browser.

Don't forget to use the Web the way your clients do: as a resource for consumers. For example, it can be less expensive to have your business cards printed by a Web-based service than to use your brokerage's service. Or you can save money, or get a more attractive version, when buying business cards online than at a store. In addition to shopping, you can use the Web to manage your bank accounts and other transactions, both business and personal.

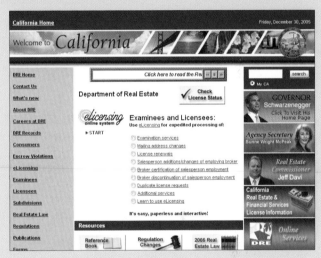

Many states, such as California, offer agents and brokers licensing and other services via the Web.

The idea is to give you a central management tool for your transactions, combining many of the technologies mentioned in this chapter into one system. That's a great concept, especially if you don't want to manage all the technology tools yourself but just want to manage the transactions.

Because it's so new, few agents are using Relay, and only a few MLSs can connect to it, so check whether it supports your MLS before you buy a service subscription. Personally, I'm leery about a Web-based service storing my transaction data, since I no longer have control over it, but then again if my computer crashes and loses data, anything stored on Relay is unaffected. Another issue to consider is that you must have an Internet connection to use it, so you couldn't work on transaction forms on your laptop during a slow open house, for example, unless you have a 3G wireless connection (as covered in Chapter 2, "The Right Connections").

However, I suspect that over time such a system will become commonplace, offered through your Realtors association (as Relay is) or as a service from your brokerage—something a few large brokerages also offer today.

 CD RESOURCES: *A link to REBT.*

Creating Digital Transaction Libraries

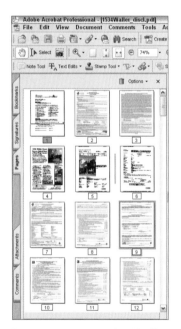

When escrow has closed and you're meeting your buyer to hand her the keys to her new home or visiting the seller to celebrate the sale of the property, consider giving the client something extra: a CD or DVD that has PDF files of all the transaction documents on it. (Oh, and make one for your own archives as well.)

A disc takes little room, holds a lot of data, is easy to store, and is convenient to use. (I use a CD, since almost any computer can read this type of disc. Older computers often don't have DVD-compatible drives.) You will have given the client paper copies of all the documents as the transaction progresses, but if the client has a disc, she can put that stack of paper in a box in the basement or garage and not have to dig it out later if a question comes up about the transaction. Instead, she can just put the disc in her computer and peruse the contents in a matter of minutes.

Chapters 1 and 3 cover the tools available to create PDF files and burn them to disc. But there are a few special considerations for creating a disc archive that I didn't cover in those chapters.

You can rearrange pages in a PDF file by clicking and dragging page icons in the Pages pane of Adobe's Acrobat Professional.

Organizing the Files

One consideration is deciding whether to combine all the documents into one large PDF file or to provide them as separate files. Having several files may sound like a great idea initially, but how do you decide how many documents to produce: a separate docu-

ment for each form? a grouping of forms by topic? And will
the filenames you use for each
document make sense to a
client? After all, he is not a real
estate professional and may not
understand what each contains.

I prefer creating one
complete file and using the
ability in Adobe's Acrobat
Professional PDF editing
software to add the electronic
equivalent of folder tabs, labeling each section. (Docudesk's
DeskPDF Professional offers
similar capabilities.)

You add and edit bookmarks—electronic file tabs—in the Bookmarks pane of Adobe's Acrobat Professional.

I first merge all the documents into one file by opening
the first document and saving
it as a new "master" file, naming it with the property address
(such as 123Main.pdf). I then import all the other files by choosing Document > Insert Pages and select a file to insert. I repeat
this for each file, saving the
master file each time.

Next, I rearrange the document's pages into what I consider
to be a logical order. For example, I might put all the marketing
materials together, the listing agreement and related disclosures
together, the various agency and legal disclosure forms I provided together, the pages from the accepted offer together, all
the escrow and title pages together, and so on. Be sure the Pages
pane is open at the left of the screen—double-click its tab to
open it if it's closed. To move pages around, select the pages you
want to move—click the first page and then Shift-click to select
a range of pages, or Ctrl-click (⌘-click on the Mac) each page to
select a set of nonadjacent individual pages—then drag the pages
to the new location in the Pages pane.

Then I create the electronic file tabs, which Adobe Acrobat
calls bookmarks. To do this, open the Bookmarks tab by double-
clicking its tab on the left side of the screen. Now go to the page
where you want the bookmark to be placed—you may need to
switch back and forth between the Pages and Bookmarks panes
as you navigate to each page to be bookmarked. In the Pages

pane's Options menu, select New Bookmark. You'll see a rectangle appear in the pane; type in the text you want to use as the bookmark. Repeat this for every bookmark you want to create. (Don't forget to save the file periodically and when you're finished.)

When your client opens the PDF file, she will see the bookmarks if she double-clicks the Bookmarks tab in Adobe Reader or Acrobat Professional. All she has to do is double-click the bookmark text for Reader or Acrobat to automatically jump to that page.

CD RESOURCES: For PDF creation software, links to Adobe, Docudesk, and ScanSoft.

Creating the Disc

With the PDF file (or files) finished, you're almost ready to create the disc. But first, see if there are any other files you might want to include, such as the digital photos you took of the property. I'd also include a text file containing a letter from me thanking them for their business and include my contact information, so they can reach me easily with questions or, I hope, for a later deal.

When you have all the files you want to place on the disc, use your disc burning software, as covered in Chapters 1 and 6, to copy the files to a recordable disc. Using a marker pen, write the name of the property and the date on the disc's face. (Some newer inkjet printers let you print a label directly on a disc, so if you have such a printer, use this labeling feature. The result is much more professional looking than a handwritten label.) Then place the disc in a disc sleeve or protective case (available at most office supply stores) so it won't get scratched easily, and present it to the client.

This act leaves a final, tangible impression that you're the kind of agent who goes the extra mile for client service and who has the know-how to do it right. That's ultimately what technology is supposed to help you accomplish, after all.

CD RESOURCES: For burning software, links to Nero and Roxio.

Tying It All Together

PART 5

Digital Workflow for Marketing

To make the most of technology in marketing yourself and your listings, adapt the following workflow to reflect the technology you use and the marketing goals you have set for yourself. Chapter 1 and Chapters 3 through 7 cover the tools and techniques involved in technology-based marketing.

Plan the Campaign

Map out a schedule for your marketing campaign using either an electronic calendar tool such as Microsoft Outlook, Now Up-to-Date and Contact, or a handheld organizer. For example, if you send postcards to your "farm" every month, or an e-mail newsletter every month, or test a new type of marketing or advertising twice a year, schedule these as well as the deadlines for producing these materials. With a schedule, you'll know they happen on time every time.

Similarly, when marketing a listing, schedule the open houses plus the deadlines for creating the flyers and newspaper ad copy, for e-mail or postcard mailings advertising the lists to your "farm" or contact list, and for distributing flyers to other agents.

Don't forget to schedule in time to update your contact lists periodically. Even if you add new contacts as they come in, you need to remove "cold" leads, opt-out requests, bounced e-mail addresses, and so forth on a regular basis. You should plan to review your contact list twice a year or once a quarter to understand whom you are marketing to so you can assess whether you need to change the mix.

Also, schedule time—once or twice a year—to assess your marketing efforts and fine-tune your business plan.

Create and Distribute the Materials

The tools used for your marketing materials will depend on the collaterals you create:

- **Print and PDF materials:** Microsoft Word, Microsoft Publisher, and Adobe InDesign are perfect for postcards, open house flyers, sign-up sheets, disclosure lists, neighborhood comps, listing presentations, and ads.

- **E-mail and Web materials:** Adobe Macromedia Dreamweaver is the best tool for professional and semiprofessional users, while Microsoft's Windows-only FrontPage is good for beginners and semiprofessional users. Make sure e-mail materials are correct by sending yourself a test message before scheduling the bulk delivery. And transfer any Web files to your server so they are available on your Web site when or before any ads appear for properties you are listing.

- **Images:** Adobe Photoshop Elements can help you retouch, enhance, crop, and resize images for use in your materials. Your photos should come from a digital camera or be processed onto a CD from a film camera.

Once created, publish the materials for distribution. You have several options to print and distribute your materials, for example:

- Print open house flyers on an inkjet printer at your home office, and then make enough copies at your local copy shop for the for-sale sign's document box, for distribution to other agents, and for use at open houses.

- Take the disc with the flyer files to a printing business like FedEx Kinko's and have it print the flyers for you.

- Print all the flyers you need on your inkjet printer—although that's usually about as expensive as having them copied and can be a time-consuming hassle if you're printing more than a dozen at a time.

- Print a copy for the local service that distributes flyers to other agents. This saves you from having to drive around to distribute them to the agents.

- Use a Web-based printing and distribution service, like NetPost Online, to do the actual printing and mailing from your files. This is often the priciest option, but it is also the most convenient.

- Generate PDF versions of your printed flyers to include on your Web site and the local MLS database's listing.

CHECKLIST
MARKETING TOOLKIT

A basic technology toolkit for real estate marketing would include the following:

- **Microsoft Office:** To produce flyers, listing presentations, checklists, neighborhood comps, and postcards using Word; to track marketing campaigns' effectiveness using Excel; to manage contacts and schedules using Outlook; and perhaps to create sales-style presentations using PowerPoint.

- **Microsoft FrontPage:** To produce your Web pages. (On the Mac, you need to choose a different tool, such as Adobe Macromedia Dreamweaver, since FrontPage works only in Windows.)

- **Adobe Acrobat Professional:** To create and edit PDF materials.

- **Adobe Photoshop Elements:** To work with digital images.

- **A digital camera:** To take pictures of your listings and of properties buyers might be interested in.

If you're comfortable using more complicated but powerful software tools, adjust the preceding list as follows by using these tools:

- **Microsoft Publisher or Adobe InDesign** (in addition to Microsoft Office): To create many of your printed materials.

- **Macromedia Dreamweaver** (in place of Microsoft FrontPage): For your Web materials, and a file-transfer program such as Ipswitch's WS_FTP Pro for Windows or Fetch Softworks' Fetch for Mac.

- **G-Lock EasyMail Pro:** To send out e-mail campaigns.

- **Tools for creating animations and virtual tours:** As described in Chapter 6, "High-Tech Marketing Collaterals." Remember: Give yourself plenty of time to create these materials the first time, since the process can be tricky.

Feel free to use different tools than those recommended here—as long as they do the job you need, of course.

Evaluate Your Campaign

Track the effectiveness of your marketing activities by recording the number of responses you get to various campaigns. Microsoft Excel is very useful for tracking expenses and responses for each marketing effort. Don't forget to use the results to refine your marketing strategy going forward.

Digital Workflow for Serving Buyers

To provide your buyers with great service, use technology throughout the buying process to improve communication and simplify the transaction management. Chapters 1, 3, and 8 through 10 cover the tools and techniques for applying technology to client service.

Educate the Buyer

Use your local MLS system to create market comps and analyze price trends. You can then produce a summary of this information for your buyer, customized for her home-buying goals and parameters. Today's MLS systems usually can generate market comps and report sales prices based on criteria such as neighborhood, number of bedrooms, amenities such as pools, and so on.

Take the insight you've gleaned from the MLS and your everyday experience in the market and use it to educate your client using appropriate technology tools: an e-mail summary, a printed or PDF document, or a spreadsheet.

With the initial market education handled, use automatic property screening tools in your local MLS to be notified of new listings that match your buyer's criteria, and have them sent directly via e-mail to either the buyer for consideration or just to you so you can screen the listings first. If you screen the properties (which I recommend, to deliver better service), consider posting the ones you think the buyer should consider to a client Web page as links to their own Web pages or to PDF flyers.

Because buyers often think agents try to sell them a more expensive house than they can afford, many buyers give you a lowball estimate, limiting what you'll find. Some buyers target a certain area and don't want you to look elsewhere. In both cases, buyers often use the Internet to check out alternative properties "just in case." Help them do their research by providing a link to the public section of your local MLS. If your MLS offers an IDX service that lets you integrate a search into your own Web site, use it, because this will keep your client coming back to your site and thus reinforce your role as the primary househunting resource.

Provide other basic education via e-mail, paper document, or PDF file, for example, a checklist of steps the buyer must make (such as getting preapproved and ensuring the down payment funds are accessible), information on mortgage rates and costs, neighborhood resources, and so on. These educational materials should be based on a master template file that you then customize for each client rather than starting from scratch each time. In some cases, these resources will be Web-based that you provide as links copied into an e-mail or accessed through your Web site. For example, you could provide a link to your city's housing office for information on rent control rules, condo conversion procedures, permit history order forms, or first-time buyers programs.

Communicate Better

Stay in touch with your client using e-mail and telephone. If long stretches go by with no appropriate properties, check in just to let the client know you're still actively working for her.

Keep the number of contact points manageable—one or two phone numbers, one fax number, and one e-mail address, for example. Consider having a fax machine at your home office or an Internet-based fax service to send and receive faxes. By having a home office fax or using an Internet-based fax service, you don't have to go to the office to send a fax, and you don't have to worry about faxes sent to the office getting mixed up with other agents' faxes.

Follow up verbal discussions with a summary e-mail, both to give your client the pertinent information and advice in a document she can refer to as needed and to protect yourself from claims that you said something you didn't or that you failed to disclose key information.

Use a client Web page to post relevant documents in one convenient place. A client Web page is also a handy venue for large files such as disclosure packages available to the client that her e-mail system might reject if you sent it as a file attachment. If you're a do-it-yourselfer, you can create and update these Web

CHECKLIST

BUYER SERVICE TOOLKIT

A basic technology toolkit for serving real estate buyers would include the following:

- **An MLS system account:** To track properties and sales trends.
- **Microsoft Office:** To produce checklists, neighborhood comps, and other educational materials using Word; to run mortgage and price calculations and comparisons using Excel, and to manage e-mail messages using Outlook.
- **Microsoft FrontPage:** To produce your Web pages. (On the Mac, you would need to choose a different tool, such as Adobe Macromedia Dreamweaver, since FrontPage works only in Windows.)
- **Adobe Acrobat Professional:** To create and edit PDF materials.
- **Electronic forms software:** To fill in transaction forms. Your local Realtors association typically chooses which company makes its forms available electronically.

As you get more comfortable using technology tools, consider using the following tools as well:

- **Microsoft Publisher or Adobe InDesign** (in addition to Microsoft Office): To create many of your printed materials.
- **Macromedia Dreamweaver** (in place of Microsoft FrontPage): For your Web materials, as well as a file-transfer program such as Ipswitch's WS_FTP Pro for Windows or Fetch Softworks' Fetch for Mac.
- **REBT's Relay Transaction System:** To provide a single tool to manage communications and document exchange. (In this case, you might not need your own Web-creation software.)
- **A digital camera:** To take images of the properties to preview them to your buyer.
- **Fax system:** A home-office fax machine or an Internet-based fax service.
- **Software such as Nero or Roxio Media Creator:** To write files to CDs and DVDs.

Feel free to use different tools than those recommended here—as long as they do the job you need, of course.

pages yourself and upload them to a Web server, using tools like Microsoft FrontPage or Adobe Macromedia Dreamweaver. If you're not interested in using technology at such a hands-on level, either hire someone else to do this or subscribe to a service that provides a simple Web-based interface for posting content to the Web, such as the REBT Relay Transaction System.

Manage the Transaction

Create checklists in Microsoft Word or use checklists provided by your broker or programs such as RE FormsNet's Winforms and Zipforms to track the various documents in the transaction, to ensure that all are accounted for and complete.

Use electronic forms software such as Winforms and Zipforms to fill in the purchase offer, disclosures, receipt acknowledgment, and other transaction forms. Consider sending blank or draft copies of these forms to your buyer ahead of time, so she can review them before you meet to sign.

Post copies of all documents to a client Web page, so there is a central repository available to you and the client no matter where you happen to be. But also protect your client's privacy (and that of the sellers) by requiring a password to open any sensitive documents—something you can do in Microsoft Word, Adobe Acrobat Professional, and Docudesk DeskPDF Professional.

When the transaction is complete, collect all the documents involved and create PDF versions of them. Then create a CD or DVD that contains all these documents so the buyer has a convenient copy. (Note that this disc should not replace the paper copies you give a client.)

Digital Workflow for Serving Sellers

To provide your sellers with great service, use technology throughout the buying process to improve communication and simplify the transaction management. Chapters 1, 3, and 8 through 10 cover the tools and techniques for applying technology to client service. Note that the workflow and tools described here are similar to those you use for buyers, as covered in Appendix B. This should not be a surprise, since buyers and sellers are parties to the same transaction, just with different roles. Also note that Appendix A covers tools and techniques for your marketing efforts, including those to help sell specific listings.

Educate the Seller

Your local MLS system has the information needed to create market comps and analyze price trends. Use that information to produce a summary of this information for your seller, customized for his sales goals. Many MLS systems can generate the reports for you based on criteria such as neighborhood, number of bedrooms, square footage, and so on.

You can take the insight gleaned from the MLS and your everyday experience in the market and use it to educate your client in any of several ways, using appropriate technology tools: an e-mail summary, a printed or PDF document, or a spreadsheet. Often, this information is used in a formal listing presentation, produced in Microsoft Word or PowerPoint, but even if you don't make a formal presentation, the seller will want to know this.

With the initial market education handled, offer the sellers the option of getting automatic e-mail notifications as other properties come on the market in their neighborhood. Sellers are naturally curious about the competition, so help them satisfy that curiosity and see how you've in fact helped price their property appropriately. (If you're talking to prospective sellers, also offer this service to help them track the market so they're properly educated about the actual conditions when they're ready to sell.) Your local MLS system typically offers such notification capability, as do some larger brokerages.

Don't forget to provide other basic education via e-mail, paper document, or PDF file, such as a checklist of steps the seller must make to prepare the house, disclosure requirements, transfer taxes, and so on. These educational materials should be based on a master template file that you then customize for each client rather than starting from scratch each time. In some cases, you can provide Web-based resources as links copied into an e-mail or through your Web site. For example, provide a link to your city's housing office for information on rent control rules, condo conversion procedures, permit history order forms, or transfer tax rates.

Communicate Better

When working with sellers, it's easy to lose touch during those marketing stretches when you have the information you need but don't yet have buyer queries or offers to coordinate. Don't let long stretches go by; stay in touch with at least an e-mail or telephone check-in just to let the client know you're still actively working for him.

Help the seller stay in touch with you by providing a manageable set of contacts for you—one or two phone numbers, one fax number, and one e-mail address, for example. Consider having a fax machine at your home office or an Internet-based fax service to send and receive faxes, so you don't have to go to the office to receive or send a fax, and you don't have to worry about faxes sent to the office getting mixed up with other agents' faxes.

Follow up verbal discussions with a summary e-mail, both to give your client the pertinent information and advice in a document he can refer to as needed and to protect yourself from claims that you said something you didn't or that you failed to disclose key information.

Use a client Web page to post relevant documents in one convenient place. For example, you could post checklists, forms, and other such materials for the seller

CHECKLIST

SELLER SERVICE TOOLKIT

A basic technology toolkit for serving real estate sellers would include the following:

- **An MLS system account:** To track properties and sales trends.
- **Microsoft Office:** To produce checklists, neighborhood comps, and other educational materials using Word; to run net-sales calculations and comparisons using Excel, and to manage e-mail messages using Outlook.
- **Microsoft FrontPage:** To produce your Web pages. (On the Mac, you would need to choose a different tool, such as Adobe Macromedia Dreamweaver, since FrontPage works only in Windows.)
- **Adobe Acrobat Professional:** To create and edit PDF materials.
- **Electronic forms software:** To fill in transaction forms. Your local Realtors association typically chooses which company makes its forms available electronically.
- **A digital camera:** To take images of the property for use in marketing, as well as image-editing software such as Adobe Photoshop Elements.

As you get more comfortable using technology tools, consider using the following tools as well:

- **Adobe Macromedia Dreamweaver** (in place of Microsoft FrontPage): For your Web materials, as well as file-transfer programs such as Ipswitch's WS_FTP Pro for Windows or Fetch Softworks' Fetch for Mac.
- **REBT's Relay Transaction System:** To provide a single tool to manage communications and document exchange. (In this case, you might not need your own Web-creation software.)
- **Fax system:** A home-office fax machine or an Internet-based fax service.
- **Software such as Nero or Roxio Media Creator:** To write files to CDs and DVDs.

Feel free to use different tools than those recommended here—as long as they do the job you need, of course.

to have access to whenever he wanted. (Consider converting any such printed materials to PDF format so they can be posted to the Web.) Even if the seller doesn't want to print various forms himself, he can still review them online before you drop off the paper copies. If you're a do-it-yourselfer, you can create and update these Web pages yourself and upload them to a Web server, using tools like Microsoft FrontPage or Adobe Macromedia Dreamweaver. If you'd prefer not to do so much technology work yourself, either hire someone else to do this or subscribe to a service that provides a simple Web-based interface for posting content to the Web, such as the REBT Relay Transaction System.

Manage the Transaction

Use checklists created in Microsoft Word or provided by your broker or programs such as RE FormsNet's Winforms and Zipforms to track the various documents in the transaction. This tracking will help ensure that all needed documents are accounted for and complete.

Use electronic forms software such as Winforms and Zipforms to fill in the listing agreement, any counteroffers, disclosures, receipt acknowledgments, and other transaction forms. Consider sending blank or draft copies of these forms to your seller ahead of time, so he can review them before you meet to discuss or sign.

When the transaction is complete, collect all the documents involved and create PDF versions of them. Then create a CD or DVD that contains all these documents so the seller has a convenient copy for his archives. (Note that this disc should not replace the paper copies you give a client.)

Defining Terms

Techies love lingo. And as you adopt technology in your real estate business, you'll encounter a lot of these terms. (And real estate has its own lingo, which newer agents may not know, either.) This appendix defines the technology and real estate terms used in the book, so you can always refresh your memory when needed.

10BaseT: A standard that lets data be sent and received at speeds of up to 10 Mbps over an Ethernet network. *See also* **Ethernet; Mbps.**

100BaseT: A standard that lets data be sent and received at speeds of up to 100 Mbps over an Ethernet network. *See also* **Ethernet; Mbps.**

1XRTT: *See* **CDMA2000 1XRTT.**

3G: Third-generation cellular network service that sends and receives both data and voice, providing data connection speeds of about 100 Kbps to 500 Kbps to a laptop or handheld device over a cellular network. (The laptop or handheld needs a special 3G card or built-in 3G radio that is compatible with the specific service you subscribe to.) There are several types of 3G service: the slower CDMA2000 1XRTT, GPRS, and EDGE services, and the faster CDMA2000 EVDO and HSDPA services. *See also* **CDMA2000 1XRTT; CDMA2000 EVDO; cellular network; EDGE; GPRS; HSDPA; radio.**

802.11: A family of standards for wireless networks that generally can transmit data in a radius of about 100 feet inside a building and up to 300 feet in an open area: *802.11a* transmits data at up to 54 Mbps, *802.11b* transmits data at up to 11 Mbps, and *802.11g* transmits data at up to 54 Mbps. 802.11a uses a different portion of the radio spectrum than 802.11g, so it's less prone to interference from common household radios such as those in some cordless phones and garage door openers, but few products are based on 802.11a. Note that 802.11g and 802.11b use the same radio spectrum and that both types of equipment can communicate with each other, although even a single 802.11b device on a wireless network will force all the 802.11g equipment on the network to slow down to 802.11b speeds. *See also* **Mbps; Wi-Fi.**

802.11i: A security standard for wireless networks that provides a secure way to transmit the user's password, so a hacker can't intercept it and log on as you. *See also* **WPA.**

802.1x: A security standard for networks, both wired and wireless, that helps verify that a device trying to log into the network is who it claims to be. This security is usually turned on automatically if you enable the firewall in your router or in your operating system. *See also* **firewall; router.**

AIFF (Apple Audio Interchange Format File): AIFF is the Mac OS X standard format for sound and music files. *See also* **MP3; WAV.**

bit: The smallest unit of measurement for data. A bit is an individual digit (0 or 1) in the sequence of digits that makes up computer data. Conceptually, a bit is like a letter in a human alphabet. *See also* **byte; Kbps; Mbps.**

BlackBerry: A handheld device from Research in Motion that allows access to e-mail almost anywhere; some versions add a personal organizer, cell phone, and/or Internet access. *See also* **smartphone.**

blog: Short for *Web log*, it is essentially an opinion page you publish on the Web that readers can add their own comments to.

bookmark: A link to another Web page or to another page within a PDF file. It is essentially a shortcut that you can create for easy access to pages you want to go to repeatedly. *See also* **browser; link; PDF.**

broadband: High-speed connections, typically to the Internet, using technology such as DSL and cable modems. *See also* **DSL; cable modem.**

browser: A software program that displays Web pages. *See also* **HTML.**

burn: Slang for writing data to a recordable CD or DVD. It's called *burn* because a laser beam etches the data onto the disc, using its high heat to do so. *See also* **CD-R; CD-RW; DVD-R; DVD-RW.**

byte: A set of eight bits, a byte is the standard measurement for data size. Data is typically segmented into bytes by computers and networks; much like human language is segmented into words. *See also* **bit; K; MB.**

cable modem: A device that connects computers to the Internet over cable TV lines. Typically, digital cable service is required to use a cable modem, and there is usually an extra fee for the Internet access as well.

campaign: An effort to reach current, past, and potential customers through a series of marketing efforts such as placing ads, sending e-mails, and mailing postcards. A campaign is something that you plan and then execute over a period of time in stages rather than a one-shot effort.

cascading style sheets (CSS): These files define the formatting of text and other parts of your Web page, so visitors see a consistent design for your site no matter how their browser is set. Each Web page contains a link to the CSS file on your Web server so the browser can read the CSS formatting and apply them to your pages.

CDMA2000 1XRTT: One of the technologies used to provide 3G data service on cellular networks. Often shortened to 1XRTT, the spelled-out version of this term (Code Division Multiplex Access First-Generation Radio Transmission Technology) is never used and makes sense only to a super techie. This technology is fairly slow, providing about 30 Kbps to 80 Kbps, and is being replaced with a technology called CDMA2000 1XEVDO. Of the major U.S. carriers, both Sprint Nextel and Verizon Wireless offer 1XRTT service (Sprint calls the service PCS Vision, while Verizon calls it NationalAccess). *See also* **3G; CDMA2000 1XEVDO.**

CDMA2000 1XEVDO: One of the technologies used to provide 3G data service on cellular networks. Often shortened to EVDO, the spelled-out version of this term is never used and makes sense only to a super techie. This technology offers data speeds of about 100 Kbps to 300 Kbps. Of the major U.S. carriers, both Sprint Nextel and Verizon Wireless offer 1XRTT service (Sprint calls the service PCS Mobile Broadband, while Verizon calls it BroadbandAccess). *See also* **3G; CDMA2000 1XRTT.**

CD-R: A recordable CD. You cannot change any data written to the CD. In some cases, you can write more than once to a CD (called a *multisession disc*), but each session will appear as if it were a separate CD on the user's computer. *See also* **burn; CD-RW; DVD-R; DVD-RW.**

CD-RW: A rewritable CD. You can erase and rewrite data on the CD just as you can on a hard drive, although after a certain number of rewrites (the number of rewrites will vary based on the type and brand of CD-RW disc), the CD-RW may not allow any further changes. *See also* **burn; CD-R; DVD-R; and DVD-RW.**

cellular network: The system that lets cellular phones, also called *mobile phones*, communicate with each other. The phones send and receive radio signals to and from each other through a series of radio towers that pass signals along. *See also* **3G; radio frequency.**

CGI (Common Gateway Interface): CGI is a protocol by which your Web site can run programs on Web pages, such as processing forms that users complete. The most common languages for such programs are Perl and PHP. *See also* **JavaScript.**

clickthrough: A measurement of how many times a specific link on a Web page is clicked by users. It is used to gauge how effective specific links, especially those in Web-based ads, are in attracting people.

comma-separated value (CSV): A file format in which each item is arranged consistently in the list and separated by a comma, so the program opening the file knows where each item begins and ends. It is typically used for lists and databases, such as a mailing list. For example, each line of a mailing list might be arranged *first,last,address,city,state,zip.*

CompactFlash (CF): *See* **memory card.**

compression: A mathematical technique to make information take less space in a computer file. Some forms of compression are *lossy*, meaning that some details are removed to reduce the file size. (For example, the JPEG image format uses lossy compression, while the TIFF image format does not.) Compression can be applied to any kind of information including text, graphics, sounds, and video. *See also* **JPEG; TIFF.**

crop: To remove outside portions of an image, usually by drawing a rectangle around what you want to keep and then telling the software program to delete, or crop out, the material outside the rectangle.

CRT (cathode ray tube): A CRT is the technology used in many TV sets and computer monitors. An electronic gun sends light rays onto a screen, which then glows where the rays hit to present the picture you see. CRTs, often just called "monitors," are usually at least as deep as they are high, taking up a foot or more of space on your desk. *See also* **LCD.**

CSS: *See* **cascading style sheet.**

CSV: *See* **comma-separated value.**

dialog box: Also referred to simply as a *dialog*, an interface element commonly used in software programs to provide various options that you select and then apply by clicking a button such as OK or Apply.

dialup: *See* **modem.**

digital zoom: A mathematical way to enlarge an image. Rather than actually get more detail by using a more powerful lens (called *optical zoom*), the device or software essentially guesses at what the details would look like when making the image bigger. These guesses are based on common patterns.

DNS (domain name server): A DNS contains a list of Web site addresses, so when a user types a URL into a browser, the DNS looks up which Web server contains that Web site and then connects the browser to that Web server. *See also* **domain; URL.**

domain: A location on the Web or on a network that contains one or more files. Typically, a domain is a specific Web address, such as www.grumanhomes.com, that contains a set of Web pages and other resources. (It can also be a similar location within a corporate network.)

download: To bring information from a device (such as a handheld or the Internet) into the computer or device you are using. *See also* **upload.**

DPI (dots per inch): Digital images are stored in a grid, with each grid point being a dot. The dpi value is the number of points that make up an image when the image is printed. (The term *ppi* is used when the image is displayed on-screen.) The higher the dpi, the more realistic the image looks, since the human eye blends the individual dots into a continuous image. *See also* **ppi**.

DSL (Digital Subscriber Line): DSL technology lets standard phone lines be used to transmit data for connections to the Internet. Typically, a converter device, called a *DSL modem* or *DSL router*, is needed to enable the connection. Note that there is usually an extra fee for the Internet access in addition to the phone service charges. *See also* **cable modem; modem; router.**

DVD-R: A recordable DVD. You cannot change any data recorded on to the DVD. In some cases, you can write more than once to a DVD (called a *multisession disc*), but each session will appear as if it were a separate DVD on the user's computer. *See also* **burn; CD-R; CD-RW; DVD-RW.**

DVD-RW: A rewritable DVD. You can erase and rewrite data on the DVD just as you can on a hard drive, although after a certain number of rewrites (the number will vary based on the type and brand of DVD-RW disc), the DVD-RW may not allow any further changes. *See also* **burn; CD-R; CD-RW; DVD-R.**

EDGE: One of the technologies used to provide 3G data service on cellular networks. The full name is Enhanced Data for GSM Evolution (GSM is the Global System for Mobile Communications, one of the two basic types of cellular networks), but no one ever uses its full name. This technology is fairly slow, providing about 70 Kbps to 130 Kbps, and is being replaced with a technology called HSDPA. Of the major U.S. carriers, only Cingular Wireless/AT&T Wireless offers EDGE service (in its Wireless Data Connect service). *See also* **3G; GPRS; HSDPA.**

Ethernet: A standard for wired networks. It is the near-universal type of wired network in use today; for all practical purposes, this term is synonymous with *wired network*. *See also* **10BaseT; 100BaseT.**

export: To deliver information from a program, database, or file into another program, database, or file without retyping it. *See also* **import.**

EVDO: *See* **CDMA2000 1XEVDO.**

flash memory card: *See* **memory card.**

farm: A set of potential customers with whom you repeatedly market your services. Typically, a farm is a geographic area, such as a neighborhood, but it could also be a group of people with like interests, such as members of a club or profession.

filename extension: Both Windows and Mac OS X add a three- or four-letter code at the end of a filename, called a filename extension. This code appears after a period; for example, the filename extension in *mylist.doc* is *doc*, which is the code for a Microsoft Word document. These filename extensions are often not displayed when you open folders on your computer; instead, you see an icon that gives you a visual representation of the filename extension.

firewall: A device or software program that blocks unauthorized access to your computer or network.

Flash: A file format from Adobe Systems' Macromedia division for animation files. Adobe also provides the Flash Player to display these files and the Flash Professional software to create and edit them. People often refer to all of these as simply "Flash." *See also* **QuickTime.**

flat panel: *See* **LCD.**

format: A specific representation, such as the font applied to text or the way data is stored in a file. The word is used to describe the act of applying attributes to text, graphics, and other objects in a print layout or in a Web page, as well as to describe the arrangement of data in a computer file (such as the PDF file format or the TIFF file format).

GB (gigabyte): A gigabyte, or 1,024 megabytes, is the same as 1,048,576 (1024×1024) K, or 1,073,741,824 bytes—roughly 1 billion bytes. *See also* **byte; MB.**

GHz (gigahertz): Gigahertz is a measurement of processing speed in chips. 1 GHz is 1,024 megahertz, and 1 hertz is a single computation per second.

GIF (Graphics Interchange Format): GIF is a common format for Web graphics and can be opened directly by any browser.

GPRS: One of the technologies used to provide 3G data service on cellular networks. The full name is Global Packet Radio Service, but no one ever uses its full name. This technology is very slow, providing about 30 Kbps to 50 Kbps, and has largely been replaced with a technology called EDGE, which is now being replaced with a technology called HSDPA. Of the major U.S. carriers, only Cingular Wireless/AT&T Wireless offers GPRS service (in its Wireless Data Connect service). *See also* **3G; EDGE; HSDPA.**

hacker: A person who tries to access computers and networks without authorization, usually to steal information or cause damage.

handheld: A small device that can be held in one hand and typically includes electronic calendar and address book capabilities. Some models also provide e-mail access, phone service, Web browsing, and/or basic word processing and spreadsheet capabilities. *See also* **PDA; smartphone.**

hardware: Physical technology devices such as computers, phones, modems, monitors, printers, and cards.

high-speed connection: Typically used to describe fast connections to the Internet using technologies such as cable modems and DSL, and is often called *broadband*. What constitutes "high-speed" changes over time, but when this book was published in 2006, any connection to the Internet over 300 Kbps was considered high-speed, although most broadband connections available to urban and suburban customers are three to 20 times faster than that.

HELO domain: The domain from which e-mail is being sent; essentially, the sender's domain. HELO is used by e-mail servers to identify potential spam by helping to verify that e-mail is coming from the actual sender rather than by someone pretending to be the sender. Bulk e-mail delivery programs typically let you enter the HELO domain information so e-mail servers can cross-check that against the actual source of e-mails they receive.

hot spot: A location that provides Wi-Fi wireless Internet service, usually for a per-use or monthly fee. *See* **Wi-Fi.**

HSDPA: One of the technologies used to provide 3G data service on cellular networks. The full name is High Speed Downlink Packet Access, but no one ever uses its full name. This technology offers data speeds of 300 Kbps to 500 Kbps. Of the major U.S. carriers, only Cingular Wireless offers HSPDA service (in its BroadbandConnect service). *See also* **3G.**

HTML (Hypertext Markup Language): HTML is the set of codes used to create Web pages. Browsers read that code and then translate it into the pages they display.

hues: Shades of colors.

hyperlink: *See* **link.**

IDX (Internet Data Exchange): IDX is an access method to an MLS that lets agents and brokers provide Web site visitors limited access to the MLS database. Typically, visitors can search only current listings but not get the full details. The idea is that visitors can educate themselves about the market but will still need to rely on agents as the source of detailed property information and of past sales information used to help assess appropriate listing and offer prices. *See also* **VOW.**

image advertising: Advertising that promotes a brand or person to raise public awareness of that brand or person rather than to sell a specific product. For example, an ad promoting a specific agent is image advertising, while an ad promoting a specific listing is not.

image resolution: The degree of detail in an image; the greater the resolution, the more detail is stored in the image file. *See also* **DPI; pixel; PPI.**

import: To bring information into a program, database, or file from another program, database, or file without retyping it. *See also* **export.**

Internet Protocol (IP): The standard by which computers connect to the Internet and exchange data over it.

IP: *See* **Internet Protocol.**

ISP (Internet service provider): An ISP delivers access to the Internet, usually through a subscription service.

JavaScript: A programming language you can use to embed programs in your Web pages. These programs run in the browsers of your visitors, not on your server, so their access to data is more limited than CGI programs, which run on the Web server. (Note that JavaScript is a different language than Java, which professional programmers use to create custom applications for large companies.) *See also* **CGI.**

JPEG (Joint Photographers Expert Group): The JPEG format is a common image format for Web graphics that can be opened by any browser. Unlike other image formats for the Web, JPEG images can have lower quality due to the use of compression to make images take less space and download faster. Image-editing programs often let you control the trade-off between quality and file size.

K (kilobyte): A kilobyte is 1,024 bytes—roughly a thousand bytes. File sizes are often measured in K. *See also* **bit; byte; MB.**

Kbps (kilobits per second): A measure of how fast data is sent and received. Because there are eight bits in a byte, a 1K file would contain 8,000 bits and at a speed of 300 Kbps would take about 26.7 seconds to transmit. *See also* **bit; byte; K; MB; Mbps.**

keylogger: A program that is secretly running on a computer to capture the user's keystrokes in the hopes of detecting passwords, account numbers, and other valuable information for use by data thieves. *See also* **malware.**

LAN (local area network): A LAN is a set of devices (such as computers and printers) connected using wired or wireless technology so they can exchange data with each other. LANs are typically confined to a common space such as an office or building. *See also* **WAN.**

layout tool: Software that you use to arrange items (such as text, buttons, and images) on a page and apply formatting such as font and color to those items. Examples include Adobe InDesign, Microsoft Publisher, and QuarkXPress.

LCD (liquid crystal display): LCD is the technology that permits the creation of flat screens an inch or so thick that also use less power than conventional CRT (cathode ray tube) monitors. LCDs are used in laptops, in handheld devices, and in flat-panel monitors that connect to desktop PCs. *See also* **CRT.**

link: Also called a *hyperlink*, this is a method by which a user can click a piece of text or an image on a Web page and be taken to another Web page. You implement a link using an HTML <A HREF> tag. *See also* **HTML; tag**.

lossy: A form of compression that removes data and thus quality. *See also* **Compression**.

mailing list: A file containing a list of addresses, such as e-mail addresses or postal addresses.

malware: Any form of software that is designed to steal data, corrupt files, or hijack your computer to send out spam. Various forms include keyloggers, Trojan horses, spyware, and viruses. Most are attached to data files (such as music) or programs that are downloaded from the Internet, but they can also be secretly attached to e-mails and Web pages. *See also* **keylogger; spyware; Trojan horse; virus**.

MB (megabyte): A megabyte is 1,024 K, or 1,048,576 (1,024×1,024) bytes—roughly 1 million bytes. *See also* **byte; K.**

Mbps (megabits per second): A measure of transmission speed. Because there are eight bits in a byte, a 1 MB file would contain 80,000 bits and at a speed of 300 Kbps would take about 267 seconds to transmit.

megapixel: A megapixel is 1,024 pixels—a unit of measurement for image resolution capability of devices such as digital cameras. It refers to the actual number of pixels that the camera can detect per image. *See also* **pixel.**

memory card: A small storage device, usually the size of a dime or quarter, that needs no power to store data. (The technology that allows such storage retention without power is called *flash memory*.) It's typically used in digital cameras. There are several formats of memory cards, so memory card readers that you attach or have in your computer typically have several slots, one for each of the popular card types. Popular card types include CompactFlash (CF), Memory Stick, Multimedia Card (MMC), Secure Digital (SD), and Smart Memory (SM).

Memory Stick: *See* **memory card.**

META: The META tag is a specific instruction used in HTML code to include identifying information in a Web page. Examples include keywords used by search engines. *See also* **HTML; tag**.

MHz (megahertz): A standard measurement of processing speed in chips. 1 MHz is 1,024 hertz, and 1 hertz is a single computation per second.

MLS (Multiple Listing Service): The MLS is a private database of past and current residential property listings for a specific area of a state. MLSs are often run by a local Realtors association or offered exclusively to members of such an association as part of membership dues or as an extra-cost service. An MLS is meant to help agents exchange information on properties for sale, so buyer's agents can easily identify possible properties for their clients. Most MLS systems now provide access through the Internet, and many offer a portion of their data at no charge to the general public to help promote the listings. *See also* **IDX; VOW**.

modem: Short for *modulator/demodulator*, a device that connects a computer to another computer or to a network. When used by itself, the word *modem* typically means a device that lets a computer use a standard phone line to connect to another computer (called *dial-up access*). The word *modem* is usually used as part of a phrase, such as *cable modem* or *DSL modem*. *See also* **cable modem; DSL**.

moderator: A person who monitors comments posted at a public or private bulletin board, chat room, or forum and who edits or removes inappropriate comments. This person may also have the authority to decide who has posting privileges.

MP3: The MPEG-1 Audio Layer 3 format is a standard file format for sound and music files on a variety of playback devices such as iPods; it is also supported on Windows and Mac OS X PCs as a sort of universal audio format. (Even though MPEG is a file format for video, the MP3 variant of this format uses its highly efficient compression technology to make sound files small, enabling an MP3 CD to hold the equivalent of six or more regular CDs.) *See also* **AIFF; MPEG; WAV**.

MPEG (Moving Pictures Expert Group): MPEG is a format for video files and is a standard on Windows and Mac OS X computers.

Multimedia Card (MMC): *See* **memory card.**

Multisession disc: A CD or DVD that has several partitions, or sections, of data. Each partition appears on the computer as if it were a separate disc. *See also* **CD-R; DVD-R; partition**.

network: A set of connections among devices to exchange data. *See also* **LAN; wireless network.**

optical zoom: The use of a lens to get more detail, such as in a camera or pair of binoculars. This type of zoom (as compared to digital zoom) provides the best details for photography. *See also* **digital zoom.**

pane: In a software program, a pane is a portion of a dialog box. A dialog box might have several panes, each with a label inside a *tab* (it looks just like a tab in a paper file folder). When you click a tab, its pane comes to the front of the dialog box, obscuring the others. Panes let software creators stuff lots of features into a single dialog box, typically grouping related functions together so the user can switch among them within the same dialog box.

partition: A virtual disc on a hard drive, CD, or DVD, a partition appears as if it were a physically separate drive or disc, even though it is stored with other partitions on the same drive or disc. *See also* **CD-R; DVD-R**.

PDA (personal digital assistant): A PDA is a handheld device that typically offers personal organizer functions such as a calendar and address book. The best-known PDAs are the various models from Palm and Hewlett-Packard's iPaq. *See also* **handheld; smartphone.**

PDF (Portable Document Format): PDF, developed by Adobe Systems, is a file format for documents that can be created by a variety of programs and be read by most browsers and by the free Adobe Reader program. PDF has thus become a standard way to deliver documents to people by e-mail, over the Web, and on disc.

Perl: A popular programming language used to create CGI scripts. *See also* **CGI.**

PHP: A popular programming language used to create CGI scripts. *See also* **CGI.**

pixel: A picture element, the individual dot in a digital image. Similar to a bit, it is the smallest building block of a digital image. *See also* **bit; DPI; PPI.**

PPI (pixels per inch): Digital images are stored in a grid, with each grid point being a point or dot. The ppi value is the number of points that make up an image when displayed on-screen. (The term *dpi* is used when the image is printed.) *See* **DPI.**

prospect: A person you are marketing to or engaging with in the hopes the person will become a client. The term is short for "prospective client."

QuickTime: A format for video and animation files from Apple Computer. *QuickTime VR* is a companion format for 360-degree images that users can pan through; the "VR" stands for *virtual reality*. Apple also offers the QuickTime Player software to display QuickTime files as well as the QuickTime Pro software to create and edit them. People often refer to all of these as simply *QuickTime*. *See also* **Flash.**

radio: A device that sends and receives signals, such as for cellular phones, wireless networks, television, and talking houses. The radio signals can travel over different radio frequencies, just as different colors of light travel over different light frequencies. The government has decided which radio frequencies can be used for what kind of signals to ensure compatibility between devices and reduce interference between different kinds of devices. *See also* **cellular network; talking house; wireless network.**

resample: A mathematical technique to adjust the number of pixels in an image as the image is enlarged or shrunk. The goal is to add or delete pixels so the resized image ends up with the same PPI (and DPI) as the original, despite its new size, so the image resolution on the monitor or printer remains consistent. When an image is enlarged, pixels are added; when an image is shrunk, pixels are removed. *See also* **DPI; pixel; PPI.**

RJ11: The name of the standard for phone plugs.

RJ45: The name of the standard for Ethernet plugs. *See also* **Ethernet.**

robot: *See* **spider.**

router: A device that manages the communication among devices on a network or between networks. A router is typically used to connect computers on a LAN to the Internet.

RSS (Real Simple Syndication): RSS technology lets users' computers automatically collect information from Web sites and present it to the user in a single program, similar to an electronic clipping service. The Web sites have to be RSS-enabled so the RSS clients know what information to collect, and users must specify which sites they want to collect the RSS information from, usually through subscription services or via an RSS sign-up link on a Web site.

search bot: *See* **spider.**

search engine: A computer system and database that lets users enter a phrase or set of words and returns a list of Web pages whose content seems to match the words. Google is perhaps the best known of these search engines. *See also* **spider.**

search robot: *See* **spider.**

Secure Digital (SD): *See* **memory card.**

server: A device that contains and delivers ("serves up") files, typically over a network. When such a device is connected to the Internet and provides access to Web pages, it is called a *Web server.*

SLR camera: A single lens reflex camera is what most people think of when they visualize a camera: one with a lens that protrudes from the front. With an SLR camera, the photographer sees exactly the same image that is exposed to the film and can adjust everything by turning dials and clicking buttons.

Smart Memory (SM): *See* **memory card.**

smartphone: A cell phone that also includes personal organizer functions such as a calendar and address book as well as basic e-mail and Web access. *See also* **BlackBerry; PDA; Treo.**

software: Computer programs that accomplish specific sets of tasks, such as reading e-mail, editing text, or formatting Web pages.

spam: Unwanted e-mail, usually delivered in bulk and often promoting sham products or services. Often sent by people who mask their identity so they cannot be traced.

spider: A program that traverses the Web looking for pages to add to search engines' indexes of available content. Also called a *search robot* or *search bot*. *See also* **search engine.**

spyware: A program secretly installed on a computer that typically monitors what the user does or captures personal information and then sends that information on to someone else. *See also* **malware.**

SSID (service set identifier): The SSID is essentially the name given to a wireless access point or router, so users can tell what they're connecting to when they initiate a Wi-Fi wireless connection. Wi-Fi access points and routers typically come with software to configure them, including their SSID; if left unconfigured, the SSID is usually Default or the model number of the device. *See also* **802.11; Wi-Fi.**

tag: An HTML command. Examples of tags include <A HREF> for defining hyperlinks, <META> for embedding information about a Web page, <B> for making text bold, and <FONT COLOR> for specifying text color. Browsers read these tags to get the instructions on how to display the Web page, and Web creation software lets you write such tags directly (in code view) or creates them for you based on how you format page components using dialog boxes and menus (in design view).

talking house: A radio transmitter placed at a property listed for sale that plays a marketing message about the property. Visitors tune their car radios to a radio frequency usually listed on the for-sale sign so they can hear it.

templates: Documents used as the basis for other documents. They contain the basic elements of, for example, a printed document or Web document, so users don't have to re-create those elements each time they create a page. Instead, they open a template, save a copy with a new name, and then modify and add to the elements supplied in the template as needed for that new page's contents.

text frame: A container for text in a layout program.

TIFF (Tagged Image File Format): A format for images such as photographs. Most layout programs can open and display TIFF files, so they are commonly used in print layouts. But because TIFF files cannot be displayed by Web browsers, you must typically convert them to the GIF or JPEG format for use on the Web.

transaction: A specific real estate deal, such as selling a specific property to a particular buyer.

Treo: A handheld device from Palm that combines a personal organizer with a cell phone and that also can access the Internet from almost anywhere. *See also* **smartphone.**

Trojan horse: A destructive program that is secretly attached to or embedded in another seemingly legitimate program. *See also* **malware.**

UDF (Universal Disk Format): The standard for storing files on a DVD on both Windows and Mac OS X computers.

unified messaging: A set of technologies that lets voice mail, faxes, and even e-mails be received through a central e-mail or Web account. Typically, you pay for these services as a monthly subscription.

upload: To send information from a device (such as a handheld) or computer you are using to another device, another computer, or the Internet. *See also* **download.**

virtual phone number: A phone number that routes incoming calls to a different phone number. The difference between *call forwarding* and a virtual phone number is that call forwarding transfers a call from one phone to another, while a virtual phone number is not actually connected to a phone. Instead, it is like a shortcut or alias to another phone number, so you could, for example, have a phone number in three different area codes that all ring through to the same phone. *See also* **VoIP.**

virus: A destructive program that is secretly attached to or embedded in a seemingly legitimate file or e-mail. *See also* **malware.**

VoIP (Voice over Internet Protocol): VoIP technology routes phone calls over the same networks that carry Internet and Web traffic, bypassing the standard phone networks. Using VoIP can lower costs, plus allows the phone calls to contain more than voice information; they can also transmit faxes, for example. Because the phone calls are converted into audio files while traversing the Internet, messages can be forwarded via e-mail to others and even stored on your PC. (If you listen to the message or call on a phone, the phone converts that audio file back to sound, so you would never have known that it traveled as an audio file.)

VOW (virtual office Web site): A service that agents and brokers can use to communicate with their clients. While there is no standard definition, generally speaking, VOWs are accessible only by clients, not the public at large, and provide services such as MLS search, disclosure files, and transaction histories. However, in practice, the term *VOW* is often used to mean an IDX. *See also* **IDX.**

WAN (wide area network): A network that is accessible over a large geographic area. It typically means a subscription-based network such as a dial-up network, a cellular network, or a broadband network as opposed to a private, local network managed by a company such as your broker for internal use. *See also* **broadband; LAN; network.**

WAV: The Microsoft Windows standard format for sound and music files. It comes from the term *wave file* to mean a file that records the sound-wave patterns in audio recordings. *See also* **AIFF; MP3.**

Web site domain: *See* **domain.**

WEP (Wired Equivalency Protocol): A security mechanism to protect login passwords when connecting over a wireless network. Provided with early 802.11 equipment, it was not very secure, so most 802.11 equipment built since 2004 uses the improved WPA technology. *See also* **802.11; WPA.**

Wi-Fi: An industry standard that ensures the interoperability of 802.11 standards-based equipment. Although only equipment certified to be interoperable should use the label Wi-Fi, the term has become synonymous with 802.11, which is the set of standards that enable wireless networking. Technically speaking, 802.11 components from different vendors aren't guaranteed to work with each other unless they are Wi-Fi–certified. *See also* **802.11.**

wireless network: A set of connections between devices such as computers and handhelds using radio frequencies instead of wires to send and receive data. The most well-known type of wireless network uses the 802.11 standard and is popularly called Wi-Fi. *See also* **3G; 802.11; LAN; network; radio; Wi-Fi.**

WPA (Wi-Fi Protected Access): Sometimes called WPA-PSK (pre-shared key), the WPA protocol is a security mechanism to protect login passwords when connecting over a wireless network. It is based on the 802.11i standard, although the WPA designation assures compatibility with other WPA-labeled products, while the 802.11i designation doesn't guarantee compatibility with other vendors' products. *See also* **802.11i.**

zoom: *See also* **digital zoom; optical zoom.**

The CD

On the CD included with the book, you'll find lots of technology resources to make it easy to put together the right technology pieces for your real estate business. The CD works on both Windows and Mac OS X computers.

Folder Contents

The CD's folders and contents are as follows:

- **Top-level folder (what you see when you first open the CD):** The start_here.html "home page" (to open in your browser), plus the read_me_first.txt file (you can open this file in any text editor such as the WordPad program that comes with Windows or the TextEdit program that comes with Mac OS X or use any word processor such a Microsoft Word or WordPerfect), which provides the same instructions as found in this appendix.

- **Document Templates folder:** Sample flyer, listing presentation, marketing postcard, and other marketing documents in a variety of formats, including Microsoft Word, Microsoft PowerPoint, and Adobe InDesign. You can use these as the basis for your own materials.

- **Online Templates folder:** Sample Web pages and style sheets to use as the basis of your own Web site. There are both standard HTML versions that any Web creation program can open and Microsoft FrontPage 2003 files designed specifically for editing in that program.

- **Tryout Software folder:** Included are programs you might want to purchase for your real estate work; these programs have been provided by their creators on a limited-functionality or limited-time version for you to try. Each program comes with setup instructions in a text file. Installation varies from program to program. You install some of these programs, such as those from Eurekaware, Real Estate Power Tools, and 3DVista, by double-clicking a file named SETUP.EXE (in Windows only; these programs have no Mac OS X counterparts and so will not display if you open the CD on a Macintosh). The ZangoTaxQ calculator is available for both Windows and Mac OS X; you open and work with it in Microsoft Excel.

- **Free Software folder:** I have created three free Excel-based calculators that you may find handy in your real estate work. You open and work with them in Microsoft Excel.

- **Web Site Code Snippets folder:** The text files include both instructions at the top and the actual HTML code below. To use the code in actual Web pages, copy and paste the HTML code (while working in code view of your Web creation program) into your page. You will need to change some of the code, such as providing actual Web page and image names rather than using the place-holder names in these snippets. Open these snippets in a text editor such as WordPad or TextEdit. You might be able to open them in a word processor, but do not open them in Miccrosoft Word, as Word will try to format the code, which makes it unusable.

- **Chapter Quizzes folder:** To help trainers and other educators—as well as individual readers who simply want to review what they've learned after reading the book—I have included a PDF file containing multiple-choice quizzes for each chapter of the book. A separate PDF file contains the answers.

- **Ergonomics How-To folder:** This folder contains a PDF file of an article from *Macworld* magazine that shows you how to set up your work environment to avoid injury while working on your computer.

- **--CD internal resources-- folder:** These are internal files used by the CD's Web pages. There is nothing in this folder for you to access directly. (In Windows, this folder may be hidden.)

CHECKLIST

SOFTWARE YOU MAY NEED

To use the template files to create your own materials, you will need one or more of the following software programs, depending on which templates you want to use. Unless noted, the files can be used on a Windows or Mac OS X computer:

- Adobe InDesign CS or later for any files with the filename extension .indd.

- Microsoft Publisher 2000 or later (Windows only) for any files with the filename extension .pub.

- Microsoft Word 2000 or later (Windows) or Word X or later (Mac OS X) for any files with the filename extension .doc.

- Microsoft PowerPoint 2000 or later (Windows) or PowerPoint X or later (Mac OS X) for any files with the filename extension .ppt.

- Microsoft Excel 2000 or later (Windows) or Excel X or later (Mac OS X) for any files with the filename extension .xls.

- Microsoft FrontPage 2003 or later (Windows only) for the FrontPage HTML templates.

- Any Web creation program, such as Macromedia Dreamweaver or Adobe GoLive, for the generic HTML templates.

You'll need a Web browser such as Microsoft Internet Explorer, Mozilla Firefox, Apple Safari, or Netscape Browser to open the Web pages. And you'll need the free Adobe Reader to read and print the PDF documents. (You can also use a PDF editing program such as Adobe Acrobat Professional, Docudesk DeskPDF, or ScanSoft PaperPort to read and print the PDF documents.)

How to Use the CD

You can access the contents of the CD in two ways:

■ **Through your Web browser:** Start by double-clicking the start_here.html file to open the CD's home page in your browser. You'll see links to the CD's contents as well as to resources on the Web.

■ **Through the CD's folders:** Open the CD by double-clicking the CD drive icon in My Computer (Windows) or on the Desktop (Mac OS X). You'll see folders that contain various documents. You open the folders and their contents by double-clicking the files or by dragging them to your computer (to the desktop or to a folder) and opening them from there. You need the appropriate applications on your computer to open these files. For example, to work with the InDesign document templates, you'll need a copy of Adobe's InDesign CS or later.

I recommend that you use your Web browser to access the CD's many links to Web sites that contain product information and services, and that you open the CD's folders to access content such as templates to experiment with on your computer. Some resources, such as the chapter quizzes and ergonomics guide, are just as easy to access via your Web browser as they are to open from their folders, so do whatever is easiest for you.

The home page for the book's companion CD.

Web Page Contents

When you double-click the start_here.html file, you open a home page for the CD in your Web browser. The home page provides links to the following pages:

- **Web Resource Links:** This section of the home page displays a group of links to individual pages containing the four main types of resources: hardware (computer and peripheral equipment), software (programs and calculators), services available over the Web (such as fax-to-PDF conversion and domain registration), and recommended books that cover the technologies I mention in this book. The book link is to a page on the Web, not on the CD, so you'll need an Internet connection to access it. (You can order any of the books from that page.)

- **Templates:** This section contains links to pages listing the print and Web template files included on the CD. If you have the appropriate software installed on your computer, you simply click a link from these pages to open a template file. However, you'll probably want to copy the templates files from the CD's folders to your computer.

- **Software on the CD:** This section contains links to pages listing the free and trial software and Excel calculators included on the CD, as well as a link to the page containing HTML code snippets you can use in your Web pages. You can install the software from the CD, either double-click the setup program from the CD itself or click its link from the CD's software Web page. You can open the Excel spreadsheet-based tools the same way, but I recommend copying them first to your hard drive so you can then save any data you enter into them.

- **Other CD Resources:** This section contains links to pages that list the PDF content on the CD: the chapter quizzes and the ergonomics how-to file. Just click the links to open the files in your Web browser. Alternately, you can open these files in Adobe Reader or another PDF-compatible program directly from the CD.

INDEX